LANGUAGE, DISCOURSE, SC
General Editors: Stephen Heath

Selected published titles:

Norman Bryson
VISION AND PAINTING: The Logic of the Gaze

Elizabeth Cowie
REPRESENTING THE WOMAN: Cinema and Psychoanalysis

Theresa de Lauretis
TECHNOLOGIES OF GENDER: Essays on Theory, Film and Fiction

Mary Ann Doane
THE DESIRE TO DESIRE: The Woman's Film of the 1940s

Alan Durant
CONDITIONS OF MUSIC

Jane Gallop
FEMINISM AND PSYCHOANALYSIS: The Daughter's Seduction

Peter Gidal
UNDERSTANDING BECKETT: A Study of Monologue and Gesture in the Works of Samuel Beckett

Alan Hunt
GOVERNANCE OF THE CONSUMING PASSIONS: A History of Sumptuary Law

Ian Hunter
CULTURE AND GOVERNMENT: The Emergence of Literary Education

Jeffrey Minson
GENEALOGIES OF MORALS: Nietzsche, Foucault, Donzelot and the Eccentricity of Ethics

Laura Mulvey
VISUAL AND OTHER PLEASURES

List continued overleaf

List continued from previous page

Christopher Norris
RESOURCES OF REALISM: Prospects for 'Post-Analytic' Philosophy

Denise Riley
'AM I THAT NAME?': Feminism and the Category of 'Women' in History

Jacqueline Rose
PETER PAN, OR THE IMPOSSIBILITY OF CHILDREN'S FICTION

Raymond Tallis
NOT SAUSSURE: A Critique of Post-Saussurean Literary Theory

David Trotter
THE MAKING OF THE READER: Language and Subjectivity in Modern American, English and Irish Poetry

Geoffrey Ward
STATUTES OF LIBERTY: The New York School of Poets

The Destructive Element

British Psychoanalysis and Modernism

Lyndsey Stonebridge
Lecturer in English
University of East Anglia

First published 1998 by
MACMILLAN PRESS LTD
Houndmills, Basingstoke, Hampshire RG21 6XS
and London
Companies and representatives
throughout the world

ISBN 0–333–67837–0 hardcover
ISBN 0–333–67838–9 paperback

A catalogue record for this book is available from the British Library.

This book is printed on paper suitable for recycling and made from fully managed and sustained forest sources.

10 9 8 7 6 5 4 3 2 1
07 06 05 04 03 02 01 00 99 98

Printed and bound in Great Britain by
Antony Rowe Ltd, Chippenham, Wiltshire

For Andy Carpenter and Jean McCaig

Contents

Preface

> In violent times the moral acts of the individual seem quite unrelated to the immense social changes going on all around him. He looks at civilization and does not see his own quiet image reflected there at all, but the face of something fierce and threatening, that may destroy him. It may seem foreign and yet resemble his own face.
>
> Stephen Spender, *The Destructive Element*[1]

In 1925 I.A. Richards, borrowing from Conrad's *Lord Jim*, appends a footnote to his reading of Eliot's *The Waste Land*. Eliot's strength in this poem, he remarks, is to have realized the central void of belief that confronts his generation: '"In the destructive element immerse ... that was the way"'.[2] By providing 'the perfect emotive description' of an epistemological crisis, Eliot's poem demonstrates that only by immersing oneself in the modern world of destruction can the modern writer reclaim some form of cultural authority and integrity. Richards dipped in the destructive element only to surface and breathe in the cool air of psychological utilitarianism. His famous footnote, however, retains an evocative quality. Valentine Cunningham goes so far as to suggest that this is 'perhaps twentieth century literature's mightiest footnote'.[3] Where Richards forged a modern and practical criticism out of the destructive element, others had a more pessimistic diagnosis of the twentieth century's fascination with destruction. Some years later, Erich Auerbach, writing in enforced exile in Istanbul during World War Two, closes his remarkable *Mimesis* with the following description of modern writing: 'We not infrequently find a turning away from the practical will to live, or delight in portraying it under its most brutal forms. There is hatred of culture and civilization, brought out by means of the subtlest stylistic devices which culture and civilization have developed, and often a radical and fanatical urge to destroy'.[4] Turning against culture with the resources of culture itself, the modern writer discovers the pleasures of an anti-cultural aggression.

In 1931 the British psychoanalyst, Edward Glover, makes a similar point in his paper, 'Sublimation, Substitution and Social

Anxiety'. Many 'cultural productions', he suggests, generate an amount of aggressivity that is so great 'as to suggest that they provide a more or less direct outlet for destructive impulses'. This is especially so, he adds, in the case of literary criticism where 'tendencies of wit and recompense of style (technique) help to conceal or extenuate the more primitive interests'.[5] Glover's paper is a summary and attempted synthesis of psychoanalytic theories of sublimation (which is why, Lacan says, it is so riddled with contradictions).[6] In this paper, Glover provides Auerbach's worries about the destructive tendencies of modern writing with a metapsychological underpinning. Freud, says Glover, shows how the identifications that constitute our cultural being bring with them a form of aggressive psychic protest – the 'Destruktionsneigung' that forms the core of civilization's discontents. Glover translates that 'destructive inclination' as 'the whole of the destructive elements'. Like Freud, and like Melanie Klein who had arrived in England six years earlier, Glover recognizes that sublimation is not only a manifestation of the pleasure principle, but is inextricably caught up with those destructive elements, with the death drive and with the anxiety and guilt associated with the social requirement to make good, not only sexuality (as in earlier accounts of sublimation), but an erotic component that, in Freud's words, 'is released in the form of an inclination to aggression and destruction'.[7]

For both psychoanalysis and literary criticism the destructive element surfaces through a confusion of tongues: where Richards quotes the words of the Bavarian Stein from the multi-lingual Conrad, Glover translates Freud. Caught up in the apocalyptic rhetoric of inter-war England, both destructive elements are foreign imports domesticated for the purpose of articulating a sense of national, social, cultural and psychic crisis. This book follows the course of the destructive element through some versions of modernism and through psychoanalysis in Britain and, back-paddling through its depths and shallows, attempts to sketch out a specific and shared trajectory between the two traditions. Central to both is the emergence of a mythology in which writers represent themselves as coming face to face with the potential violence – historical, epistemological and psychic – of modernity in order to transcend it. If these attempts at transcendence ultimately falter, it is because neither psychoanalysis nor literary modernism can resist the implication that culture itself finds something satisfying in the production of its own destructive elements. Pushing both psychoanalysis and literary modernism to their limits, 'the destructive element', in this context, can be read as marking a moment where efforts to transcend modernity are forced into new forms of engagement with it.

* * *

An earlier version of this book was submitted as a PhD thesis at the University of London in 1995. I had the good fortune to be supervised by Jacqueline Rose, first at the University of Sussex and later at Queen Mary and Westfield College, London. I owe a tremendous amount to her wisdom, criticism and unfailing support. I also wish to thank my examiners Stephen Bann and Denise Riley for their careful reading, and Malcolm Bowie for his advice during the earlier stages of the thesis. Especial thanks are due to Denise Riley for extending her role as examiner to that of editor with such good grace, and for much pleasurable companionship. My work on Adrian Stokes was made possible by the kind assistance of Ann and Ian Angus and by the librarians at the Tate Gallery Archive. Bet Inglis at the University of Sussex and the librarians at the Tavistock Centre, the Anna Freud Centre and the Wellcome Institute all provided invaluable help. Many people have helped me write this book, be it through friendship and encouragement or intellectual advice and suggestions. I should like to thank: Claire Buck, Howard Caygill, Jon Cook, Hugh Haughton, Laura Marcus, Judith Mehta, John Mepham, Drew Milne, Peter Nicholls, Ian Patterson, David Peters-Corbett, John Phillips, Rachel Potter, Suzanne Raitt, David Rogers, Victor Sage and Trudi Tate. I am particularly grateful to Geoffrey Gilbert for reading through everything and for being so smart. Finally, my thanks, and much more, to Anika Carpenter and Sue Jones who patiently ensured that I kept my head above water throughout.

Lyndsey Stonebridge

Acknowledgements

Chapter 3, 'Rhythm: Breaking the Illusion' was originally published in *New Essays on Virginia Woolf*, ed. Helen Wussow, Dallas: Contemporary Research Press, 1995 and a version of Chapter 5 was published as 'Taking care of ourselves and looking after the subject: Marion Milner's autobiographical acts' in *Paragraph*, vol. 17, no. 2, July 1994. The author and publisher also gratefully acknowledge permission to quote from the following:

W.H. Auden, 'In Praise of Limestone', *Selected Poems*, London: Faber and Faber, 1988. Copyright by the Estate of W.H. Auden.

W.H. Auden, Unpublished Correspondence to Adrian Stokes from the Adrian Stokes archives, held at the Tate Gallery Archive. Copyright by the Estate of W.H. Auden.

Melanie Klein, Extract from 'Klein's letters to the Boulagers', Copyright The Melanie Klein Trust.

Osbert Sitwell, Extracts from Letters by Osbert Sitwell, Copyright 1988 Frank Margo'.

Adrian Stokes, Extracts from the 'Notebooks of Adrian Stokes', printed by permission of the literary executors of the late Adrian Stokes.

Adrian Stokes, Extracts from 'Freud's views concerning culture in *The Future of an Illusion* and in *Civilization and Its Discontents*', printed by permission of the literary executors of the late Adrian Stokes.

Acknowledgements

Introduction: From Bokhara to Samarra: Psychoanalysis and Modernism

The destructive element, the death drive, aggressivity – there is something persistent and compelling about the way these terms curl around our consciousness of the early twentieth century. Expressive and evocative enough to give a general sense of the historical affects of the period, the terms also have enough theoretical suppleness to promise a more nuanced understanding of the discontents they at the same time describe. We hold on to our destructive elements because – and this is a tradition to which both the modernist and psychoanalytic writers explored in this book attest – we feel we have something to gain by them. For Lionel Trilling in his famous 1955 lecture, 'Freud and the Crisis of our Culture', what is to be gained is a modern sense of self. Freud, in his account, is modern in the sense that Joyce, Kafka, Proust and E.M. Forster are modern:

> [Freud] needed to believe that there was some point at which it was possible to stand beyond the reach of culture. Perhaps his formulation of the death instinct is to be interpreted as the expression of this need. "Death destroys a man" says E.M. Forster "but the idea of death saves him". Saves him from what? From the entire submission of himself – of his self to life in culture.[1]

For Trilling the death drive is a redemptive thesis which, because it affirms 'a biological sense of self', leaves a triumphant 'residue of human quality beyond the reach of cultural control'.[2] Like literature, the function of psychoanalysis is to make us see 'the high authority of the self in its quarrel with society and culture'.[3] Through one of the bleakest of Freud's insights, the self momentarily wins this quarrel.

Compare Trilling's argument with more recent readings of the relation between modernism and psychoanalysis, and this affirmation of the self perhaps begins to look like a too hastily claimed victory for humanist criticism in a quarrel which is by no means over. Leo Bersani's *The Culture of Redemption* in many ways provides an implicit critique of Trilling's paradigm.[4] For Bersani, a reading of modernism in which the self transcends the realm of culture is not an affirmation of human existence, but an insidious downgrading of historical experience. The redemptive hypothesis in both modernist rhetoric and theory attempts to paste the universal over the particular, and so affirms art over experience at a historical juncture when the frontiers between the two are at their most precarious. For Bersani, it is precisely when Freud bolsters up the 'high authority' of the self, as in *On Narcissism* (1914), that that self most readily legitimates the culture from which, in Trilling's account, it is set apart. The very notion of the self is authorized by and authorizes a culture based on the 'sacrosanct values' of individuality. But Trilling and Bersani are not quite as far apart as this sketch suggests. As two commentators have recently argued, Perry Meisel in the context of canonical modernism and Jacqueline Rose with reference to the political and psychic challenges of studying and teaching literature today, Trilling's lecture is cut through with a set of difficulties, paradoxes and ironies that make him as modern as the writers he is talking about.[5] At the same moment that Trilling calls on Freud's death drive to proclaim a humanist integrity against culture, he also cancels that proposition. 'It can of course be said', he notes, 'that the indignation which an individual directs upon his culture is itself culturally conditioned. Culture may be thought of as a Kismet – we flee from Bokhara to escape its decrees, only to fulfill them in Samarra'.[6] The idea of transcending culture, in other words, is an illusion that is sustained and enabled by culture itself. The 'intense conviction of the existence of the self apart from culture is', says Trilling, with a melancholy twist, 'as culture well knows, its noblest and most generous achievement'.[7] At the same moment as psychoanalysis and modernism appear to take us beyond culture, then, we find that in effect we have never really left its grasp. Of course, what Trilling sees as a noble and generous gift is, for Bersani, one of culture's most insidious tricks; for him, there is nothing very edifying about the way culture gives us the notion of the self only to legitimate its own authority. What I want to emphasize here is Trilling's and Bersani's shared notion of some kind of double-bind or impasse: a kind of paradoxical relation whereby the attempt to separate the self from culture results in the knowledge of their intractable relatedness, and which, in each case, although divided by at least thirty years of critical thought, is derived from a reading of both psychoanalysis and modernism.

This impasse or irony is well documented in Perry Meisel's 1987 study, *The Myth of the Modern*. For him, modernism 'makes it new' only to the extent that it is encumbered by its own literary and cultural past. 'Modernism', he writes,

> is a way of adjusting to the belatedness that is its precondition. If what enables also wounds, what empowers also makes for anxiety, then we should ask how well our canonical modernists manage this dilemma that gives them life while threatening them with death.[8]

The present study also asks how well some canonical modernists, and some non-canonical modernists, manage the dilemma whereby culture both threatens and enables an articulation of the modern. In this book, however, I am less concerned with the paradoxes and burdens of canonical modernism than with a different, more historically local and specific context; one which, in fact, is also present in Trilling's lecture. Summing up, Trilling concludes with a reference, not to Freud, Joyce or Proust, but to Anna Freud's Freud Memorial Lecture, 'Psychoanalysis and Education', given one year before Trilling's own. Anna Freud begins her lecture by describing two phases in the psychoanalytic study of the child. First, she argues, the idea that infantile anxiety could be curtailed by modifying parental behaviour produced a period of optimism in the psychoanalysis of children. In fact, this is a lightly veiled reference to Anna Freud's own earlier Utopian views of child analysis.[9] In this account, the child's guilt and anxiety is put down to a failure of the parental super-ego. The child's super-ego fails because the parent's super-ego also failed: modify the behaviour of the parent and you can save the child. By 1954, however, Anna Freud concedes that this initial optimism has been transformed into a period of pessimism. There are, she now says, a variety of 'inevitable' factors, such as primordial ambivalence, which cause the child's guilt and anxiety. Child psychoanalysis, accordingly, acknowledges that the neuroses cannot be educated. Trilling seizes on this period of pessimism with all the ardour of a good liberal sceptic. For him, the idea of an innate and inevitable psychical conflict is further evidence of psychoanalysis' on-going affirmation of 'the *non*-cultural part of our destiny'.[10]

But there is another story waiting to be told here. Anna Freud's description of a shift from optimism to pessimism also rehearses the central themes of her battle with Melanie Klein that tore apart the English psychoanalytic community during World War Two and which culminated in the acrimonious 'Controversial Discussions'. In that fiercely fought debate, it was Klein's theory of an early and inexorable super-ego which *cannot* be educated by outside interference that the Anna Freudians rejected, not only because of its pessimism, but also because of Klein's uncompromising image of the destructive origins of human life and the way her analysis of children delved into the theoretically shadowy and hazardous depths of the psyche.[11] When Anna Freud suggests that psychoanalysis now has a more pessimistic view of the relation between the psyche and culture, she is also beginning to venture into, or at the very least acknowledge, an area where only Melanie Klein had dared to go before. As she says in a discussion after her lecture 'the study of this darkest of all ages has never been my predilection...In no other realm of psychoanalysis does speculation need to run quite as free, as far, and as wild'.[12]

If, as Meisel suggests, Trilling's 1955 lecture 'remains as clear a definition as we have had of what is axiomatic in our assumptions about the modern',[13] ought we not to ask, not only canonical modernists, but also the women who are working in the back-room of Trilling's lecture, how well they managed the dilemma between the self and culture? What happens if we read the psychoanalysts of the British Psycho-Analytical Society not as simply affirming a redemptive thesis of a life beyond culture, but – speculating wildly and freely – as caught up in the dilemmas and ironies that Trilling and Bersani propose in their accounts of modernism? If British psychoanalysts can be demonstrated to produce their own 'Kismet', how can their writings be read in dialogue with the rhetoric and theory of Anglo-American modernism? What would the battle between the self and culture look like if it were placed back into the context of the relation between the British Society and early twentieth-century literature?

* * *

Why return to British psychoanalysis? What, if anything, have I.A. Richards' pronouncements in *The Criterion*, the writings of

Roger Fry, Virginia Woolf, Ezra Pound, W.H. Auden and Stevie Smith, to do with the thinking of the British Psycho-Analytical Society, presided over mainly by women who spent their working days in analytic play rooms and who endlessly speculated on the psychic hinterlands of 'that darkest of all ages', early oedipality? How is it possible to connect what is often regarded as this century's most far-reaching challenge to aesthetics with what has been aptly termed the 'war in the nursery'? ('We often say, half-jokingly' noted Anna Freud and Dorothy Burlingham in *Young Children in War-Time* 'that there is a continual war raging in the nursery').[14] In *War in the Nursery: Theories of the Child and Mother*, Denise Riley gives the example of a friend who asks her why, instead of exploring the ideas of Freud and Jacques Lacan, she is studying 'second-rate' thinkers such as Klein and John Bowlby.[15] Riley answers as a historian. The reason why Klein and Bowlby are important is that theirs were the ideas which acquired ideological currency at the time; it was their theories, and not those of say Reich, that were popularized in war-time Britain. Similarly, my concern here is to register the historical presence of psychoanalysis in British culture in the period leading up to and including World War Two. But this is not an historical study and nor is it, properly speaking, a work of psychoanalytic theory: rather it falls – or fails – between the two. Psychoanalysis has (at least) two histories. It emerges as a social and aesthetic discourse at the same time as it is shaped and helps shape cultural and social history itself. This causes problems. On one hand, to be seduced by psychoanalytic theory is to run the risk of producing a psychoanalysis without the transference; the sort of psychoanalysis that has a concept of a 'political unconscious', for example, but frequently forgets that psychoanalysis itself has a cultural and institutional history. On the other hand, a history of psychoanalysis that forgets that psychoanalysis itself has had some very important things to say about how histories get told, fails to do justice to the extent to which concepts such as fantasy and the unconscious have helped redefine the historical field. This study is primarily concerned with the development of psychoanalysis, particularly in its Kleinian forms, as a social and aesthetic discourse. Following 1990s etiquette, I allow myself to be seduced, but I do try to make enquiries about the history of my seducer. This has many instructive perils: the seducer lies, the destructive element, like Freud's death drive, gestures towards an ahistoricism which, as Trilling's paradoxes illustrate so clearly, is historically and culturally bound. To forget this is to risk an aestheticization of the destructive element which is potentially as politically grievous as the valorizing tendencies of some of the writers I discuss here.

Leaving aside the extensive and important work that has been done on Freud 'as a modernist', until relatively recently many psychoanalytic readings of modernism have tended to lean on French psychoanalytic theory. The relation between modernism and psychoanalysis in France has, of course, its own history which, from Breton through to the *Tel Quel* group and Julia Kristeva's *Revolution in Poetic Language*, is characterized by a continual affirmation of the radical potential both of the avant-garde and psychoanalysis. In the 1980s critical readings produced through this trajectory were successful not only in removing Anglo-American modernism from a New Critical stranglehold, but also in drawing attention to issues surrounding writing and sexuality, subjectivity and ideology: Kristevan readings of Virginia Woolf, which helped set a new feminist agenda for her work in the 1980s, are a case in point – however much one might want to question that agenda.[16] But while the theoretical questions which produced and sustained the French alliance between psychoanalysis and the avant-garde are, as we will see, in some ways also pertinent to the British context, there are problems in the wholesale importation across the Channel of this particular genealogy. Psychoanalysis runs the risk of becoming the un-historicized ghost at the banquet – responsible for pointing out, for example, how Anglo-American modernism, in spite of itself, is more avant-garde than it will dare admit, or has had the insight to recognize. Likewise, importing the privileging of the aesthetic which tends to distinguish, for example, Kristeva's view of modernism, can obscure the frequently self-conscious debates about the status of the aesthetic within British modernism and psychoanalysis. To be seduced too quickly by the interpretative allure of contemporary French psychoanalysis is to bequeath to Anglo-American modernism a heritage which is not, strictly speaking, its own.

To begin with, therefore, it seems more helpful not to presume an analogous relation between the French avant-garde psychoanalytic heritage and British psychoanalysis' relation to modernism, but rather to explore what structural homologies exist between them. In the second volume of her invaluable study of the history of French psychoanalysis, Elisabeth Roudinesco writes:

> In 1929, the lure of death resulted in Freud's observation of a fundamental discontent in civilization. A certain 'golden age' of

> psychoanalysis had disappeared in the torment of war, but, beyond the disaster, a hope subsisted: the renunciation of murderous instincts could engender sublimation.[17]

1929 marked the publication of the first chapter of Freud's *Civilization and Its Discontents*. To an extent, the 'golden age' of psychoanalysis had already begun to disappear in 1920 with Freud's presentation of the death drive in *Beyond the Pleasure Principle*. As Maud Ellmann has demonstrated, this text is as much the product of the destructive elements of World War One as Eliot's *The Waste Land*.[18] In *Civilization and its Discontents* Freud twists the screw still further. It is not only that the subject begins life spilling over with erotic and murderous drives, and it is not only that the price we pay for civilization is the renunciation of those drives: the scandal of *Civilization and Its Discontents*, as with Freud's second topography more generally, rests with his image of a super-ego which does not simply repress murderous desires but draws from them and repeats their ferocity with all the violence that it at the same time prohibits. This, then, is Freud's own brutal version of a cultural 'Kismet'. As Lacan, among others, has pointed out, the social law in *Civilization* is a perverse law which is as potentially destructive as the destructive desires it asks us to renounce.[19]

Within the French context, the impasses of the second topography precipitate what Roudinesco terms a 'fracture' between the avant-garde and French institutional psychoanalysis. In the 1920s and 1930s there was, she argues, an 'incommunicability' between the reception of Freud's ideas by the French psychoanalytic establishment and his influence on the avant-garde. In this account, Surrealism grabs the radical mantle of the ideas that the psychoanalytic movement was simultaneously energizing and yet trying to contain within the parameters of scientific respectability. 'Contemporaneous with a dynamism whose authority it contested', Roudinesco argues, 'Surrealism contributed nothing less than [the French psychiatro-psychoanalytic movement's] apotheosis by supplying the weapons needed for its generation. Without the Surrealist scandal, the second psychoanalytic generation would have spent its energy without hearing any echo of the new battle'.[20] It was, of course, Lacan who picked up that echo and turned into a battle cry. In the 1920s and 1930s, while Surrealism was sowing the seeds for a radicalized psychoanalysis, the French psychoanalytic movement, by contrast, closed ranks under the influence of Ernest

Jones' (president of the International Psycho-Analytic Association from 1932–1949) reaction against the occultism of Rank and Jung. While the International Association attempted to maintain the frontier between madness and science through an appeal to pathology, Surrealism used psychoanalysis to claim the unconscious as a revolutionizing expressive form. And while the psychoanalytic establishment continued to see art as a superior form of symptom formation, for Surrealism sublimation was at best, a non-issue and, at worst, a reactionary concept with little theoretical yield.

The French response to Freud's *Civilization* is crucial in Roudinesco's account in so far as it provides a test-case for the differing political and theoretical trajectories of the psychoanalytic movement and the avant-garde. Roudinesco credits Surrealism with single-mindedly taking on Freud's notion of the death drive. As she puts it:

> The Surrealists were not 'influenced' by the publication of ... *Beyond the Pleasure Principle*. And yet the lure of death, which has traversed the writing of poetry from the time of its inception, constituted an advantageous terrain for the implantation of the Freudian notion of the death instinct. That notion was refused simultaneously by the psychoanalytic movement, by Freudo-Marxism and by Communist discourse.[21]

It was left to the Surrealist cult of death, sex and suicide to carry Freud's discovery through to a 'veritable "theory" of morbid energy'. While Surrealism takes on Freud's death drive, it also goes one stage further by rejecting his theory of the sublimation of murderous instincts. With this, Surrealism's reading of psychoanalysis contributes its development of a negative critique. Citing the cult that grew up in 1933 around the parricide Violette Nozière, 'mythmonger' and natural heir to the famous Papin sisters, Roudinesco argues that 'through an exacerbated representation of the female, the "generation of refusal" no longer sought the exile of sleep within, but, in the negative idealization of crime, finally discovered the means to struggle against a society reviled from every quarter'.[22] Through Surrealism, then, Freud's pessimism about the destructive element located at the heart of the relation between the individual and culture is transformed into an aesthetic and social protest.

Switch now to the reception of Freud's ideas in Britain and a very different picture seems to emerge. Far from taking on and radically energizing psychoanalysis, the modernist vanguard roundly rejected it. 'The *Lunatic*, or the *Demented*, and the *Child*' notes Wyndham Lewis, in *The Art of Being Ruled*, to give an example of the depth of modernist unease, 'are linked together by psychoanalysis, the link being its dogma of the Unconscious'.[23] What this 'dogma' represents for Lewis, hideously manifest in the 'lunatic' and child-like writings of Gertrude Stein, is an unhealthy nostalgia for the 'central problems of subjectivity'.[24] Psychoanalysis reaffirms interiority and, as such, supports a narcissistic, effeminate and decadent culture based on a regressive and degenerate notion of the self. Like Richards, Lewis is a proponent of the destructive element. '[W]e have lost our sense of reality': what we need, he says, 'is a world of negation'.[25] But for Lewis, psychoanalysis does not (as it does for Surrealism) articulate this negativity, but is a false messiah offering 'topical unreality' in the place of radical negation. For D.H. Lawrence, a writer who took psychoanalysis very seriously indeed, the difficulty with Freud was that he emasculated psychoanalysis through the theory of repression, hence blocking Lawrence's desired return to a culture of pagan and sexual rejuvenation.[26] The problem with psychoanalysis for British modernism, one senses, was that it either took you too far or not far enough in the battle with culture: too far back into the self, in Lewis' case, but not far back enough to liberate that self, in Lawrence's.

As the rhetorical nuances of Lewis' and Lawrence's critiques might suggest, if there is 'fracture' in the reception of Freud's ideas in Anglo-American modernism it falls along gendered lines. Where the 'Men of 1914' repudiated psychoanalysis on the grounds of its emasculating emphasis on interiority or its counter-revolutionary belief in repression, women writers associated with the modernist vanguard embraced it. May Sinclair, for example, and most notably, H.D., both seized upon psychoanalysis for its potential as a critique of gender and sexuality. This is one area where historical connections between psychoanalysis and modernism have been thoroughly researched in recent years.[27] But women modernists' enthusiastic reception of psychoanalysis is less, it seems to me, a case of the 'gender of modernism' (a category which is a little too wide for successful historical navigation), than part of the on-going history of psychoanalysis and feminism. The work of Sinclair and H.D, for instance, is contemporaneous with the famous 'femininity debates' of the 1920s and 1930s. When Ernest Jones was invited to Venice to lecture on the growing differences between the British and Viennese psychoanalytic schools in 1935, he chose female sexuality as his subject. Psychoanalytic feminism in the early 1980s turned to that earlier debate in order to argue the case for a return to Freud through Lacan. The recent return to Klein – who was once dismissed on the grounds of her belief in an innate sexuality – it might be suggested, is another chapter in that history.[28]

Modernist genealogies, then, run in uneasy parallel with the history of psychoanalysis and feminism. The cultural group that did take on psychoanalysis in Britain was, of course, Bloomsbury – the political and aesthetic negative image, one could say, of French Surrealism. The connections between Bloomsbury and psychoanalysis are plentiful: Virginia Woolf's and Leonard Woolf's Hogarth Press published both Freud and Klein, James and Alix Strachey were Freud's translators, Adrian Stephen, Woolf's brother and his wife Karin, became psychoanalysts, and famously, in a story laden with suggestiveness, Freud apparently presented Virginia Woolf with a narcissus when they met in 1939. Where the modernist vanguard rejected psychoanalysis and where women writers took on its critique of sexuality, Bloomsbury not only popularized psychoanalysis for the British intelligentsia, but also domesticated it by incorporating psychoanalysis within its over-arching liberal ethos of the 'free and civilized individual'. Or at least that is what it may look like. In his essay on the cultural formation of Bloomsbury, Raymond Williams notes:

> The different positions which the Bloomsbury Group assembled, and which they effectively disseminated as the contents of the mind of a modern, educated civilized individual, are all in effect *alternatives* to a general theory. We do not need to ask, while this impression holds, whether Freud's generalizations on aggression are compatible with single-minded work for the League of Nations ... we do not need to ask because the effective integration has already taken place, at the level of the 'civilized individual' ... The social conscience, in the end, is to protect the private consciousness.[29]

Psychoanalysis, by this reading, settles into the folds of English liberal modernism and hence joins with that British tradition of radicals who challenge the orthodoxy of their culture in order, when all is said and done, to preserve the authority of that culture itself. But this, as Williams says, is just an impression. What happens if we do ask whether Freud's generalizations on aggression are, in fact, commensurate with the ideals of social conscience as a form of private consciousness?

Inserting the work of Kleinian psychoanalysts into this context is one way of beginning to challenge this impression – one way of beginning to ask questions. While, in contrast to Surrealism, the English modernist vanguard was rejecting psychoanalysis, and while the French psychoanalytic movement was simultaneously rejecting Freud's theory of the death drive, the British psychoanalytic movement, under the influence of Melanie Klein and a close group of predominantly women followers, whole-heartedly embraced the death drive and placed Freud's vision of a persecutory cultural super-ego at the heart of their theories. If psychoanalysis in France contributed to the Surrealist critique through an idealization of crime in the figure of the transgressive woman and the male homosexual, across the Channel we have the image of a group of women who, although far from idealizing crime, continually theorized the violence of the tie between the individual and culture which Freud outlined in *Civilization*. Indeed, the debate between Melanie Klein and Anna Freud in World War Two was precisely a battle about the super-ego; about the limits of violence and criminality in a psychic world which, from the Kleinian perspective, at least, was awash with the destructive element.

If we look, for example, at the rhetoric of Joan Rivière's description of early infancy, we might wonder who, in the case of the British reception of psychoanalysis, comes closest to the 'veritable "theory" of morbid energy' that Roudinesco associates with Surrealism:

> Loose motions, flatus and urine are all felt to be burning, corroding and poisoning agents. Not only the excretory but all other physical functions are pressed into the service of the need for aggressive (sadistic) discharge in phantasy. Limbs shall trample, kick and hit; lips, fingers and hands shall suck, twist, pinch; teeth shall bite, gnaw, mangle and cut; mouth shall devour, swallow and "kill" (annihilate); eyes kill by a look, pierce and penetrate; breath and mouth hurt by noise, as the child's own sensitive ears have experienced.[30]

There is an uneasy tension in this passage between its function as a description of the violence of early phantasy and a sense that the writer has got caught up inside this violence. The use of the imperative ('Limbs *shall* trample'), for example, has the effect of suggesting not merely an account of an early stage of psychic life, but a command that this 'shall' be so. (Where, we might ask, can we locate the super-ego in Rivière's writing?) Likewise, the dismembered syntax and the way the literal is confused with the metaphoric ('eyes shall kill') has the effect of repeating, on the level of writing, the destruction which Rivière is at the same time describing. It is, perhaps, not surprising to find Rivière three years later reading *The Waste Land* as a contemporary instance of the projection of destructive desire, and Apollinaire's *Alcools* as a supreme example of the 'concrete realism' of phantasy'.[31]

Whereas in France the psychoanalytic movement dismissed Freud's death drive, in Britain those who were influenced by the work of Melanie Klein (who arrived in England in 1926) were quick to latch on to her all-encompassing thesis of aggressivity. The rhetoric of E.F.M. Durbin's and John Bowlby's 1938 essay, 'Personal Aggressiveness and War', to give another example, is as inflected with aggressivity as the infectious cruelty they posit as the bedrock of biological, psychological and anthropological constitution. 'Cruelty knows no boundary or party creed' they say. 'It wears every kind of shirt'.[32] For Bowlby and Durbin, there is a direct analogy between the way female apes on Monkey Hill, in the Regent's Park Zoo, are torn limb from limb, the sadistic relish with which the children described in work of Susan Isaacs tear up their toys, and the brutality of late 1930s international politics. On page after page, Bowlby and Durbin accrue more examples of psychic, biological and political violence. An essay which is indeed immersed in the destructive element, there is something more than a little disturbing about the sheer weight and repetitiveness of the morbid energy which runs across this text. This British 'negative idealization' of aggressivity was not, of course, a struggle against a reviled society, but part of an argument that attempted to reform it. Socialism is not the answer, say Durbin and Bowlby in this anti-Communist text, but the eradication of brutality in a culture that condones violence in the name of civilized values. If children 'were allowed to express desire and anger more freely' they conclude, 'it should follow that they would make more happy, more peaceful, and more social adults'.[33]

To suggest that a shared interest in the death drive means that Kleinian psychoanalysis has an affinity with the French avant-garde is, of course, a provocation. Nonetheless, as much as it is true to say (and it is a partial truth) that Kleinism belongs to the ethos of Bloomsbury, its history and its theoretical challenges do brush up against the more radicalized version of psychoanalysis that we have come to associate with Lacan. As Elisabeth Roudinesco points out in her first volume on the history of psychoanalysis in France, despite their theoretical differences, Lacan's project is directly linked to Klein's. The Lacanian scandals that rocked the French psychoanalytic establishment between 1953 and 1963 followed a path that was already marked out by the Controversial Discussions: 'There is a historical continuation between the two movements' she writes, 'the one is the anticipation of the other, a prelude'.[34] Combative and revolutionary, Klein (Roudinesco argues) represents the first, tentative return to the meaning of Freudian teaching in the history of the psychoanalytic movement. The younger Lacan was clearly influenced by Klein, as texts such as 'Les complexes familiaux dans la formation del' individu' (1938) and the later 'L'aggressivité en psychanalyse' (1948) attest. Lacan agreed to translate Klein's first book, *The Psychoanalysis of Children* (1932) when they met in 1949. He failed to do so and incurred Klein's wrath: 'still', she noted in a letter to her new translators the Boulagers in 1952, 'it is no good crying over spilt milk',[35] a phrase which, in retrospect, alludes suggestively both to the maternal corporeality that figures so heavily in Klein's work and to Lacan's theoretical debts to Klein that, perhaps, spill out of those containers in his famous experiment with the inverted vase in his 1954 seminar on technique, in which Lacan used Klein's essay on Little Dick ('The Importance of Symbol Formation in the Development of the Ego', 1930) in order to elucidate the topic of the imaginary. What Klein shows us, Lacan argued there, is that 'if, in the human world, objects become variegated, develop, with the luxuriance that makes for its originality, it is to the extent that they make their appearance within a process of expulsion linked to the instinct of primitive destruction'.[36] This is Klein's negativity which, as Jacqueline Rose has recently demonstrated, not only has a proximity to Lacan's reading of the negating logic of the symbolic function, the alienation at the core of the constitution of the subject, but makes it difficult to sustain the charge that the death drive in Klein is some kind of instinctual reductionism.[37] It is also difficult to see how this version of the psyche can be wedded to the promotion of the values of individual consciousness propounded by more conservative elements of English modernism: much of what follows is about the measure of that difficulty.

'Trop, c'est Trop' is the title of a recent essay on Melanie Klein by André Green.[38] For many it is the excessiveness of Klein's theory and practice that troubles. She is much too much, say her critics: too ready to posit an anxiety-driven aggressivity at the core of psychic life; too dogmatic in her insistence on the early development of the super-ego; too quick to interpret the contents of infantile phantasy with devastating literal-mindedness; too eager to enter into that infant's phantasy world without paying due attention to environmental influences (for the Anna Freudians) or to the existence of the signifier (for Lacan). Klein, it seems, churns out a theory of morbid energy that does not fail to disturb. It is not for nothing that Edward Glover, her most vehement detractor, once accused Klein of compounding the errors of Rank and Jung – thus consigning her to the margins of psychoanalytic scientific respectability and casting her into the hinterlands of wild speculation.[39] By inverting Glover's judgements, it is not too difficult to produce an image of Klein as grabbing the radical mantle of psychoanalysis in the 1930s and 1940s, by recasting phantasy into an expressive form so forceful that it took her to the limits of psychic and institutional legitimacy. But Glover, for all his sustained efforts, did not by any means succeed in making a maverick out of Klein: her theories were, and still are, very much close to (if not exactly at the centre of) the heart of the British psychoanalytic establishment. The legacy of Klein's theoretical daring, as Roudinesco has argued, splits on a paradox: at the same moment that Klein and her followers revolutionized psychoanalysis, they also established the parameters for a medico-psychiatric version of object-relations theory that today is renowned more for its conservatism than any radicalizing potential (John Bowlby's post-war work on infantile separation anxiety is a case in point).[40]

To return to Klein today, then, is to traverse a twisting path between different, and frequently conflicting, traditions and genealogies: her work and that of her followers needs to be read as (at least) double, as both conservative and radical. The destructive elements at the heart of Klein's version of psychic life pull in both directions at once. The flow of morbid energy that runs across Kleinian texts often verges on toppling into a form of cultural complicity with the violence they describe: in this the Kleinians share much with some of their modernist contemporaries. The compass of Kleinian phantasy seems limitless, and the destructive drives that propel it appear as an inevitable component of psychic life. Edward Glover, in his widely read *War, Sadism and Pacifism: Three Essays*, based on lectures he gave to a League of Nations Summer School in 1931 (a good place to start if we want to find out whether Freud's generalized theories on aggression are indeed compatible with 'single-mind work for the League Nations') seems to know where the boundaries between phantasy and life begin and end. 'After all', he counsels, 'the infant can neither swallow its mother whole in an access of love, nor tear her to shreds in an access of hate. It is only on battlefields that people can be blown to bits deliberately with the manifest approval of some of the onlookers.'[41] The scandal of the Kleinian account is that, for the infant at least, this distinction does not hold quite so securely. Of course it is only on the battlefield that people can actually be blown to bits; but what 'blown to bits' *means* in psychic terms, or what it feels like to have torn the mother to shreds in phantasy, will not be resolved by direct appeals to empirical reality; indeed it is often that reality itself which fuels the dynamics of phantasy.[42] Small wonder, perhaps, that when Glover turns against Klein two years after the publication of *War, Sadism and Pacifism*, it is on the grounds that she has dared to roam into the field of the psychoses – the mental states which produce the most profound rupture between the ego and reality.[43]

But while the Kleinian account of the destructive elements of the psyche is often as uncompromising, and certainly as troubling, as the theories of more notably radical avatars of the death drive, at the same time British Kleinians did have a distinct, if implicit, cultural and social agenda. Most significantly, in terms of the homologies I've been drawing here, the French and the British responses to Freud's analysis of culture's discontents part dramatically on the question of sublimation. Where French Surrealism rejected sublimation (for the Kleinian art critic Adrian Stokes this was precisely its problem), Kleinian psychoanalysis both avows the destructive element *and* attempts to sublimate it and with the theory of reparation tries to redeem a fundamentally negative view of early psychic life. One reason for the relative marginalization of Kleinian psychoanalysis in literary studies, rests with what is often perceived as, at best, a lack of daring when it comes to questions of aesthetics or, at worst, an ideologically normative and conservative reading of the relation between art and psychic processes. Freudian and post-Freudian accounts of sublimation as an unwieldy displacement of the libido on to cultural production are seen to produce a subversive view of art and culture (in which aesthetic processes are, like the unconscious, another scene that usurps the privileges of consciousness as socially lived).[44] On the other hand, the Kleinian account of reparation, in which art is produced from a loving attempt to repair and restore objects damaged through destructive anxiety, is perceived as too quickly sewing up the radical force of unconscious phantasy and, as Lacan argues, blind to the extent to which aesthetic production is dependent upon social recognition.[45] Indeed to read Christopher Lasch in 1986 extolling the values of Kleinian analysis as returning us 'to the ethics of pre-Enlightenment morality', in a way which is 'good' for both state and country, is to be sufficiently warned of the troubling political trajectories into which Kleinism can be harnessed.[46] But to shed Kleinian and post-Kleinian theories of art of their history, to read, for instance, the theory of reparation as complete and detached from the historical and theoretical debates out of which it is born, is equivalent to not reading psychoanalysis at all. Reparation may well be the answer to the Kleinian account of infantile aggressivity, may be what the Kleinians have to gain by holding onto the destructive element so tenaciously; but if art and creativity are the redemptive answer to Kleinian discontents, as we will see, Kleinian and post-Kleinian aesthetics remain as entangled in the dilemmas of their age as their modernist and literary contemporaries.

Psychoanalysis in Britain does not share the political drive or verve of French Surrealism or, indeed, of the second generation of French psychoanalysis. It does, however, cross the same theoretical and aesthetic domain with an equally energizing rhetorical and theoretical force. The women and men in the back room of Trilling's thesis do more than merely supply us with an interdisciplinary background to the debates and dilemmas of the early twentieth century. They, as much as others, contribute to an on-going quarrel with culture. This is not to say that British psychoanalysis, any more than literary modernism, eventually succeeds in establishing a realm beyond culture. Instead, what we find in both fields is a tension between an initial promise of aesthetic transcendence and a growing knowledge of the intractable complicity between the destructive element within and cultural and social violence without.

* * *

This book does not offer a comprehensive history of either British psychoanalysis or literary culture in the early twentieth century, let alone the manifold connections between them. Nor does it offer an adequate account of the tricky domain between the development of psychoanalysis in Britain and inter-war history (what relation, if any, for example, is there between the theorists of the depressive position and the Depression?). These urgent areas for study require two different kinds of book. Space and self-imposed historical parameters have also prevented any in-depth exploration of two of the most powerful and influential thinkers of British psychoanalysis: D.W. Winnicott, whose work on psychic and cultural space profoundly re-figured conceptions of the relation between self and culture in post-war England, and W.R. Bion whose theoretical brilliance casts a long shadow over avant-garde writers such as, most famously, Samuel Beckett. It is perhaps Bion who finally puts paid to the image of a conservative British psychoanalytic movement lagging behind its more adventurous French counterpart. A further chapter of this history would have not only to include Bion, but also to examine the impact of psychoanalysis on later modernist theories of the visual arts, such as, most notably, those of Anton Ehrenzweig.[47]

Rather than attempt a general or discursive history, this book collects together five readings of moments of potential dialogue between British psychoanalysis and selected contemporary criticism and literature. Sometimes these dialogues are sustained by biographical and historical evidence (as in the relation between Fry's modernism, Virginia Woolf and Kleinian theories of art, for instance, or the art critic Adrian Stokes' biographical and theoretical journey between Ezra Pound and Melanie Klein). Sometimes they are not. Each reading is concerned with a version or a working through of Trilling's 'Kismet' – a moment when an aesthetic or psychic retreat from culture is exposed as culturally bound and predicated. What unites these writers is the effort to salvage something of value, in particular of aesthetic value, out of the destructive elements they all, in various ways, hold on to. Some of them make for very strange bedfellows. I.A. Richards and Melanie Klein, for example, seem to have absolutely nothing in common aside from the fact that they were writing at the same time (the 'historicism' of weak coincidence). Chapter 1, however, returns to Richards' dip in the destructive element to ask how his efforts to construct a moral theory of value shadow equivalent psychoanalytic attempts to harness a theory of destructive phantasy to aesthetic and moral purposes. To recognize the destructive element, as Richards, Empson and Klein demonstrate, is also to unleash it both as a rhetorical force and as a theoretical problem. Consequently, the paradoxes and dilemmas between self and culture, value and life, soon begin to multiply. Far from affirming 'the non-cultural part of our destinies', what is produced is a cultural 'Kismet' – a fateful complicity between the psyche and culture – which challenges more redemptive hypotheses.

Virginia Woolf's writing, among all modernists, seems most readily conducive to a Kleinian reading of art. 'I suppose', she said famously of *To the Lighthouse*, 'I did for myself what psychoanalysts do for their patients. I expressed some very long felt and deeply felt emotion. And in expressing it I explained it and then laid it to rest'.[48] For Woolf here, art is not only a transcendent form, it also offers transcendence as a form of therapy. If we add Roger Fry's aestheticism to this account, which is precisely what both Woolf and Kleinian analysts did, the domestication of Kleinian insights into the ethos of Bloomsbury's liberal sensibility might seem complete. Chapter 2 argues that what makes this impression incomplete, and hence hard to sustain, is the question of sex, especially of female sexuality, and its relation to violence. For the Kleinians, civilization's discontents have a special proximity to their analysis of femininity's discontents. Read Woolf alongside this trajectory, and her treatment of Fry's formalism becomes instructive. For Woolf, to immerse oneself in the destructive element is not, as it is for Trilling and Richards, to affirm a new cultural authority for the self, but rather to witness the dissolution of its protective frontiers. This is not the melancholy fate of the woman writer for whom modernist aesthetics fails to provide an adequate means of representation, but a crucial part of Woolf's later critique of an aesthetics of transcendence that marks a significant, albeit ambivalent, re-alignment of the relation between art and experience in her writing during World War Two.

Chapter Three continues to explore this realignment in Woolf's writing but this time reads it alongside a similar shift in thinking by another analyst working with some of Klein's ideas. Rhythm has long been seen as central to Woolf's writing and, in recent neo-Kristevan readings of her work, frequently figures as the central trope by which Woolf uses modernist practice to construct an alternative, potentially liberating, space for the articulation of subjectivity and sexual difference. At the same time, Woolf's brother's analyst, Ella Freeman Sharpe, was also concerning herself with the political and poetic potential of the rhythms of the unconscious. This can be read as an attempt on the part of psychoanalysis to find an account of sublimation amid what, by the 1930s, appears as a political culture bent on celebrating its own destructive elements. Taking Woolf's and Sharpe's writings on rhythm together, a pattern emerges. For both, rhythm, as a liminal figure, brings new possibilities for artistic and unconscious creativity. Yet because these writers locate rhythm with an alterity that cannot be mastered by traditional modes of representation, rhythm is also presented as harbouring a more sinister psycho-political legacy. So, for Sharpe, it is because rhythm is associated with the deepest unconscious drives that it can also celebrate fundamentally conservative fantasies of non-separation and non-differentiation. And, for Woolf, it is because such fantasies covertly beat their seductive rhythms across our cultural tableaux – in drama and poetry – that it can reach out to what she (like so many of her contemporaries) calls the 'herd instinct'. For each, as much as rhythm is a transgressive poetic category, it is also potentially and dangerously aligned with the most regressive of political fantasies.

The work of Adrian Stokes, examined in Chapter 4, represents, I think, one of the most important transitional moments in the history of Anglo-American modernism and its relation to British psychoanalysis. Stokes' break with Ezra Pound in the 1930s and his turn to Kleinian psychoanalysis has been seen as a retreat into the psyche in an effort to salvage the aesthetic for an authentic humanism from within which to confront the horrors of fascism and World War Two. Following this reading, it would be possible to place Stokes in the same line of heritage as Trilling. Stokes' engagement with psychoanalysis, however, does not finally remove him from the cultural and political impasses of his earlier allegiances. But by this very failure, and by re-figuring his earlier aesthetics through Kleinian and post-Kleinian accounts of phantasy, he produces one of the most challenging psychoanalytic accounts of the precariousness of the frontier between aesthetics and ideology. Stokes' desire to maintain the aesthetic as a cultural category is both balanced and put into question by his extraordinarily attentive eye for the complexity of psychic experience and fidelity to the means of artistic expression. Far from simply using art to escape the grasp of a morbid political culture, Stokes' interest also lies in the prospect of an art form that can express the 'restlessness, refusal and dissatisfaction' which, for him, psychically underpins the modern battle between the self and culture.

Adrian Stokes represents part of a movement within English psychoanalytic thought which both developed and questioned Klein's reparative hypothesis. For Stokes' contemporary, the psychoanalyst Marion Milner, art is not a secondary act of reparation but is the product of a psychic space in which the relation between the self and culture is worked through. Reading her work alongside Stevie Smith's *Over the Frontier* in the final chapter, we reach a point in both British psychoanalysis and literature where the line of severance between the destructive element within and its manifestation without is at its most precarious. Both Smith and Milner are interested in the frontier that separates phantasy in art from the totalitarian spectacles of mass phantasy which they witnessed in the 1930s. Phantasy is less a question of insides and outsides, of the self as opposed to culture, than a question of strategies of narration brought on to master an ever-slippery mimetic identification between self and other. Milner constructs a narrative 'frame' in which to contain a potentially dangerous slippage between inner and outer destructive elements. Smith, by contrast, structures her novel through the figure of a parabola. As soon as the destructive element is seen to be contained in some aesthetic moment by reference to, for example, Georg Grosz's paintings which are the central *mise-en-abîme* of the novel, Smith dissolves the frontier between fantasy in art and fantasy in life and between the self and culture. For Smith, to be immersed in the destructive element in 1938 is finally and inescapably to be in Bokhara and Samarra.

A parabola might be an apt metaphor by which to describe where, finally, psychoanalysis and modernism might take us: not beyond culture, but to a recognition of the intractable inter-relation of the self and culture; not through, and therefore out of the destructive element, but into something more like a 'vicious circle', to borrow one of Klein's favourite phrases, whereby the effort to transcend culture, or to make an aesthetic or moral out of its violence, is rewarded by the knowledge that you have never really left its grasp. At a time when the European theatricals of psychic cruelty which so perturbed both psychoanalysts and writers are once more being played out, and at a moment in contemporary

British culture when a politics of reparation (preserving the 'good') seems to have acquired a curious new legitimacy, the failure of writers and analysts of the early part of the century to extricate themselves from their own cultural 'Kismet' remains as instructive for us now as it was then.

1

Sticks for Dahlias: The Destructive Element in Literary Criticism and Melanie Klein

The waste remains, the waste remains and kills.

William Empson, 'Missing Dates'

'In the destructive element immerse...that was the way'. When Richards found the right phrase to describe Eliot's *The Waste Land* in Conrad's *Lord Jim* it was, in part, with reference to psychoanalysis. In 'A Background for Contemporary Poetry' Richards identifies psychoanalysis as one of the causes of the epistemological violence that has been waged upon the 'Magical View of Nature'. Nature, for Richards, is already something like an English suburban garden, as his somewhat breathless indictment of horticultural malaise suggests in the passage which inspires the footnote on Eliot:

> Over whole tracts of natural emotional response we are to-day like a bed of dahlias whose sticks have been removed. And this effect of the neutralisation of nature is only in its beginnings. Consider the probable effects in the near future of the kind of enquiry into basic human constitution exemplified by psychoanalysis.
>
> A sense of desolation, of uncertainty, of futility, of the baselessness of aspirations, of the vanity of endeavour, and a thirst for life-giving water which seems suddenly to have failed, are the signs in consciousness of this necessary reorganisation of our lives. Our attitudes and impulses are being compelled to become self-supporting; they are being driven back upon their biological justification, made once again sufficient to themselves. And the

> only impulses which seem strong enough to continue unflagging are commonly so crude that to more finely developed individuals, they seem hardly worth having.[1]

Small wonder, perhaps, that it was the footnote and not the main body of Richards' text which acquired such notoriety. ('The answer to that', Stephen Spender ripostes impatiently ten years later, 'is "Don't be a dahlia, and you won't need a stick!"').[2] The vandal in the garden is psychoanalysis which has removed the stick of belief by uncovering unconscious drive-invested impulses so crude, Richards notes, that 'they seem hardly worth having'.

Where Trilling will later make a virtue out of the fact that psychoanalysis drives us back to our 'biological justification', Richards, who once said that he began his study of physiology with the intention of becoming a psychoanalyst, is more troubled by the cultural implications of desire.[3] Even when psychoanalytic 'stories are duly discounted', he argues in 'A Psychological Theory of Value', 'enough which is verifiable remains for *infans polypervers* to present a truly impressive figure dominating all future inquiry into value.'[4] One way to read Richards' footnote, then, is as a possible solution to this threat to value posed, in part, by psychoanalysis. Eliot, says Richards, 'by effecting a complete severance between his poetry and *all* beliefs [...] has shown the way to the only solution of these difficulties. "In the destructive element...that was the way."'[5] *The Waste Land* offers a 'perfect emotive description' of a crisis of value that psychoanalysis, among other sciences, has laid bare: a 'pseudo-statement' which because it relinquishes any claim to belief, can order and, thereby, transcend the damage that it at the same time diagnoses. To suggest that Richards developed his own theory of value in response to psychoanalysis' threat to value would be to misconstrue his project; yet there remains a noteworthy tension here between psychoanalysis and the construction of Richards' own literary principles which can shed light on how the question of value in each discourse became inextricable from shifting definitions of the destructive element.

Far from overtly inflating the value of art, Practical Criticism prided itself in its attacks on traditional notions of aesthetic value. In *Principles of Literary Criticism* Richards puts paid to the 'phantom of the aesthetic state' by proposing what looks like a thoroughly democratic theory of pleasure and value. Richards wants a psychology of value which will dispense with idealism and offer an alternative to Fry's and Bell's aestheticism. Value, hence, is not to be defined via the category of the aesthetic; rather, as with Freud, and similarly following G.T. Fechner, Richards proposes an economic theory that equates value with the reduction of tension: 'anything is valuable which satisfies an appetency.'[6] The key to satisfying an appetency lies in the development of an organized system that can keep conflicting impulses in balance. Against the implied totalitarianism of an 'aesthetic state' a well-ordered individual psychology acts as a microcosm of the balanced liberal state. Like Freud, Richards recognizes that such an organization of impulses on a cultural level requires a sacrifice on the part of the individual. But where Freud is pessimistic about the exorbitant price to be paid for this entrance into culture (as in *Civilization and Its Discontents*), Richards, owing more to Bentham (like his collaborator C.K. Ogden), is more sanguine: 'By the extent of the loss, the range of impulses thwarted or starved, and their degree of importance, the merit of a systematization is judged. That organization which is least wasteful of human possibilities is, in short, the best'.[7] No use crying over the milk spilt by the *infans polypervers* in its journey, in Richards' terms, to the acquisition of value: waste not, want not.

But phantoms of the aesthetic state are not only illusory; like other ghosts they also have a habit of returning to haunt the site of their supposed exorcism. As Steven Connor has argued, Richards' apparent continuum between disorganized appetencies and aversions, and their development towards equipoise and organization, quickly hardens into an opposition between good and bad art.[8] While he maintains that aesthetic experiences are 'only a further development, a finer organization of ordinary experiences, and not in the least a new or different kind of thing',[9] this finer organization of art also offers an economy that is not available in common experience: 'the experiences which the arts offer are not obtainable, or but rarely, elsewhere. Would that they were! They are not incomplete; they might be better described as ordinary experiences completed'.[10] Art completes, because of its superior organization of impulses, what ordinary experience leaves unfinished. The value of *The Waste Land*, therefore, lies in nothing so snobbish as its intellectual allusions, but 'in the unified response which this interaction creates in the right reader'.[11] This is the poetically correct reader of Practical Criticism (the *bête noire* of anyone who has struggled to demonstrate Richards' point in the course of their literary education). To be immersed in the destructive element in this sense is to subscribe to a view that redeems waste through a critical economy that transmutes conflict into balanced equipoise. Or, as Richards puts it in his revised version of the footnote in his later *Science and Poetry,* Eliot finds a 'new order through the contemplation and exhibition of disorder'.[12]

Dahlias, then, have nothing to lose but their sticks, as Practical Criticism begins to put right the damage done by psychoanalysis in the garden of value. But removing the sticks of belief, like banishing the ghost of aesthetic idealism, is easier said than done. Richards bases his claims on a thoroughly modern theory of value: 'The view that what we need in this tempestuous turmoil of change is a Rock to shelter under or to cling to, rather than an efficient aeroplane to ride it, is comprehensible, but mistaken.'[13] But the rhetoric of redemption is never far away. In his appendix to *Principles of Literary Criticism,* 'The Poetry of T.S Eliot', Richards revises his earlier reading of the poem. Not only does the poem immerse us in the destructive element, here Richards also introduces Eliot's 'persistent concern with sex, the problem of our generation, as religion was the problem of the last'.[14] Perhaps in the light of this new association with sex, Richards, no doubt also responding to Eliot's own corrective complaints, ends with an implicit qualification of his earlier reading:

> There are those who think that [Eliot] merely takes his readers into the Waste Land and leaves them there, that in this last poem he confesses his impotence to release the healing waters. The reply is that some readers find in his poetry not only a clearer, fuller realization of their plight, the plight of a whole generation, than they find elsewhere, but also through the very energies set free in that realization a return of the saving passion.[15]

The rhetoric of redemption here might quite reasonably be said to belong not to Richards but to his – carefully placed – 'some readers'. Notwithstanding, Richards' language correlates eloquently with a thesis that sees art as completing experience and as thereby restoring value in a world gripped by a crisis in belief. It is as if, finally, the 'impressive figure' of the polymorphously perverse infant has been promoted to the status of the aesthetically and culturally valuable: the baselessness of contemporary life that this figure signifies is refracted back to us through poetry, not only as a monument to our desolation, but as an icon of possible salvation through suffering. Something, it might be said, has just crawled under a rock; or as Eliot later says of Richards' criticism, drawing the obvious parallel with Arnold, this is ultimately 'salvation by poetry'.[16]

While it is true to say that Richards, in contrast to Eliot and American New Criticism, is reconciled to producing a form of scientific criticism for a secular culture, something perhaps of that unconscious Christianity that Eliot wanted criticism to preserve remains here.[17] This is precisely the point that William Empson, steadfastly opposed to religious criticism throughout his career (particularly in his later work), makes in his astute appendix on value in *The Structure of Complex Words* (dedicated to Richards '[w]ho is the source of all ideas in this book, even the minor ones arrived at by disagreeing with him'). Richards, says Empson, 'need not be as secure against the religions as he intended to be'.[18] It is the lack of qualification in Richards' theory of value, Empson argues, that issues a back-door invitation to the kinds of dangerous idealism that Richards wants to get rid of. Once again this debate about value is caught up in a conversation with psychoanalysis. Empson points out that by defining value as the achievement of equilibrium through the reduction of tension, Richards runs tantalizingly close to reproducing a version of Freud's death drive. As Empson puts it in an apparently un-posted letter to Richards from Peking in 1933: 'Freud's dim but rich concept of death wishes come in here: one sense of it is certainly that all impulses are reactions to a stimulus aiming at the removal of the stimulus'.[19] As long as value is defined solely in terms of the achievement of equilibrium, the democratic balance Richards aims for risks carrying with it a more deathly proposition. And if this is the case, there is nothing to stop the *infans polypervers* from re-emerging as a problem for value. Richards' claims about the sublimatory values of 'balanced' impulses, says Empson, 'still [don't] face the issue that this may be done badly: it is just this process that sends energy into perverse desires that give pain when unsatisfied and no pleasure when satisfied'.[20] As Empson reintroduces psychoanalysis into the debate he also exposes the internal limits of Richards' version of the destructive element: immersing oneself in a world of no belief armed only with a stoically utilitarian theory of value is finally no protection from those other, less civilized, destructive elements identified by psychoanalysis. The waste, that surplus of thwarted and starved impulses that Richards wanted to channel into his version of a useful life, remains.

Far from offering a solution to the crisis of value, Richards leaves us with a question that elsewhere Empson identifies as pertaining to psychoanalysis: 'what version of a perversion is to be admired'?[21] This is the question that Empson addresses to himself in 'Death and Its Desires' which he drafted in the same year as his letter to Richards. It is not (it could hardly be) perversion *per se* that worries Empson here, but the extent to which death wishes in art degenerate into forms of weak mysticism and unwarranted pessimism – corrupted versions of the destructive element which Richards' theory of value, by implication, cannot guard against. Empson finds the purest version of the destructive element, or the death wish, like Eliot before him, in the Fire Sermon of the Buddha, and describes Nirvana in terms which directly recall Richards' praise of Eliot: 'The main effect of the doctrine ... is to remove *all* doctrinal props about immortality and still claim that death is somehow of the highest value'.[22] Empson particularly relishes the way the Fire Sermon achieves this without Christianity's morbid fascination with spectacles of sacrificial death – his is a dip in the destructive element without a voyeuristic pay-off. Elsewhere Empson thinks of this distinction in terms of the difference between the 'return to a narcissistic state of being' (Nirvana) and 'corpse lust' (voyeuristic sadism) and notes how irritating it is not to be sure which version of the death wish a work of art is offering you – which version of perversion (*The Waste Land* might be a case in point).[23] It is difficult (although probably wrong-headed) not to suspect that Empson is engaged in some irreverent shadow-boxing with Richards here. Where Richards chooses the scene out of *Lord Jim* in which the Bavarian butterfly collector and trader, Stein, lectures Marlow on the ways of non-being ('with the exertions of your hands and feet in the water make the deep, deep sea keep you up')[24] in order to register the profundity of Eliot's disassociation of belief, Empson offers us English pastoral in the form of T.F. Powys ('death like the clown is a sort of perverse figure of pastoral'). In 'John Pardy and the Waves', Powys' Molloy-like tramp character concludes his search for happiness by immersing himself in the waves. Empson paraphrases:

> Passing on to count the waves of the sea he was told by the waves that if he joined them he could not only destroy himself

> but become one of the great elements of destruction and perhaps take part in a typhoon to destroy a city.[25]

'In the destructive element...'. Because it is pastoral, what's important to Empson is the extent to which the genre mystifies or normalizes existing social and economic relations. Such is the case with Powys' treatment of death; 'this indefatigable game of talking about death must be a mere blind; the use of death wishes in such literature is only to protect something else'.[26] Powys domesticates the destructive element, and on these grounds Empson charges him with something like bad faith. In the same paper Empson makes a similar charge against R.E. Money-Kyrle, the psychoanalyst who was to become one of Melanie Klein's most trustworthy and steadfast supporters. It is Money-Kyrle, perhaps, who by driving the death instinct to its logical and extreme conclusion, also produces the most grotesque parody of Richards' theory of value: 'the quickest and most final method by which an individual can remove his needs' he advises 'is to put his head in a gas-oven'.[27]

Empson and Richards remind us that while Valentine Cunningham is right to argue that the destructive element is caught up within a general apocalyptic rhetoric of the 1920s and 1930s, the phrase also has a specific theoretical and moral history. For Richards the struggle was to find a model of criticism that could redeem a world out of step with its own values; 'redeem' both in the sense of atone, and in the economic sense of to reclaim what's yours, or to make good the waste. In his 1935 revision of *Science and Poetry*, he increases the political stakes of his theory of value: the Treaty of Versailles, Richards notes, is no longer sustainable, what we need is 'a League of Nations for the moral ordering of the impulses; a new order based on conciliation, not on attempted suppression'.[28] World War Two blasted that illusion apart (notoriously, literary studies took somewhat longer to wake up to the ideological anachronisms of Practical Criticism). Empson, by contrast, cautions against the valorization of the destructive element, all too aware, perhaps, that the apparent fair-mindedness of a League of Nations, pushed to its conclusion, offers scant protection against the punitive moralities of 1919. As such, Empson moves beyond the impasses of Richards' individualist psychology and shifts to what we could cautiously read as a more 'properly' psychoanalytic critical terrain.

Perhaps the best example of this is Empson's wonderful reading of Herbert's 'The Sacrifice' in *Seven Types of Ambiguity*. Empson's debt to Freud is overt in his chapter on the seventh type of ambiguity. Empson's seventh type bears a mark of repression so that, in his words, the ambiguity both carries the 'notion of what you want and involves the notion that you must not take it'.[29] In Empson's deft hands, Herbert's doctrinal monologue on the suffering of Christ has, thus, to be read double. What emerges in his exemplary reading of the poem is a fusion of both 'the love of Christ' *and* 'the vindictive terrors of the sacrificial idea': Christ's suffering is at the same time the suffering of his betrayers; his agony also translates as a desire for retribution, a wished for agony of his torturers; 'I may *cleave their hearts* with my tenderness or with their despair'; Christ is both sinless and a criminal. In other words the founding act of New Testament law is built upon a love that can barely conceal the hate and vindictiveness that sustain it. It 'is true that George Herbert is a cricket in the sunshine', Empson concludes, 'but one is accustomed to be shocked on discovering the habits of such creatures; they are more savage than they seem'.[30] The idea that civilization is more savage than it seems was, of course, precisely the point that Freud made in *Civilization and Its Discontents* (published in the same year as *Seven Types*). The command that one should 'Love thy neighbour', Freud points out, is built upon the hostility we feel for our neighbours ('*Homo homini lupus*'). By signing up to Christian ethics, civilization puts 'a positive premium on being bad.'[31] It is this version of the destructive element, of a violence at the core of culture, that concerns Klein (Freud footnotes Klein twice in *Civilization*), and will later come to dominate debates within British psychoanalysis during World War Two. In 1930 Empson adds a timely literary codicil to Freud's thesis. 'Herbert', he concludes, 'deals in this poem, on the scale and by the methods necessary to it, with the most complicated and deeply-rooted notion of the human mind.'[32] Neither Freud nor Klein would have disagreed.

Empson, on the other hand, would not have agreed that in his reading of Herbert he was moving on to a more 'properly' psychoanalytic domain. In his 1947 preface to *Seven Types* he regrets that 'the topical interest of Freud distracted [him]'. The reading of Herbert, Empson now claims, was not 'concerned with neurotic disunion but with a fully public theological poem'[33] (Freud, for one, might have replied that it was precisely the coming together of personal neurosis and the publicly theological that was at issue). To some extent, Empson's disclaiming caveats are a typical expression of British modernism's tendency to fix psychoanalysis as a form of regressive individualism which must be resisted at all costs. (Wyndham Lewis, for example, discounts Richards on the grounds of this stereotype: 'Mr. Richards is after all a psycho-analyst: and everything in the psycho-analyst promotes self-consciousness.')[34] Writing in 1947, seventeen years after *Seven Types* and *Civilization*, Empson's characterization of the relation between psychoanalysis and modernist criticism is typical: 'Some literary critics at the time were prepared to "collaborate" with the invading psycho-analysts, whereas the honest majority who were prepared to fight in the streets either learned fire-watching technique or drilled with the Home Guard'.[35] Typically perhaps for Empson, this disclaimer of psychoanalysis is curiously psychoanalytic: compare Freud's description of the ego as 'a kind of frontier-station with a mixed garrison' that may or may not collaborate with the symptom, the 'foreign body'.[36] The passage is also anachronistic: Empson pastes the rhetoric of World War Two over an earlier historical moment (while psychoanalytic ideas invaded the English intellectual scene throughout the 1920s, the psychoanalysts themselves did not really begin to 'invade' until the 1930s). It is as if the in-fighting of modernist criticism can only be couched in the language of war-time Britain: psychoanalysis is the alien invader, English literary criticism is the plucky Home Guard. The components of England's national culture, one senses, are already beginning to harden. What happens to this picture of modernist criticism and psychoanalysis if, taking a cue from Empson's more pro-psychoanalytic moments, we re-read the aesthetics of the destructive element in collaboration with psychoanalysis? Do the destructive elements of psychoanalysis, as Richards feared, present a threat to cultural value? Or is psychoanalysis too, as Leo Bersani has recently suggested, ultimately complicit with attempts to redeem and transcend the crisis of the modern with a form of aesthetic compensation? These are the questions I want to look at in the rest of this chapter by turning to the work of Klein who, at the same time that Richards was drilling us in the ordering of the impulses, was working her own extraordinary way through the destructive element.

* * *

> All creation is really a re-creation of a once loved and once whole, but now lost and ruined object, a ruined internal world and self. It is when the world within us is destroyed, when it is

> dead and loveless, when our loved ones are in fragments, and we ourselves in helpless despair – it is then that we must re-create our world anew, reassemble the pieces, infuse life into the dead fragments, re-create life.
>
> Hanna Segal, 'A Psycho-Analytical Approach to Aesthetics'[37]

This is how Hanna Segal, Klein's most influential interpreter, reads Proust in the light of a Kleinian approach to aesthetics in the first paper she presented to the British Psycho-Analytical Society. Twenty years on it is as if Richards' reading of Eliot creating 'a new order through the contemplation of disorder' ends up precisely where Lewis suspected it would – in the internal world of the 'self'. For Segal, Proust's writing exemplifies the aesthetic at the heart of Klein's concept of reparation in which sublimation and creativity are seen as the end products of a process whereby the subject attempts to restore and make good the violence it has done to its objects in phantasy. Writing just after the war and after Klein's relatively successful battle with Anna Freud in the 1940s, Segal gives a theoretical coherence to her mentor's work. This seeming coherence of Klein's reparative theories has, until very recently, led on the one hand, to its being praised for the extent to which Klein stresses the therapeutic nature of the arts and, among some feminists, for her mother-centred view of creativity whilst, on the other, its being criticized for its theoretical crudity and ideological normativity.[38] But Klein's writing is not a seamless and coherent whole. Spanning forty years, her work on unconscious phantasy and early oedipality, and her insistence on the primacy of aggression and later envy, testifies to a body of theory in constant struggle with the psychoanalytic concepts Klein is attempting to reformulate.[39] In other words, even though today the concept of reparation might suggest a reductive and normative view of the place of the psyche in cultural production, the history of the theoretical processes of Klein's thinking tells a very different story.

This story is not, of course, solely caught up in the history of psychoanalysis. Just as Richards called upon the League of Nations to provide a political model for his psychological theory of value, so too does Kleinism traffic with the rhetoric of the inter-war years. This traffic can no more simply be described as proof that psychoanalysis may be understood as the sum of historical contingencies that produced it (which is true), than it can be put forward as testament to the efficacy of psychoanalysis as a form of historical interpretation (which is also true): the relation between psychoanalysis and history is, notoriously and rightly, more knotted and complex. One such knot ties itself around the word 'reparation'. Like redemption, reparation carries with it both the spiritual sense of salvation and atonement and economic connotations of compensation and dues collected. When in 1919 reparation entered the European vocabulary with a new political charge, it also took on two more meanings: first, as the OED puts it 'compensation for war damage owed by the aggressor' and second, as a direct result of the former, reparation, in an Empsonian manner, began to haemorrhage into almost the opposite of the rightful justice it was supposed to connote. For vocal if not ultimately influential sections of the European intelligentsia as well as for those suffering under the terms of the treaty, reparation came to mean something exorbitant, excessive and punitive, in short, an invitation to more aggression. Re-read those passages from Keynes' *The Economic Consequences of the Peace* (1919) where he talks of the 'imbecile greed' of the 'Reparation Chapter' in the Treaty of Versailles and of the shame that any one involved in its writing should undoubtedly feel,[40] and then fast-forward to 1936 when Melanie Klein, Austrian emigrant, begins *Love, Guilt and Reparation*, her part of the public lectures she gave with Joan Rivière (*The Emotional Life of Civilized Men and Women*), by pointing out that 'only when consideration has been given to the part destructive impulses play in the interaction of hate and love, is it possible to show the ways in which feelings of love and tendencies to reparation develop in connection with aggressive impulses.'[41] In the period between the wars, reparation, in a Kleinian as well as Empsonian sense, is pregnant with the destructive element.

Such associations are worth bearing in mind in the context of Leo Bersani's provocative reading of modernism and psychoanalysis. In the essay which opens *The Culture of Redemption*, Bersani reads Klein alongside Proust (in, perhaps, irreverent homage to Segal). Klein, he argues, 'makes normative' Proust's mortuary aesthetics; in other words, Kleinism is ultimately complicit with what Bersani sees as the dominant morality of the redemptive ethos behind literary modernism. His argument is worth looking at in some detail both because it sheds light on some of the redemptive strategies I have been tracing so far, and because Bersani raises the question of the extent to which psychoanalysis can indeed be seen as attempting to achieve a kind of moral transcendence out of the destructive elements that were, by the 1920s and 1930s, quickly forming the bedrock of contemporary Kleinism.

Where Segal reads death in Proust as a metaphor for the psychic recreation of the self, Bersani reveals a more ambivalent aesthetic at the heart of Proust's writing, which he then reads across to psychoanalysis' own troubled relation to the question of sublimation. On the one hand, death for Proust potentially marks the loss of self-authority, in so far as the death of the other marks the loss of our image in their minds, thus rupturing the dream of self-representation and recreating the world – not as a rediscovery of order within the self – but in terms of our absence from it. On the other hand, death in *A la recherche du temps perdu* is a completely self-appropriating gesture: once our loved ones are in fragments, to re-phrase Segal, only our image of the lost one remains and the authority to make or re-make them goes uncontested. With this reading Bersani makes explicit the relation between literary representation and the authority of the self which Segal appears to leave mute. Such undecidability – self-possession or self-annihilation – is repeated in the novel's infamous autobiographical and narrative complexity and, argues Bersani, is produced and sustained by a dominant conception in Proust's writing of 'art as a remedial completion of life'. As for Richards, for Proust too this working through of the relation between art and experience newly figures the truth value of art. Within the Proustian narrative, says Bersani,

> Art ... is 'real' to the degree that it discovers and expresses a pre-existent truth; it is 'factitious' to the extent that it produces a 'truth' of its own, a 'truth' derived from the conditions and constraints of literary performance.[42]

Art derives truths from experience from which it then produces a new version of experience. It is something of a pseudo-statement; as in Richards, here too art is real to the extent that it begins with 'ordinary experience' and factitious in so far as it can only be believed on its own terms. Art thus redeems experience and hence brings it, for Bersani, under the 'corrective will' of the ego: identity triumphs over difference, as death 'permits the resurrection of others as redemptive truths'[43] – the cult of the ego, which Empson, as well as Lewis, once suspected might be found lurking in Richards' theory of value, now shows its true colours.[44] But Bersani, and of course Proust, are both far more wily than this implies. Because in Proust to recreate the other for the self also introduces the possibility of an end to self-authority, his version of the redemptive hypothesis has the potential for a different model of literary representation: one in which, as Bersani demonstrates through a close reading of *Sodome et Gomorrhe*, 'the unprecedented visibility of past appearances' is allowed free play, and through which contact with the phenomenal world is renewed. In this model, experience is not redeemed through art, rather art itself is the precondition for a re-emergence of difference.

In what ways, then, is psychoanalysis complicit with Proust's double-edged redemptive aesthetic? At its most simple, sublimation is presumed to take place when an instinct has been diverted to a new, non-sexual and socially valued aim. This is a thesis which, once put into practice, frequently succumbs to the temptation to read works of art as if they were simply culturally valued symptoms and one that, by stressing art's compensatory function, is readily pressed into the service of the most normative accounts of the relation between sexuality and art. For Bersani, however, psychoanalytic readings of art are themselves symptoms of the theory's difficult relation to its own more radical propositions about the relation between sexuality and culture. In the case of Klein, Bersani detects one such radical proposition in her 1923 paper on inhibition and sublimation, 'Early Analysis'. Typically, an inhibition takes place when a strong primary pleasure has been repressed due to its sexual content. What Bersani finds so radical about Klein here is her insistence that inhibition can only occur when an ego-tendency has already been sublimated. This originary sublimation is not the result of repression, but is defined by Klein in terms of a '"superfluous libido in a cathexis of ego-tendencies"'.[45] Sublimation, in this version, is hence propelled by a type of 'libidinal economy' unfettered, so it appears, by the tyranny of culturally redemptive symbol formations. As a consequence, art can no longer be seen as a form of compensation or substitution because, for Bersani, Klein displaces the very category of representation (whereby one sign – 'athletic movements of all kinds', to borrow an example from Klein – is substituted for another 'stand in for penetrating the mother'), that is commonly presumed by the theory of sublimation. Accordingly, it is not symbol formation, in the sense that one non-sexual activity replaces an originary pleasure on the basis of similarity that underpins this cathexis of ego-tendencies here, but a promiscuous non-referential form of identification. 'In sublimation, the ego activities become "symbols" in the sense that the most diverse cultural activities "symbolize" the libidinal energy with which they are invested'. That waste of drives and impulses which worried Richards becomes, in Bersani's reading, the basis of Klein's anti-redemptive thesis: in his words, 'the drive in question would be, precisely, an aimless one, a kind of floating signifier of sexual energy.'[46]

This 'libidinal' Klein, proffering a theory of psychic expenditure without return, is a far cry from the popular image of the child analyst absorbed in the destructive elements of the human psyche and the omnipresence of a super-moral guilt. For Bersani, it is precisely Klein's growing interest in aggression and anxiety that turns her earlier transgressive theory of sublimation into what will later become a discourse of cultural redemption. Like many of her critics, what bothers Bersani about the later Klein is her insistence on the primacy of phantasy. It is through phantasy that, in what Klein eventually calls the 'paranoid-schizoid position', the premature ego will attempt to defend itself from the anxiety provoked by its own aggression projected onto its terrifyingly persecutory and impossibly idealized objects. It is through phantasy, in the 'depressive position', that the infant will recognize and introject its parents, not as fragments, but as whole objects which the infant fears may be lost as a consequence of its own sadism. Again, it is through phantasy that the infant will attempt to repair, to restore and make good the violence that it imagines it has done to these phantasmagoric objects; and it is at this point that sublimation, in the now dominant reparative model, comes into play. What Bersani finds so objectionable about the later Klein is the way that this notion of a 'sexuality that is *born* as aggression' precipitates a theory of reparation as a mode of defence.[47] In flight from its own aggressivity, anxiety, as opposed to Klein's earlier notion of the repetition of pleasure, comes to dominate the infant's identifications. Symbol formation is figured as a means of deflecting this anxiety, leading the infant to make and re-make equations between objects which, increasingly, are not only several removes from the infant's first sexual tie to an object (the breast) but are, crucially in Bersani's account, '*restored versions* of the former.'[48]

Klein then re-joins Proust at this point since for both 'sublimations integrate, unify and restore'. Moreover, what the infant restores is, as with Proust, a qualitatively improved version of what has been lost.

> If the sublimated object is by definition an idealized object – both a mental construct and a 'better' (repaired and made whole) version of an originally dangerous, injured, and fragmented object – we can also say that sublimation is disguised as transcendence.[49]

Read this way, Klein shares not only with Proust, but also with Richards, a contemporary drive towards the valorization of art: the universal law triumphs over the particular, as unification and restoration assure an aesthetic continuity in a world racked by its own aggression. Bersani puts it more forcefully: 'in the culture of redemption, sexuality is consecrated as violence by virtue of the very definition of culture as an unceasing effort to make life whole, to repair a world attacked by desire.'[50]

Once more the spectre of the 'aesthetic state' threatens to re-emerge; this time in the playrooms of child psychoanalysis (Richards, it seems, need not have been so perturbed by the values of the *infans polypervers* after all). On the one hand, this all seems to add up to a pretty damning indictment of two influential currents in inter-war British culture: despite their differences, both Practical Criticism and Kleinian psychoanalysis seem bent on a moralistic endeavour to secure the legitimacy of culture deriving from a shared prognosis of culture's discontents. At the same time, it could be countered that Bersani's version of a more radical anti-redemptive, wasteful, Klein runs her work ahead into a set of recent and less historically localized contexts that were simply not available, or only barely present, to British psychoanalysis in the inter-war period. What happens if we read Klein's version of sublimation as reparation, not so much as depicting a relation between sexuality and the law (which are the key terms for recent post-structuralist psychoanalytic criticism) but as telling a contemporary story about the *social* passage of the destructive element? Further, what happens to the hypothesis of the culture of redemption if we read Klein not as having achieved a form of transcendence for art, but as failing, at crucial moments, to make a moral out of the aggression which is so central to her theory?

* * *

I want to begin with two equally Kleinian propositions concerning the nature of sublimation. The first is from her 1952 essay, 'Some Theoretical Conclusions on the Emotional Life of the Infant'. Klein is describing the desired result of a successful passage through the depressive position which, here, is linked to the growth of genital trends. The *infans polypervers*, in other words, is about to grow up and take its place in a world of sexual difference and cultural value.

> In the interplay between progression and regression, which is strongly influenced by anxiety, genital trends gradually gain the ascendant. As a result, the capacity for reparation increases, its range widens and sublimations gain in strength and stability; for on a genital level they are bound up with the most creative urge of man. Genital sublimations in the feminine position are linked with fertility – the power to give life – and thus with the re-creation of lost or injured objects. In the male position, the element of life-giving is re-inforced by the phantasies of fertilizing and thus restoring or reviving the injured or destroyed mother. The genital, therefore, represents not only the organ of procreation but also the means of creating anew.[51]

The way that sublimation in this passage aids the collapse of a distinction between a psychically positioned sexual difference and the most banal of gender stereotypes reveals Klein at her most notoriously normative. Note here, however, Klein's emphasis on anxiety as a precipitating factor in this sublimation, and also the stress on phantasy and representation in the twin sublimatory myths she offers.

In a much earlier discussion in *The Psychoanalysis of Children* (1932), Klein footnotes Freud to support her claims, central to her entire theory, about the importance of internal destructive impulses in the formation of the super-ego. In this extraordinary passage from *The Ego and the Id* Freud presents sublimation not only in terms of 'de-sexualized Eros', as in his earlier account of sublimation, but in the context of that initial identification with the father from which the super-ego is formed.

> Every such identification is in the nature of a desexualization or even of a sublimation. It now seems as though when a transformation of this kind takes place, an instinctual defusion occurs at the same time. After sublimation the erotic component no

> longer has the power to bind the whole of the destructiveness [Destruktionsneigung] that was combined with it, and this is released in the form of an inclination to aggression and destruction. This defusion would be the source of the general character of the harshness and cruelty exhibited by the ideal – the dictatorial 'Thou Shalt'.[52]

This is the same passage that Edward Glover quotes in his 1931 paper on sublimation where he translates 'the whole of destructiveness' ('Destruktionsneigung') as 'the whole of the destructive elements'. Where Klein's first description of sublimation secured the child's arrival in a world of cultural value (with each gender equipped with its own reparative talents), here sublimation, in the form of identification with the super-ego, signals a loss of authority and the setting loose of aggression and destruction. For Klein, it is as if to take on the law, to sublimate, is at the same time to be immersed in the destructive element.

How is it possible to reconcile these two very different emphases on the value and function of sublimation in Klein? How is it possible to see sublimation as *both* a culturally valued reparation of phantasized destruction and the precipitate of an inclination to violence and aggressivity? What Bersani finds 'redemptive' in Klein is her massive claim for the role of phantasy in the development of the child. Yet, as much as phantasy in Klein provides a narrative of child development and, correspondingly, a model for object relations, it is also the concept through which the ideal of development is undone and, crucially, by which Kleinian analysis troubles any straightforward distinction between subject and object, psyche and culture, transgression and the law. One of the key terms, perhaps *the* key term, which underpins both of these directions in Klein's writing is, as Bersani says, anxiety. It is worth noting that in 1946 Klein, distinguishing her work from Fairbairn's, insists that while 'Fairbairn's approach was largely from the angle of ego-development in relation to objects', hers 'was predominantly from the angle of anxieties and their vicissitudes'.[53] The narrative that leads the infantile ego from a state of indiscretion to self-possession by a gradual modification of its relation to objects that is so often associated with Klein is not, as far as she is concerned, what is at issue in her work.

For Bersani, it is this emphasis on what he calls 'anxious desire' that supports the hypothesis of sublimation as a mode of defence and, hence, leads to the progressive de-realization and consecration of sexuality in Klein. Yet even in 'Early Analysis', in so far as anxiety leads to the inhibition of primary libidinally invested sublimation, it is equally true to say that it is only through the reactivation of anxiety that inhibition can be lifted: 'The fact that the removing of these inhibitions and symptoms takes place by way of anxiety', notes Klein, 'surely shows that anxiety is their source'.[54] Anxiety thus emerges as both a cause *and* an effect of inhibition. This 'doubling' of anxiety, whereby the term emerges as a form of 'prime mover' in psychic processes, is a legacy which Klein inherits from Freud. As with Freud, anxiety has an ambiguous status in Klein's discourse, both motivating her theoretical conclusions and checking them at significant points in a manner very similar to that described by Samuel Weber in his reading of Freud's *Inhibitions, Symptoms and Anxiety*. The question that Weber sees anxiety posing for Freud is one that can equally be applied to Klein's work: 'Is anxiety a constitutive process by which the psyche maintains its coherence and identity or does it ultimately entail their dissolution?'[55] In other words, while anxiety ensures that the ego defends itself, guaranteeing its integrity against a world of difference, it also shatters the coherence of the ego and de-possesses it of authority. For Klein it is anxiety which while 'pre-eminently an inhibiting agency in the development of the individual is at the same time a fundamental factor of importance in promoting the growth of his ego and sexual life'.[56] For Klein, the individual does not so much develop in a straight line from 'A' to 'B' (from the destructive element, for instance, to its transcendence through psychic reparation), but is constantly defined and redefined by the vicissitudes of anxiety.

Freud, as is well known, began by conceptualizing anxiety as an effect of the transformation of libido but, with the advent of the second topography, later moved onto a much more complex reading of anxiety in which he sought to understand the way in which the ego constituted itself, erected its frontiers, through its anxious relations with the outside world. Klein directly engages with this departure in a very dense and detailed discussion of anxiety in *The Psychoanalysis of Children*. In what looks like an argument for the innate primacy of the death drive in the infant (the death drive as provoking anxiety), Klein seizes on the difficulty Freud has in reconciling the fact that while anxiety is a threat which emanates from the *outside* of the psyche, it is also fundamentally experienced as an *internal* threat by the ego. Anxiety arises first from need, a 'situation of helplessness', provoked by absence. This, then, is a relation of exteriority forcing the premature ego to recognize its own helplessness in relation to the outside world. For Klein, this exteriority is repeated internally within the psyche as a response to the death drive: 'We know ... that the destructive instinct is directed against the organism itself and must therefore be regarded by the ego as a danger. I believe it is this danger which is felt by the individual as anxiety.'[57] But although this may look like an argument for the innate primacy of the death drive, it is in fact the phenomenology of that drive, exemplified in Freud's 'Economic Theory of Masochism' (1924), that Klein is drawing on here. So while it might seem as if Klein is simply claiming a monadic autonomy for the psyche, the apparent interiority she sets up within is marked and produced by a crucial dialectic between inside and outside. As such, anxiety focuses attention on a kind of primary masochism of the ego as a condition of its possibility. Discussing the way in which the infant masters its anxiety, Klein states:

> It seems to me that the ego has yet another means of mastering those destructive impulses which still remain in the organism. It can mobilize one part of them as a defence against the other part. In this way the id will undergo a split which is, I think, the first step in the formation of instinctual inhibitions and of the superego which may be the same thing as primal repression. We may suppose that a split of this sort is rendered possible by the fact that, as soon as the process of incorporation has begun, the incorporated object becomes the vehicle of defence against the destructive impulses within the organism.[58]

Klein is laying the ground here for what will later become the 'paranoid-schizoid position'. The threat that anxiety poses is to the integrity of the ego, the *I*; yet what Klein appears to be saying is that it is only in relation to this threat that the I actually constitutes itself as such, through its splitting (primal repression). Klein's famous and scandalous proposition of an early and aggressive super-ego, therefore, does not simply offer a model of a commanding intrusion from the outside coming in to tame primary destructive impulses (the law versus its transgression). Rather anxiety in Klein sets up a model in which the inner phantasy world is marked by a prior exteriority which sets up the interiority of the psyche.

If, according to Bersani's hypothesis, anxiety and aggressivity in Klein lay the ground for an eventual and inevitable scenario of moral redemption, it is equally true to say that, at the same time, anxiety is the concept in Kleinian theory which lays bare the precarious formation of the ego. Klein focuses attention not so much (as Bersani argues) on the ego's defensive attempts to gain authority over its phantasized objects, but on an ever-fragile relation between the ego and its objects, in which what is 'outside' the ego is not only seen as prohibitive and commanding, but also as constitutive of what is felt to be 'inside'.

The imperative at this point in Klein's early work is to extricate the child from the potential solipsism of anxiety implied by this description of the genesis of the ego. This is the solipsism that Bersani is quick to note in Klein's depressive position which, indeed, suggests a model whereby sublimations emerge as the ego's last ditch defence against its own aggression and anxiety. Denial, splitting, omnipotence and idealization characterize the ego's relations to its objects at this point as, under the exacting commands of the super-ego, the desire to make good emerges as just as tyrannical as that to make bad. But, in as much as such mechanisms put the object to death (in Bersani's terms) so that the ego might achieve some integrity by idealizing the world and eradicating difference, they also *repeat* the early anxiety situations that they are supposed to modify. Once more, then, anxiety comes to check and disrupt the very unity and coherence it is meant to ensure. In this context it is worth noting that it is these mechanisms that Kristeva has identified as *destroying* any notion of truth-as-identity (integrity, unity and self-presence) in the Freudian narrative on Moses and, indeed, as characterizing the workings of modernist texts. For her these anxiety-provoked and provoking denials, splittings and disavowals reveal the subject's relation to the real to be caught within a chain of unstable and shifting signifiers which are, ambivalently, taken for the truth (in Kristeva's terms 'the true-real' – which in itself is a contemporary psychoanalytic development of Richards' pseudo-statement). Far from ensuring the authority of the speaking subject, the depressive mechanisms reveal truth to be a 'process of separation' for a subject for whom '*truth* is nothing more than language as a mechanism for displacement, negation and denegation.'[59] In as much as depressive anxiety in Klein reduces a world of potential difference down to a set of redemptive identities, it simultaneously describes the conditions by which the modern subject is deprived of any claim to authority.

It would be a mistake, however, to collapse Klein into Kristeva; whatever the latter's debts to the former, Kristeva's psychoanalytic project, like her modernism, is as culturally and historically specific as Empson's and Richards'. Klein herself never gives up on the goal of a normative arrival (for both the infant and her own theory), through sublimation and reparation, in a world of prescribed cultural values. Quite the contrary. Just as, for Freud, as Weber puts it, the imperative was to prevent his discourse on anxiety becoming itself an 'anxious discourse', so too for Klein, the concept of reparation seems to have been developed with the aim of checking the internal incoherence of her theory.[60] The fact that it is only partially successful in doing so leads us back to the double-requirement in Klein that culture be both redemptive *and* the domain where the destructive element is at its most vociferous. There are two main paths, according to Klein, by which the infant can exit the vicious circle in which anxiety entraps it: first, the ascendancy of the libidinal trends which ensure that Eros eventually triumphs over the death drive, and second, what Klein refers to as 'reality testing', whereby the child becomes better able to reconcile the difference between the inner world of violent phantasy and an outer world of real objects and cultural value. In both cases anxiety once more steps in to disrupt, in the first instance, the idea of a straightforward linear development and, in the second, to trouble the simple binarism of inner phantasies and desires and outer laws and interdicts.

In contrast to Klein's early fidelity to Freud's claim that the first identification of the super-ego means that 'after sublimation the erotic component no longer has the power to bind ... destructiveness', Klein will later insist that sublimation draws on 'libidinal phantasies and desires.'[61] Although it appears that Klein is presenting us with a narrative in which sublimation is assured as Eros gradually gains ascendancy over the death drive in a temporal progression, what in fact emerges is a scenario whereby any progression is marked by a prior, anxiety provoking, regression:

> There is an indissoluble bond between the libido and the destructive tendencies which puts the former to a great extent in the power of the latter. But the vicious circle dominated by the death-instinct in which aggression gives rise to anxiety and

> anxiety reinforces aggression can be broken by the libidinal forces when these have gained in strength; in the early stages of development, the life-instinct has to exert its power to the utmost in order to maintain itself against the death instinct. *But this very necessity stimulates sexual development* [my emphasis].[62]

No progression to libidinal binding then, without a necessary regression to destructiveness and fragmentation. This continual resurgence of anxiety into what looks like a simply developmental account is crucial because it allows us to understand how, in Klein, the law, in the form of the super-ego, not only prohibits libidinal tendencies, it *demands* them:

> the conclusion is that it is the excessive pressure by the super-ego which determines a compulsive instigation of sexual activities, just as it determines a complete suppression of them, that is to say, that anxiety and a sense of guilt reinforces libidinal fixation and heightens libidinal desires.[63]

Nor any libidinal desire then, without the anxiety provoked by the commanding super-ego. The same theoretical logic that requires the child to 'redeem' a dangerous sexuality, to make good its polymorphous sexuality, 'reinforces' and 'heightens' a libidinally invested sexuality. In other words, in as much as the strengthening of the libido guarantees Klein's reparative hypothesis, recreating love out of aggressivity, by the same logic this seemingly culturally redemptive trajectory perpetuates the 'vicious circle' it is supposed to break.

If the super-ego can appear as both the motivation for and the legislator against the libido, this is because, at one level, as the 'internal' representative' of the 'external' parents, it is experienced by the child through phantasy; hence its monstrosity, crude morality and overwhelming perversity. By measuring this phantasy world against the 'real world', Klein later argues, the child gains proof of the essential goodness of its 'real objects'; anxiety is modified and reparation in earnest can begin as the child moves away from the excesses of its polarized phantasmagoria and towards the more measured world of cultural value. But the acquisition of knowledge, in Klein, is also something of an anxious affair. The infant's original anxiety and aggressivity is directly linked with the failure of knowledge to provide an adequate account of its objects. Not only is the child's relation to the outside world already mediated through its phantasies ('the child's sadistic phantasies about the interior of his mother's body lay down for him a fundamental relation to the external world and to reality'),[64] but also, as Klein points out over and over again, knowledge and judgement are inextricable from the drives; hence the 'real' mother 'no more satisfies [the infant's] desire to know than she has satisfied his oral desires.'[65] Reality no more measures up to what Klein calls the infant's epistemological drive (*Wisstrieb*), than it satisfies his oral sadism. The absence of knowledge, the *gap* between drive and object, thus characterizes the infant's quest for reality. What Klein refers to as 'accurate observations and judgement'[66] only secure the ego's relation to the outside world to the extent that they also expose the precarious hold the infant has on reality. 'Reality testing' in Klein no more guarantees the integrity of the ego than it does the success of the supposed reparations it makes on a cultural level.

At each point in Klein's working though of her reparative hypothesis her theory is checked by its own internal inconsistency. It is as if the success of sublimation, in the form of the integration, unification and restoration of a past anxiety-provoking experience is dependent upon a *failure* to square the 'vicious circle' of anxiety, or to 'make good' the destructive element. With this reading in mind, it is possible to reply to Bersani's critique that it is not so much her early hypothesis of a libidinally unbound sexuality that troubles the notion of cultural redemption in Klein, but the way that she produces a theory which, even as it tries to secure a normative narrative of the psyche's role in cultural production, simultaneously reveals the impossibility of achieving such an aim. Indeed, 'normativity' in Klein, as we saw with her reading of the ego's coming into being via the crude morality of the super-ego, is more often than not a form of perversity itself.

If sublimation, for Klein, neither assures aesthetic continuity in a world racked by psychic violence, nor offers an aesthetic site of transgressive pleasure, what, if anything, can Klein tell us about modernism? One possible answer is that Klein pushes redemptive strategies, such as Richards', up to their limits. It was the death drive, remember, that Empson noted shadowed Richards' claims to a moral ordering of the impulses. Running with the death drive, as it were, Klein forces this to its most extreme conclusion: the culture of redemption, for Klein, ultimately testifies to the omnipresence of aggression. This is Kleinism at its bleakest but also perhaps at its strongest. In place of Richards' vision of the well-ordered psychic economy of the reader of modernism, what Klein offers is a version of the ego as continually shattered into culture by the vicissitudes of anxiety. When that anxiety becomes the ground for a thesis that turns on the solipsism of an ego bent on re-creating the world in its own image Klein comes close to endorsing a culture of the death drive. The fact that that same anxiety remains unresolved, on the other hand, opens up the potential for a different kind of reading of the destructive element. This is the legacy that Klein leaves her followers and with which much of the rest of this book is concerned.

2

Is the Room a Tomb? Virginia Woolf, Roger Fry and the Kleinians

A young woman was being conducted round the second exhibition by Roger Fry and complained that she found no beauty in the bulbous legs of three nudes. 'Yes', said Fry, 'but just look at the *gaps* they leave!'

Benedict Nicholson, 'Post-Impressionism and Roger Fry'[1]

'Slim, imperious, challenging, she stands there with a moonlight coloured shawl draped over her shoulders: she has the effect of a magnificent woman of primitive times, who could any day engage in combat with the children of the desert with her naked hands. What a chin! What force there is in the haughty gaze! The blank space has been filled'.

Karin Michaelis, quoted by Melanie Klein[2]

It's a common complaint: there is never just enough of a woman to fill the gaze, but always too little or too much. For Roger Fry in the first quotation above, you get too much woman, or too much of her excess flesh, only if you look in the wrong place. Don't look at the flesh, he instructs his female companion at the second Post-Impressionist exhibition, look at the gaps it makes. This anecdote from Benedict Nicholson exemplifies, all too literally perhaps, the disembodied gaze of Fry's modernist formalism. It is not only the bodies of women that are cancelled out by Fry, but those of the spectators of art too. As Rosalind Krauss has pointed out, Fry also forgets that the eyes that take in the 'artist's vision' are attached to bodies: Fry, she says, is an 'absence in his own field of vision', 'An eye without a body. Pure giver of form. Pure operator of the law.' Or, as Virginia Woolf noted in her biography of Fry: 'Only one subject seemed to escape his insatiable curiosity, and that was himself. Analysis seemed to stop short there.'[3] Woolf herself, by contrast, is renowned for her insatiable curiosity about the self; its depths, its limits, its seeing and its being-seen. But Woolf's selves frequently appear to be as disembodied as Fry's. Her vision of women, Elaine Showalter famously once complained, is 'as deathly as it is disembodied.'[4] Woolf, in this sense, is very much like Fry's companion at the second Post-Impressionist exhibition; she does not care too much for the flesh, but is, perhaps, attracted to the gaps, the spatial form, the negative imprints of bodies of canvas. In the first part of this chapter I argue that something happens to these gaps once they work their way into Woolf's prose. Far from affirming the disinterestedness of her mentor's modernism, Woolf tracks down formalism's phantoms, the repressed of Fry's disembodied gaze. In so doing, she inscribes her own version of the destructive element not, as with Trilling's modernists, to proclaim the authority of the self but, rather, to bear witness to the dissolution of the self's protective frontiers.

If there is too little of woman in Fry's field of vision, in the second quotation there is a little too much. This passage from Karin Michaelis' biography of Ruth Kjär is taken from Klein's 1929 paper, 'Infantile Anxiety-Situations Reflected in a Work of Art and the Creative Impulse.' As its title implies, Klein's excursion into aesthetic criticism is not, at first sight, notable for its critical sophistication. Klein reads Ravel's opera and Colette's libretto of *The Magic Word*, and Karin Michaelis' biography of the artist Ruth Kjär, not so much as works of art, but as privileged case-histories that validate her theories of infantile anxiety and psychic reparation. This is what Kjär has achieved: she has filled her blank space, which is both the blank space of canvas and a psychic space, and has thus restored to her mother the power which, in phantasy, she once robbed her of. Where Fry's aesthetics offer a theory of disembodiment, Klein puts the body back into the field of vision; or more precisely, she inscribes phantasies about the body, frequently sadistic and destructive phantasies, across the (psychic) work of art. This is an art that is born of hate as well as love: 'The daughter's wish to destroy the mother', Klein says of Ruth Kjär, 'is the cause of the need to represent her in full possession of her strength and beauty.'[5] Both art and femininity, for Klein, begin with the destructive element. It is for this reason, maybe, that there seems to be a little too much magnificence, too much of the 'primitive', too much sadism and phallic motherhood in the portrait that Kjär paints of her mother. The aggressive phantasies that the creative impulse is supposed to atone for are encrypted within Kjär's idealized portrait; making good, filling the gap, is a testament to the force of an earlier sadism.

The aesthetic implications of such sadistic remainders returned to bother Klein nearly twenty years later when she confronted William Coldstream's half-finished portrait of herself (commissioned by her ex-analysand Adrian Stokes). The portrait did not conform to Klein's own version of the mother of child psychoanalysis. It did, however, confirm her theories of art. Far from being happy and motherly, as Joan Rivière complained at the time, the Klein in the portrait looked a little too much like the embodiment of her own theories: depressive and melancholic. There were too many persecutory phantasies imbued in the picture for it to work as an accurate portrait. Troubled and disturbed by the message the picture seemed to give about her work Klein insisted on its destruction.[6] It's one thing to put the destructive element into art, it seems, but quite another to know what to do with it. It is in this kind of struggle to contain the destructive elements of phantasy, I argue in the second part of this chapter, that Kleinian writing on art and femininity begins to converge with Woolf's. Imagine, then, that Fry's companion at the second Post-Impressionist exhibition starts to stare at the gaps created by the bulbous legs of the women on the canvas: yes, but look at the psychic price paid for that disembodiment, she cries. Look at the waste.

* * *

Given the energy with which Richards attacks Roger Fry's and Clive Bell's reductive neo-Kantianism in *Principles of Literary Criticism,* it might seem odd to associate his theories of aesthetic value with those of modernist formalism.[7] Richards proposes that art can organize the unwieldy impulses and instincts uncovered by psychoanalysis into higher forms of poise and balance. Fry, on the other hand, determinedly separates 'aesthetic emotions' from what he sees as baser human instincts and emotions. Where Richards brushes up against psychoanalysis in his search for new literary principles, Fry, it seems, repudiates any psychoanalytic understanding of art as a dangerous downgrading of aesthetic value. The theorist of the formalist gaze has no time for the disturbances of vision seized upon by Freud as evidence of the sexual origins of the scopic drive.[8] Active, conscious and detached, Fry's gaze, as Krauss argues, bears the imprint of the cogito of vision beloved of modernist formalism. It is the cognitive pleasures to be found in the gaps, not the libidinal pleasures aroused by the excess of flesh, that appeal to Fry: or as Krauss puts it, Fry's is 'the utterly disinterested, disincarnated passion of the artist's vision'.[9]

Fry's disdain for psychoanalysis is nowhere more evident than in his opprobrious essay, 'The Artist and Psycho-Analysis', read to the British Psychological Society in 1924. In some senses this lecture is a continuation and confirmation of the principles that Fry had worked out in his defence of the two pre-war Post-Impressionist exhibitions. Fry's task then, as he defined it, was to discover 'the visual language of the imagination. To discover, that is, what arrangements of form and colour are calculated to stir the imagination through the stimulus given to the sense of sight.'[10] Fry's firm dismissal of psychoanalysis' tendency to dig around in the sexual origins of art, in his 1924 lecture, reads as one further endeavour to protect the autonomous realm of the visual. But while it may look as if Fry is shaking the detritus of the sexual from his feet as he takes one more step up the high formalist ladder, the background to 'The Artist and Psycho-Analysis' also points to the complex nature of the relation between Bloomsbury and psychoanalysis: 1924 was also the year in which the British Institute of Psycho-Analysis was founded, and the year in which the British Society became the joint publisher of the International Psycho-Analytic Library Series. The Society's partner in this endeavour was Virginia and Leonard Woolf's Hogarth Press. By 1924, psychoanalysis had a cultural visibility which it simply did not have in 1910 and 1911 (the London Psycho-Analytic Society was not formed until 1913). Fry's lecture was responding to psychoanalysis' increasing popularity in the inter-war years, and as with Clive Bell's more rebarbative 'Dr Freud on Art' (published in the same year in *Nation and Athenaeum*), is as polemical as it is theoretical.

In 'The Artist and Psycho-Analysis' Fry rehearses a set of formalist axioms familiar from his earlier essays. Whereas previously his task had been to defend Post-Impressionism, here his job is to defend art from psychoanalysis. The same hierarchical compulsion, the tendency to imbue the gaze with different aesthetic (and frequently moral) gradations that marked his earlier writing persists. There are two types of art, says Fry, the art of women novelists and popular culture, and a higher art concerned with the contemplation of formal relations. Psychoanalysis is rejected as a critical hermeneutic for the latter, because the emotional and instinctual relations that it uncovers are amenable only to an understanding of popular and, by implication, effeminate pleasures:

> The vast majority of people have no notion whether the form of God Save the King has been finely constructed and capable of arousing esthetic emotion or not. They have never, properly speaking, heard the form because they have passed at once into that richly varied world of racial and social emotion which has gathered around it.[11]

Although psychoanalysis, like the masses, can appreciate that 'richly varied world of racial and social emotion', it cannot account for the purely 'aesthetic emotion'. Lacking an understanding of the aesthetic, psychoanalysis threatens cultural value by confirming those 'racial and social' emotions which the majority respond to in popular art. It is as if Fry is suggesting that the majority do not need psychoanalysis because they have already 'passed at once', without the aid of analysis, into the unconscious. This looks new, but Fry had long associated unconscious instincts toward gratification with the popular pleasures of modernity. There is a practical look, he had argued in 1919, an instinctive gaze we use when we shop; it has some discrimination ('Some of us can tell Canadian cheddar at a glance, and no one was ever taken in by sham suede gloves'), but lacks the disinterested coherence of creative vision.[12] In his 1924 lecture Fry, like other modernist opponents of psychoanalysis, collapses its claims to be a science of desire into the idea that psychoanalysis promotes desire itself. Just as 'popular, commercial or impure art' subordinates the coherence of formal design to 'excitation of the emotions associated with objects', so too, for Fry, does psychoanalysis allow the libido to roam rough-shod over art: both are a threat to aesthetic value.[13]

Steven Connor has argued that in trying to maintain these distinctions between different kinds of value Fry's thesis converges with Richards'. Having aligned pleasure with value and having rejected Fry and Bell's argument that art is *sui generis*, Richards was still faced with having to distinguish those pleasures which belong to a wider socio-political field from the sphere of 'good art'. The 'aesthetic resolution', the argument that art organizes those impulses by which Richards attempts to effect this division, ultimately fails to prevent his theory from becoming caught up in the very processes of value and discrimination for which Richards is simultaneously trying to legislate.[14] No more than Richards can Fry quite prevent those condemned areas of cultural and social emotion associated with a psychoanalytic understanding of art from creeping back into his theories of modernist autonomy. 'What', asks Fry towards the end of 'The Artist and Psycho-Analysis', 'is the psychological meaning of this emotion about forms and what is its relation to the desire for truth which is the only disinterested passion we know of – what, if any, are their relations to the libido and the ego?'[15] Fry's answer, as Hanna Segal will later point out, is curiously psychoanalytic, in that it shares with psychoanalysis a notion of the repetition and spatialization of previous emotions.[16] Pure art, according to Fry, 'seems to derive an emotional energy from the very conditions of our existence by its revelation of an emotional significance in time and space'. Having allowed these presumably non-aesthetic emotions a place in his theory, Fry is quick to turn this into a form of redemptive ascesis: 'we get an echo of the emotion without the limitation and particular direction which it had in experience'.[17] Pure art is not only the repetition, but the valorized de-realization of experience. Even so, as Fry struggles to discriminate between the more brute primary pleasures of the masses and the aesthetic emotions of pure art, primary and instinctive gratifications continually re-emerge in his attempt to protect the autonomy of art. 'It will be seen, then', he had already concluded in 'An Essay in Aesthetics' (1919), that art 'arouse[s] emotions in us by playing upon what one may call the overtones of our primary physical needs'.[18]

Fry's is no straightforward formalism. As he extricates the aesthetic from psychoanalysis, his writing is a compelling testament to a familiar modernist anxiety about the relation between the emotions provoked by high art and those present in the socio-cultural field. In the attempt to demonstrate how art transcends culture, Fry continually poses the dilemmas involved in separating the purely aesthetic from the primary physical needs uncovered by psychoanalysis. It may be true to say, as the psychoanalyst Barbara Low indeed did at the time, that Fry is simply wrong about psychoanalysis; nonetheless these dilemmas remain instructive.[19] While Fry continues to fetishize the autonomous realm of the visual at the expense of the drive-invested body, what looks like a straightforward denial in his writing can also be read as a disavowal: Fry knows the aesthetic realm cannot be autonomous, but all the same he will continue to promote it as such.

It is the precarious nature of this 'all the same' that calls for further attention. In 'Some Motifs in Baudelaire', Walter Benjamin points to the way that since the end of the nineteenth century philosophy 'has made a series of attempts to lay hold of the "true experience" as opposed to the kind that manifests itself in the standardized, denatured life of the civilized masses'. For Benjamin, this distinction is as much an *effect*, as it is an understanding, of a change in the structure of experience. Philosophy's point of departure 'understandably enough' was not man's life in society. What [it] evoked was poetry, preferably nature, and, most recently, the age of myths.'[20] This is a tradition which begins with Dilthey's *Das Erlebnis und die Dichtung*, and finds its political apotheosis in the theories of Klages (the German philosopher, psychologist and exponent of vitalism and characterology) and Jung who both, says Benjamin, have a common cause with Fascism. In a different register, it is found in Bergson and Freud and is subverted in Proust and, of course, Baudelaire. Where Klages and Jung attempt to immunize a higher experience, a mythological existence for example, from contemporary social life (hence their mystificatory political danger), Proust and Baudelaire aestheticize experience in order to dramatize the way modernity atrophies experience. Where the former deny alienation, in other words, the latter display it.

Fry is clearly part of this tradition. We should not, however, be too quick to associate Fry's claims to the 'true experience' of aesthetic form with an unproblematic flight from historical, social and, in the context of his rejection of psychoanalysis, sexual experience. Although Fry's theories can indeed be read as a phobic and conservative response to the fracturing of contemporary experience, at the same time they continually bear the marks of the social and cultural forces that gave rise to them. For Fry, art permits the reflection that is denied by everyday experience. Contemporary life, with its speed and overactive mental stimuli, enforces an economy of vision. In the everyday, says Fry, 'the emotions we actually experience are too close to us to enable us to feel them clearly. They are in a sense unintelligible'. However, in the mirror of art

> it is easier to abstract ourselves completely, and look upon the changing scene as a whole. It then, at once, takes on the visionary

> quality, and we become true spectators, not selecting what we see, but seeing everything equally, and thereby we come to notice a number of appearances and relations of appearances which could have escaped our notice before, owing to that perpetual economising by selection of what impressions we will assimilate, which in life we perform by unconscious processes.[21]

Where, for Benjamin, Proust and Baudelaire offer aesthetic fragments of experience in the form of critique, Fry promotes the aesthetic as a means of solace which promises a retreat from the frenetic pace of the everyday and facilitates a reflexive grasp of experience: a cogito of vision in the autonomous aesthetic realm. Nonetheless – or perhaps 'all the same' – Fry also suggests that art is the means by which we become *conscious* of the emotions and experiences which modernity consigns to the unconscious. This is nothing like an acknowledgement of social alienation. If anything, Fry is concerned to preserve what Benjamin calls the 'aura' of aesthetic emotion. Note, however, the way that Fry praises art for its ability to demystify those processes which modernity designates as unconscious. Through art, he says, we 'come to notice a number of appearances and relations of appearances' which in life are performed 'by unconscious processes'. Is art, for Fry after all, something like a pseudo-psychoanalysis? One, perhaps, that in different hands holds out the possibility of critique?

* * *

It is well known that Woolf, Fry's biographer, devoted friend and an admirer, as well as the publisher, of 'The Artist and Psycho-Analyst', rehearses many of Fry's axioms in her writing.[22] This affinity is something that Fry himself was quick to note: Survage, he says in his 1919 review of French Art at the Mansard Gallery, does 'precisely the same thing in paint that Mrs. Woolf does in prose' (and adds 'Only I like intensely such sequences of ideas present to me in Mrs. Virginia Woolf's prose, and as yet I have a rather strong distaste for Survage's visual statements').[23] These ideas can be found in Woolf's 'The Mark on the Wall' (1917), the first text published by the Hogarth Press (in the same volume as Leonard Woolf's short story 'The Three Jews'). Fry praised Woolf's story for what he referred to as its 'plasticity'.[24] It is not only the formal qualities of the piece that would have attracted him: Woolf's aesthetic credo too would have been familiar. Life is not arranged in conformity to Edwardian realist conventions, nor can consciousness be determined by everyday appearances. Life is a dazzling array of impressions, and consciousness, likewise, a series of reflecting, transient, mirrors: 'the novelists in the future will realise more and more the importance of these reflections ... those are the depths they will explore, those the phantoms they will pursue, leaving the description of reality more and more out of their stories, taking a knowledge of it for granted'.[25] In a characteristic *mise-en-abîme,* what Woolf proposes as the novel of the future is a description of the 'The Mark', which explores the depths of one consciousness as it meditates on a puzzling mark on the wall. Not so much a story (there is even less narrative action here than there is in 'Kew Gardens' (1919), Woolf's other formalist experiment written in the same year), 'The Mark' is an essay on the pursuit of the phantoms of consciousness. Woolf's formalism, her 'plasticity', is articulated as a powerful desire for a primordial and pre-discursive state where consciousness is stripped of all socially associative meaning:

> But after life. The slow pulling down of thick green stalks so that the cup of the flower, as it turns over, deluges one with purple and red light ... There will be nothing but spaces of light and dark, intersected by thick stalks, and rather higher up perhaps, rose-shaped blots of an indistinct colour – dim pinks and blues – which will, as time goes on, become more definite, become – I don't know what....[26]

Sight and sound replace meaning and cognition. Colour, space and light, in turn, are stripped of all culturally associative connotations. Moments when consciousness strains back against itself like this are a hallmark of Woolf's prose. At the same time as they express a desire for an alternative mode of being, they also reformulate Fry's ideal aesthetic state whereby the mind is liberated from the cacophony of everyday experience and social emotions.

For Woolf, as for Fry, these moments are aesthetic revelations. But while 'The Mark' offers the possibility of aesthetic transcendence, it also ('all the same') dramatizes its impossibility. It does so, first, in Woolf's representation of her narrator's meandering consciousness which, as much as it desires to return to a state 'after life', is frequently caught up in a set of 'automatic fancies' that are on a par with Fry's 'racial and social emotions'. Impressions are economized into stereotypical and sentimental scenes and associations: ruminations about the house's previous owner's taste in furniture (the 'social' associations of the leisure culture), for example, fantasies about Shakespeare and the English love of tombs (the 'racial' associations of a vanishing Englishness) all permeate the narrator's thoughts. It is as if Woolf's narrator, like Fry's listeners to 'God Save the King', passes 'at once' into a richly varied emotional world. Although 'The Mark' promises to plumb the depths of a consciousness existing beyond everyday description and convention, the text also exposes the intransigence of socially clichéd and culturally associative impressions. Unlike Fry, Woolf does not so readily assume the existence of an autonomous aesthetic realm, but engages with the difficulty of moving beyond the standardized and denatured experience of modernity.

On the one hand, this difference is bound to emerge in the translation of an aesthetic doctrine from painting to writing. Any attempt at a straightforward analogy between Fry's theories of painting and writing is likely to expose the impotence of the analogy itself. Writing is, obviously, discursive and associative and, as Woolf knows full well, it is only through exploiting this that writing's negatives – the pre-discursive, 'pure' significance – can be evoked. And, of course, as much as Woolf admired and loved Fry, her writing does have a singular and distinct agenda. She might admire the gaps formed by bulbous legs on canvas and, indeed, her writing might conform to Fry's 'plasticity', but Woolf, of all of Fry's contemporaries, is not about to forget that bulbous legs are attached to women – however abstracted. In 'The Mark', as so often in her writing, Woolf twists Fry's search for true aesthetic experience into feminist critique. If social and racial emotions and their associative baggage are to be transcended, it is not only because they are valueless, or because their frenetic pace obscures contemplation, but also because they are oppressive: as oppressive as the ubiquitous 'Whitaker's Table of Precedency', with its obsessive hierarchies and categories:

> How peaceful it is down here, rooted in the centre of the world and gazing up through the grey waters, with their sudden gleams of light ... if it were not for Whitaker's Almanack – if it were not for the Table of Precedency!'[27]

Patricia Waugh has argued that, unlike her formalist contemporaries, Woolf does not so much retreat from the social into 'true' imaginative experience, as use the imagination to re-figure the social in gendered terms. Rather than subscribe to modernist autonomy, Waugh suggests, Woolf continually parodies the construction of pure aesthetic significance in her writing.[28] Desirable as it is to read Woolf as mastering formalism in order willfully to turn an elitist aesthetic doctrine back against itself, other moments in her writing reveal a more vexed and ambivalent relation to formalism. What Waugh sees as parody, I would hazard, is underpinned by a form of problematic irony. Woolf is a mistress of the ironic turnstile of affirmation and negation; and while indeed this frequently allows her to sport with parody, just as often Woolf's irony has a deadly serious intent. Having proposed the distinction between the oppressive world of Whitaker's Almanack and an imaginary state of pre-discursivity in 'The Mark', for example, Woolf pulls the rug from under her own feet by diagnosing her own desire for transcendence as a symptomatic response to the association-laden world she is trying to escape:

> Here is nature once more at her old game of self-preservation. This train of thought , she perceives, is threatening mere waste of energy, even some collision with reality, for who will ever be able to lift a finger against Whitaker's Table of Precedency? ... Whitaker knows, and let that, so Nature counsels, comfort you, instead of enraging you; and if you can't be comforted, if you must shatter this hour of peace, think of the mark on the wall. I understand Nature's game – her prompting to take action as a way of ending any thought that threatens to excite or to pain.[29]

What goes by the name of 'Nature' here reads as a particularly contemporary form of consciousness: one which, as in Freud's account of the psyche, takes anticipatory evasive action whenever threatened with the traumas of the real.[30] Aesthetic contemplation, the search for pure significance, is here diagnosed as a kind of 'protection against stimuli'; it is an *effect* of the way in which modern consciousness can only exist at one remove from experience. Woolf's ironic reflexivity does not so much parody Fry's formalism as inflect it with something like the negating logic which Freud, only three years later, was to ascribe to the death drive. Stripping the enigmatic mark of associative meaning, searching for pure significance, is also an attempt to reduce meaning to zero degree for a bombarded consciousness – this is 1917. For all its formalist abstraction and experimentation, 'The Mark' offers a pretty convincing idea of what might lie beyond the pleasure principle on the home front. It is not for nothing that Woolf's narrator's reverie is interrupted by the return of a male partner. It is he who puts an end to her exercise in psychic and aesthetic reduction: 'Nothing ever happens', he exclaims, 'Curse this war: God Damn this war! ... All the same, I don't see why we should have a snail on our wall.'[31]

Read this way, Woolf's early story could be said to be as imbued with the destructive element as her first really accomplished work of formal experimentation and mourning, *Jacob's Room* (1922); a text which is frequently compared to Eliot's *The Waste Land*, also published by Hogarth. Woolf's speculative and ironic turn-arounds, however, are of a different order than those of her modernist contemporaries. The fully ironic work, Cleanth Brooks noted, always 'carries within its own structure the destructive elements'.[32] According to Alan Wilde's more recent account, the modernist ironist holds on to both these destructive elements and his artistic vision through 'a conception of equal and opposed possibilities held in a state of total poise, or ... the shape of an indestructible, unresolvable paradox.'[33] The modernist ironist recognizes the intractable crisis of contemporary existence through the aesthetics of paradox. This issue is not, then, for example, whether or not the rains do actually fall in *The Waste Land*, but to what extent this paradox is mediated through formal equipoise. While Wilde's view of irony provides a good paradigm for understanding modernist strategies of mastery, and while Woolf's work too poses such unresolvable paradoxes, the outcome of such gestures is very different in her writing. Where her contemporaries might use irony to effect an authoritative closure, by World War Two at least Woolf's strategies of negation arrive at a very different position.

In his essay on Woolf, 'L'échec du démon: la vocation', Maurice Blanchot writes of the terrible price that Woolf paid for her moments of being. Woolf, he says is driven by a vocation, a demon, that demands she goes beyond appearances towards the negative limits of her own writing.

> To depend on dispersal, intermittence, bright fragments of vision, the scintillating fascination of the instant, is terrifying in the extreme ... . Is it a solution to reassemble what is dispersed,

> to make continuous the discontinuous, to make what is erratic into a unified whole?[34]

For Wilde's 'absolute ironist' the solution would be to resolve this double movement towards continuity and discontinuity by means of a formal paradox. For Blanchot, however, Woolf did not find a solution in the formal reconciliation of opposites, but in her own death. Woolf's negating moments demand a weakness (which is also a strength) that estranges her from 'natural' or conventional resources of expression. This weakness, for Blanchot, means that Woolf's suicide is as inevitable as Rhoda's in *The Waves*.[35] Negation, for Woolf, is ultimately resolved by an act of self-negation. It is not the mastery of the absolute modernist ironist that is proclaimed in her work, but a surrender of authority.

This structure, whereby the promise of aesthetic significance gives way to self-negation, cuts through one of Woolf's last texts, the autobiographical 'Sketch of the Past' (1939–40). 'Sketch', an unfinished memoir that Woolf began in 1939, was written alongside her biography of Fry and her last work of fiction, *Between the Acts*. It thus stands poised between an account of Woolf's life, a retrospective look at Fry's formalism and her own fictional practice. Woolf also began to read Freud in 1939. In spite of the memoir's confessional nature (it is here that her childhood abuse is revealed), the author of 'Freudian Fiction', an essay which lambasts the reductive seductions of psychoanalysis, is hardly likely to swallow Freud whole. In so far as Woolf engages with psychoanalysis, she takes us back to Roger Fry's 1924 repudiation, as she runs Fry's search for pure aesthetic significance into what frequently resembles an account of sublimation. It is not just the links that Woolf makes between sexuality and art in 'Sketch' that make it such a curious companion piece to her biography of Fry. More striking and more frequent are the references to the relation between art and violence (violence *as* sexuality). If Woolf's 'plasticity' in 'The Mark on the Wall' has affinities with Freud's death drive, 'Sketch' is an exploration of how that drive turns in towards the self: sublimation, for Woolf by 1939, is inextricable from masochism.

Writing as war breaks, Woolf is at pains to stress art's redemptive potential and lays out a blueprint for aesthetic significance which seems both to echo and endorse Fry. Take, for example, the following much-quoted evocation of the transcendental power of art.

> I hazard the explanation that a shock is at once in my case followed by the desire to explain it. I feel that I have had a blow; but it is not, as I thought, simply a blow from an enemy hidden behind the cotton wool of everyday life; it is or will become a revelation of some order; it is a token of some real thing behind appearances; and I make it whole by putting it into words. It is only by putting it into words that I can make it whole; this wholeness means that it has lost the power to hurt me; it gives, perhaps, because by doing so I take away the pain, a great delight to put the severed parts together … . From this I reach what I might call a philosophy; at any rate it is a constant idea of mine; that behind the cotton wool is hidden a pattern; that we – I mean all human beings are connected with this; that the whole world is a work of art; that we are parts of a work of art.[36]

This is not just redemptive; there is something urgent, manic, in this hyper-inflation of the power of art. If, as critics often assert, this is a summary of Woolf's longstanding aesthetic credo, it has never been so fraught. Revelation, for Woolf, comes not from emotions about forms but, as Bion might have put it, from a sense of catastrophe.[37] Shock is transmuted into signs; 'putting it into words', assembling the fragments, takes away the pain as the pleasure of composition ensures that Eros triumphs over Thanatos. But this mystical hope is belied by the way Woolf actually narrates the formation of such revelatory moments of being in the memoir itself. Just before this passage, Woolf describes three childhood 'shock' experiences. Out of the three, only one offers any sense of aesthetic transcendence. In the first, Woolf recalls a fight with her brother Thoby: 'We were pomelling each other with fists. Just as I raised my fist to hit him, I felt: why hurt another person? I dropped my hand instantly, and stood there, and let him beat me'. This scene of self-submission and passivity is echoed in Woolf's third memory, the suicide of Mr Valpy, a visitor to St Ives.

> The next thing I remember is being in the garden at night and walking on the path by the apple tree. It seemed to me that the apple tree was connected with the horror of Mr. Valpy's suicide. I could not pass it. I stood there looking at the grey-green creases of the bark … in a trance of horror. I seemed to be dragged down, hopelessly, into some pit of absolute despair from which I could not escape. My body seemed paralysed.[38]

Where, according to Woolf's 'philosophy', the apple tree might have offered itself as a redemptive symbol, here it refuses to yield any sense of reparative signification. Not revelation, then, but self-paralysis. Only the second memory, again of St. Ives, conforms to Woolf's promise of a reparative aesthetic.

> I was looking at a plant with a spread of leaves; and it seemed suddenly plain that the flower itself was part of the earth; that a ring enclosed what was the flower; and that was the real flower; part earth; part flower. It was a thought I put away as being likely to be useful to me later.[39]

Even here, the augured revelation is presented synecdochically; as if the signification of the moment, in spite of its redemptive appeal, will always remain, at best, contingent.

At each turn of her memoir, Woolf's attempts to put the severed shards of the past together fail to deliver a form of transcendence. Instead they continually replay scenes of trauma which exacerbate the very 'shock' experience Woolf's philosophy promises to assuage. What Blanchot accurately describes as the 'terrifying joy' of Woolf's epiphanies is invariably accompanied by scenes of self-abnegation. Look for example, at the violence portrayed in the following bath-time scene:

> Next, the other moment when the idiot boy sprang up with his hand outstretched mewing, slit-eyed, red-rimmed; and without saying a word, with a sense of horror in me, I poured into his hand a bag of Russian toffee. But it was not over, for that night in the bath the dumb horror came over me. Again, I had that hopeless sadness; that collapse I have described before as if I were passive under some sledge-hammer blow; exposed to a whole avalanche of meaning that heaped itself up and discharged itself upon me, unprotected, with nothing to ward it off, so that I huddled up at my end of the bath, motionless.[40]

'A child is being beaten' – by meaning. It is as if this particular epiphanic moment of being is born out of a collision of meaning and sexuality which, as in Freud's account of the Oedipus complex, shatters the subject into being. In her original drafts of 'Sketch' Woolf describes that avalanche of meaning as discharging itself 'up' her ('exposed to a whole avalanche of meaning that had heaped itself up and suddenly discharged itself up me'). 'Upon me' is, I assume, Jeanne Schulkind's judicious editorial correction in the Sussex University and Grafton edition of the memoirs (avalanches – unlike penises – do not discharge themselves 'up' people).[41] Amid Woolf's original semantic muddle, however, the messy syntax of 'up me' does help underscore the troubling equation which threads throughout her memoir: meaning=sexuality=violence.

'Many of these exceptional moments', then, as Woolf herself says, 'brought with them a peculiar horror and physical collapse'.[42] Charles Bernheimer, in his reading of the memoir, puts this more forcefully: 'Sketch', he argues, expresses a 'powerful masochistic impulse to fracture the self's wholeness and submit to the other's violence.' Subversive, because they give the lie to the concept of the authoritative integrity of the subject, Woolf's moments of 'self-shattering' result in what Bernheimer terms a poetics of 'ontological revelation'.[43] To an extent, we could say that Woolf's final response to both Fry and the anxious irony of her modernist contemporaries lies in this exorbitant refusal of authority. But 'ontological revelation', in this context at least, is not a neutral phrase. What does it mean to suggest that Woolf's poetics of negation finally result in a series of *mise-en-scènes* of self-negation and self-punishment? Why does the death drive turn inward in 1939? And how can we understand the suggestion that for a woman the ultimate ontological revelation is, in Bernheimer's words, to make 'subliminally manifest her unconscious desire for death?'[44]

This last question is answered in Julia Kristeva's famous allusion to Woolf's suicide in *About Chinese Women*. For Kristeva, Woolf's writing and death embodies what she sees as the 'impossible dialectic' confronting women within Western monotheistic culture. In a culture where 'woman' is posited as the unconscious other to the socio-symbolic, and is hence both its *bête noire* and guarantor, the dilemma for women is how to accede to symbolic power without renouncing the potentially subversive power of their marginal status. While the male artist, according to Kristeva, can run the risk of taking on the symbolic through poetic language, because ultimately he has the cultural authority to do so, attempts by women writers such as Woolf, Tsvetaeva and Plath to negate the social are resolved only by their own deaths:

> Once the moorings of the word, the ego, the superego, begin to slip, life itself can't hang on: death quietly moves in. Suicide

> without a cause, or sacrifice without fuss for an apparent cause which, in our age, is usually political: a woman can carry off such things without tragedy, even without drama, without the feeling that she is fleeing a well-fortified front, but rather as though it were simply a matter of making an inevitable, irresistible and self-evident transition. I think of Virginia Woolf, who sank wordlessly into the river, her pockets weighed down with stones. Haunted by voices, waves, lights, in love with colours – blue, green – and seized by a strange gaiety that would bring on the fits of strangled, screeching laughter.[45]

Counter to the absolute ironist, Woolf is figured here as a melancholic, yet exuberant, siren. Kristeva herself, I think, knows precarious the fault-line is between apparently universal psycho-sexual structures and culturally imbricated gendered terms; it is this fissure which runs, albeit uncomfortably, throughout her work. Yet to concede that Woolf's suicide is 'an inevitable, irresistible and self-evident transition' is also to risk leaving her work open to the charge made, most famously, by Elaine Showalter, that Woolf's modernism fails to provide women with any political agency. 'Refined to its essences, abstracted from its physicality and anger, denied any action, Woolf's vision of womanhood is as deadly as it disembodied'. As deadly and disembodied, perhaps, as Fry's vision of those bulbous legs in the second Post-Impressionism exhibition. 'The ultimate room of one's own', Showalter concludes, 'is the grave'.[46]

Is the room a tomb? The idea that Woolf ought to have but failed to flesh out 'a vision of womanhood' is both anachronistic and prescriptive (and I'm not the first to find something troublingly anti-political in the category of 'womanhood').[47] But substituting Showalter's bathetic lamentation for womanhood with the pathos of an 'inevitable' psychic agony of sexual difference is no less problematic. To ally Woolf's writing with her physical death is perhaps, on the one hand, to produce an image of female masochism that unsettles because it reveals an uncomfortable truth about women's relation to culture. But at the same moment, we run the risk of pathologizing women's protest (as if psychoanalytic theory begins with a concept of the pathology of culture, only to displace culture's discontents back on to the woman herself). What happens if we turn the question around and ask, not what psychoanalysis can tell us about Woolf, but in what ways Woolf's work can be read alongside contemporary psychoanalytic accounts of femininity, aesthetic form and civilization's discontents?

* * *

'I suppose', Woolf said of *To the Lighthouse,* 'that I did for myself what psycho-analysts do for their patients. I expressed some very long felt and deeply felt emotion. And in expressing it I explained it and then laid it to rest.'[48] In her excellent study of Woolf's relation to psychoanalysis, Elizabeth Abel shows how Klein's matricentric plots weave their way through Woolf's texts of the 1920s. Woolf, Abel argues, challenges Freud's rewriting of the paternal legacies of the nineteenth century and in this her project directly echoes Klein's. It was, after all, in Adrian and Karin Stephen's living room that Klein delivered her 1925 lectures. Next door sat Woolf, scribbling away at *To the Lighthouse.*[49] The parallels between Woolf's experimental elegy, Lily Briscoe's painting of Mrs Ramsay and Klein's analysis of Ruth Kjär's reparative creativity (Klein's paper on art came just two years after *To the Lighthouse*) seem irresistible. That 'slim, imperious, challenging' mother that fills Kjär's empty space, seems to bear more than a passing resemblance to the indomitable figure of Mrs Ramsay, who could any day engage in combat with the children of the beach, if not of the desert.

Direct analogies between Klein and Woolf, however, need to be treated with caution. As Abel shows, their relation is less one of influence, than of a historically, politically and culturally imbricated intertextuality. One obvious danger in making such analogies is the risk of acceding to those myths of individual creativity which are as common in some representations of Woolf as they are in certain forms of Kleinism. Abel describes the Kleinian project in the following terms:

> At the 'cross-roads' of the Kleinian narrative is not a renunciation of the mother but her imaginary generation. Integral to the Kleinian framework is a notion of art as a simultaneously formal and therapeutic project for reconstructing a fragmented inner world. For Kleinians, culture, opposed not as (paternal) law to instinct but as creativity to inner chaos, emerges from the impulse to make reparation to the mother.[50]

It is this emphasis on the imaginary regeneration of the maternal in Kleinian thought which, for many, has seemed most germane to a new understanding of the relation between sexual difference and art. But, as we saw in the last chapter, for Klein herself culture is not always connoted as a benevolent concept of creativity, but is as likely to be as cruel and forbidding as what Abel describes as 'paternal law'. What is so unsettling about Klein's theorization of psychic life is her image of an aggressivity which, as for Freud in *Civilization*, can only be repeated in a vexed and anxious relation to cultural inhibitions. It is the fascism of such a culture, accompanied by the culturally connoted return of the maternal into mass ideology that, Abel argues, eventually drove Woolf away from Klein and back to Freud in the late 1930s. With so much ambivalence around, how then does the emphasis on the formal and therapeutic fit into the Kleinian model of maternal reparation?

In part, the answer to this question takes us directly back to where I began, to the dilemmas proposed by Fry's commitment to pure aesthetic significance. For many analysts in the 1930s and 1940s, Klein's stress on the reconstruction of inner chaos readily dovetailed into Fry's concern with the purity of form. Frustrated with the inadequacies of writing as a medium, Woolf, with more than a nod to Fry, at one point states that she would have had to paint like Cézanne in order to give a real sense of Julia Stephen.[51] Hanna Segal also picks up the affinities between Klein's theories of reparation and Fry: 'What Klein says about Ruth Kjär', she argues, 'seems to echo what Fry said of Cézanne … that his aim was "not to paint attractive pictures but to work out his salvation"'.[52] Less a case of the influence of psychoanalysis on modernism within the British context it is, in fact, more appropriate to talk of the influence of high modernism on psychoanalysis.

On the one hand, this influence looks like a straightforward, not to say banal, reduction of Klein's thought.[53] To subsume psychic conflict under the rubric of aesthetic significance is a convenient way of ridding psychoanalysis of its internal theoretical conflicts. Likewise, ontologizing Fry's aestheticism as a psychic universal effectively strips the psyche, and indeed psychoanalysis itself, of any social contingency. But as psychoanalysis encounters Fry's formalism, it also invests it with a psychic drive that is imbued with that logic of negativity which we saw at work in Woolf. This drive proves difficult to contain: both for the psyche and for a theory which frequently struggles under its own moral terms. Like Woolf, the Kleinians inscribe a drive-invested body across the disinterested gaze of formalism. This is not, of course, the libidinal body of Surrealism: it is, rather, a body racked by anxiety and guilt.

Many commentators have pointed to *Civilization* as the text in which Klein and Freud are theoretically most proximate. Freud's image of a cultural super-ego which both represses aggression and demands it is one which rests at the core of Klein's work. Where for Freud in *Civilization* this is the super-ego of paternal law, Klein in 'The Early Stages of the Oedipus Conflict' (1928), written one year earlier, pushes this moment back to the child's first identifications with the mother. This is a move which Freud will later reprimand and one which, as Klein's more recent critics have pointed out, leads to a theory which presumes, rather than accounts for, sexual difference.[54] Yet as much as Klein's theory appears to engulf the child's coming into being in a world of maternal phantasy, with no apparent reference to the paternal or symbolic function, her concepts of sexual difference are as notable for their impasses as are, more famously, Freud's theories of feminine sexuality.

Anxiety, for Klein, both constitutes the psyche and entails its dissolution. In 'The Early Stages of the Oedipus Conflict', the mother's body is the locus for early oedipal anxiety. Projective identification holds sway at this point, as the immature ego both projects hostile fantasies towards the mother and simultaneously fears her retribution. As a result, both sexes turn away from the mother and take, instead, the father as the object of their desire. Swapping the mother for the father also precipitates the process of symbol formation, as the infant is now able to substitute one object for another. The first, hesitant, turn to the law is accompanied by a fragile process of metaphorization. This resolution of what Klein calls the 'femininity phase' can thus be seen as an archaic reduplication of both the Oedipus complex in Freud, and what will later become the entrance to the symbolic in Lacan. Sexual difference comes into play, for Klein, in the distinct ways by which each sex attempts to resolve the femininity phase or, more precisely in the way in which each sex *interprets* the femininity phase. For the child the 'meanings' of anatomical difference are precipitated and distorted by the presence of what Klein calls the 'epistemophilic drive'; an early questioning drive which reveals nothing to the child but the 'gap' in his or her knowledge of sexual difference. The femininity phase of the little boy is characterized by his identification and rivalry with the mother which replays the set of aggressive phantasies that led him to turn away from her in the first place. The boy is subsequently locked into an anxiety-driven turnstile whereby his fantasized aggression towards the mother is answered, first, only by the signs of what he lacks: faeces, babies and the father's penis. His epistemophilic drive, however, allows him to displace this anxiety and inadequacy up to an 'intellectual plane' through which the little boy 'deduces' that he has, in fact, like his father, got a penis. This phallic 'knowledge' substitutes for his own deficiency with regard to female reproduction, and the little boy is henceforth set on the path to a precarious and overstated form of masculinity.

The case for the little girl is not only different, but more difficult. Her epistemophilic drive does not provide a pseudo-solution to the threat of her mother but, rather, confirms her sense of deficiency: her anatomical investigations confirm that she lacks a penis. This piece of knowledge leads not, as with the boy, to gestures of overcompensation, but to more anxiety and more aggression with regard to the mother: 'She feels this lack to be a fresh cause of hatred of the mother, but at the same time her sense of guilt makes her regard it as a punishment'.[55] The little girl is thus guilty on two counts; once for her aggression, and again for the fact of her sexual difference. Eventually, says Klein, maternal rivalry and hostility will lead the daughter back to identification with the mother (the femininity phase 'proper'). But throughout this identificatory oscillation, anxiety and inhibition persist to an extent which potentially disables any firm identification between mother and daughter. The prospect of arriving at full femininity via maternity, for example, 'is weakened ... by anxiety and sense of guilt, and these may seriously damage the maternal capacity for a woman'. And further: 'It is this anxiety and a sense of guilt which is a chief cause of the repression of feelings of pride and joy in the feminine role'.[56] Despite Klein's normative pull here (what do pride and joy in the feminine role mean?), her version of femininity is as psychically precarious and, indeed, as caught up with a vexed interplay between fantasy and meaning, as Freud's.

Freud gives two reasons for what he deduces as the ethical inferiority of women: they have too much envy to have a sense of social justice, he says, and a weaker super-ego than men. Klein's response is telling: women are envious *because* their super-ego is so strong, so unremitting. For Klein, there is too much, not too little, of the destructive element about women. Bersani has argued that Freud's pessimism in *Civilization* is 'the discursive sign of a perhaps suicidal melancholy, the palely reactive *aura* of a cultural complicity with the power of an anticultural destructiveness'.[57] Freud, in other words, endorses the cultural violence of the anti-cultural super-ego which both demands and prohibits aggression. For Klein in 'The Early Stages of the Oedipus Conflict' the early super-ego both legitimates an overstated masculine aggression and demands and inhibits femininity. This, it could be said, is yet another example of Kleinian (amoral) super-morality. But is this also, perhaps, the sign of a quiescent acknowledgement, not only of an anti-cultural destructiveness, but also of the heavy burden that destructiveness places on women? What is certain is that if, as Freud suggests, guilt is the origin of civilization's discontents, for Klein this is a guilt which impacts doubly on women. How, then, is it possible to sublimate the heavy premium which the destructive element puts on women? To some degree, by 1945 Klein has performed her own theoretical sublimation, as what began as the femininity phase is eventually subsumed under the concept of the depressive position.[58] Earlier attempts by Kleinian analysts to sublimate the difficulty of women's relation to the super-ego, however, reveal more of a struggle over the concepts of art and femininity.

Paula Heimann's 1939 British Society membership paper, 'A contribution to the problem of sublimation and its relation to processes of internalization', bears both traces of this struggle and a telling indebtedness to the doctrine of pure aesthetic significance. Heimann's paper centres upon the successful analysis of a woman painter who came to her with an acute morphine addiction and an inhibition in painting. The aim of analysis, in Kleinian terms, is to persuade the patient to take responsibility for her own aggression; in this way, Heimann suggests, she can avow her own guilt and thus vanquish the persecutory demons who haunt her. Through the connecting interpretations and repetitions of the transference and counter-transference, what Heimann calls 'the design' gradually manifests itself. Born out of the architectonics of the analytic narrative, this 'design' also weaves its way into the patient's painting. The analysis is organized through a series of spatial metaphors: the 'design' is both a metaphor for the transference and, finally, becomes the governing principle of the patient's painting. Heimann's account of the analysis is strikingly similar to Fry's account of Cézanne's development (*Cézanne*, 1927).[59] Cézanne's career began with an early exuberance that produced stereotypical tendencies in his painting – he wanted to be Delacroix, really, says

Fry, and it's lucky for us that he didn't make it. This imitative urge was eventually superseded by Cézanne's art of aesthetic resolution. Likewise, Heimann looks to her patient's painting for growing evidence of formal and aesthetic mastery. As the analysis proceeds, the paintings go through three different stages. The first paintings without morphine are somewhat 'primitive' in scope and technique. By comparison, the second paintings of 'Victorian family scenes' are both satisfying and commercially successful but yet, Heimann adds, have 'an obsessional element' which interferes with their 'sublimatory value'. These stereotypical family scenes leave the analysand stuck in the past. She becomes aware of what Heimann calls their lack of 'value',

> as an anxiety that she might not be able to paint in any other manner but this and that if she were compelled to go on with this type of painting her possibilities of self-expression would be gravely restricted, if she had no other function in life but that of restoring her childhood objects, she would not attain the full range of boundless territory in which to develop herself.[60]

Art here, as in most psychoanalytic accounts, repeats and symbolizes the past. What Heimann and her patient additionally attempt to account for is the 'aesthetic value' of those repetitions. This what they discover in the third set of paintings:

> The pictures of this period showed a great advance in colour and composition. During this period her internal objects ... appeared frequently in the form of artistic problems. Her interest was thus not only more objective, but far richer and comprehending far more varied details. Her internal conflicts were objectified in terms of aesthetic and technical problems. Instead of suffering from the torments of a devilish father and mother, she struggled with the problems of 'human interest' and 'aesthetic interest' in painting.[61]

Compare Fry's comment to the effect that Cézanne was too much of an intellectual to be content with Impressionism. The energy of Cézanne's exuberance, which was also his sexual desire, says Fry, was finally harnessed in acts of brilliantly precise cognition: Cézanne stripped the object bare, shed of its stereotypical appearances, in order to see, to rediscover, what it really was. Compare too the way Lily Briscoe in *To the Lighthouse* works through the problem of depicting maternity by abstracting Mrs Ramsay and James into 'a purple triangle' ('But the picture was not of them ... By a shadow here and light there...[H]er tribute took that form').[62] Like Lily, Heimann's patient abstracts the past into a set of formal aesthetic relations. The banality of the earlier Victorian scenes are, hence, re-figured and surpassed through the formal composition of the modernist daughter. But in Heimann's account, the formalist axiom whereby the general rules of composition take precedence over the particularity of phenomena becomes a cornerstone of the analytic cure.

Where others, such as the Surrealists and Lacan, scupper the logic of the formalist gaze, Heimann bolsters claims to the moral superiority of abstraction by bestowing it with all the legitimacy of the psychoanalytic cure. However, her account of the analysis reveals a latent and more disturbing subtext which runs counter to Heimann's own formalist imperative. In a peculiar cryptography of the anxiety of influence, the Victorian mother who compels the patient to produce stereotypical family scenes proves, for both the patient and for Heimann's theory, difficult to kill off. Having presented the case history as a straightforward narrative which moves from inner persecutory chaos to sublimation as formal transcendence, Heimann muddies the coherence of her own linear account with an interpretation of the inexorable return of the 'Victorian mother' into her patient's symptomatology and painting. Following a quarrel with a woman whom Heimann analyses as standing in for the patient's mother, the previously sublimated Victorian scenes make a phantom return into the analysand's painting:

> She started the sketch, but found that there was something wrong with her drawing, both while she was working on it and when she had finished and hung it up on the wall .... When the artist who criticized the sketches came to hers, he said in surprise: 'Good God, what has happened to you? This looks like a drawing out of a Victorian family album'. My patient now realized what it was she had felt to be wrong with it. She said: 'It looked like a drawing that had been done fifty years ago'. She felt so awful about this that she had to go and have three sherries.[63]

Even three sherries are not enough to prevent the return of the Victorian Mother who, like Woolf's 'Angel of the House', returns both to inhabit and to inhibit the modernist daughter.[64] For Woolf, the phantasmagoric 'Angel' reveals that 'thinking back through our mothers' can also mean struggling with the mother's complicity with oppression. While Heimann does not share Woolf's ideological reading of the phantom mother, she does share her sense of injustice. 'There is a great difference', she notes, 'between wanting to paint Victorian family scenes and being unconsciously compelled (by an internal Victorian mother) to paint in a Victorian fashion'.[65] What better indictment of the 'penal servitude', in Heimann's words, of the woman artist for whom the psychic inheritance of the mother is as oppressive as a world dictated by the false hierarchies of 'Whitaker's Almanac'?

Heimann interprets the phantom return of the Victorian mother as 'an impaired sublimation' because 'this type of restoration has too much the character of revenge and punishment'.[66] The concept of 'faulty' sublimation suggests that the incorporation of the Victorian mother can, along with the rest of the patient's psychic ambivalence, eventually be exorcized and sublated to the status of an aesthetic problem. But while the narrative which leads from persecutory anxiety to transcendence through aesthetic significance suggests that the femininity phase can be overcome, the subtext to Heimann's paper points to a continual repetition of the anxiety and guilt that mark femininity in Klein's account. This is precisely the point Matte Blanco made in his criticism of Heimann's paper after its first reading: 'Attempts at further development are continually made by Melanie Klein and her followers, but the results seem to be nothing more than, to use a graphic French expression, *'piétiner sur place'*, moving incessantly without ever succeeding in going forward'.[67] Heimann, having footnoted Blanco in the published version of her paper, is quick to refute this charge. The 'vicious circle' which characterizes the Kleinian account of early psychic life and sexual difference is not incessant, but can be broken. Denial and expulsion are not the only mechanisms whereby the Kleinian subject comes into being: goodness, as well as badness, can be incorporated to the extent that 'the subject in his phantasies feels that he is creating his parents rather than swallowing them'.[68] But to 'create' the parents, as opposed to swallowing them whole in a phantasy of incorporation, in Heimann's terms, is to create them in terms of aesthetic interest. If this is love (and Kleinians are often quick to defend Klein against charges of morbidity by insisting that love has as much a place in her writing as hate and destruction), it's of a curiously disinterested and disembodied kind. It is as if aesthetic significance resolves the anguish and despair of both the modernist daughter's 'penal servitude', and of Heimann's legacy to Klein. Sublimatory 'value' hence is a way of repairing, or making good, an earlier, more disturbing, version of a punished and self-punishing female subjectivity which hides, cryptographically, within both the psyche of the patient and in Heimann's paper – a symptom, rather than a resolution, of the difficulty with which Kleinian thought tries to reconcile its own theory of femininity's discontents.

When Hanna Segal crosses the same theoretical terrain in 1947 in 'A Psycho-Analytical Approach to Aesthetics', it looks as though the concept of aesthetic value has come to carry the full weight of the destructive elements that Kleinism places at the heart of the constitution of subjectivity. Segal has high praise for Fry in this essay ('what Roger Fry says of post-impressionists undoubtedly applies to all genuine art') and opens her paper by repeating his distinction between aesthetic value and superficial or imitative art: 'One of the great differences between art and imitation or a superficial "pretty" achievement is that neither the imitation nor the "pretty" production ever achieves this creation of an entirely new reality'.[69] Translated into psychoanalytic terms, the 'creation of an entirely new reality' is born out of the depressive position, while 'pretty' or superficial art is a sign of the repetition of early persecutory anxiety. As with other Kleinian writers, however, Segal's evocations of persecutory anxiety seem to enact the anxiety they describe. Take, for example, this extraordinary description of woman writer's inhibition in writing:

> Using words, she said, made her break 'an endless unity into bits'. It was like 'chopping up', like 'cutting things'. It was obviously felt by her as an aggressive act. Besides, using words was 'making things infinite and separate'. To use words meant acknowledging the separateness of the world from herself, and gave her a feeling of loss. She felt that using words made her lose the illusion of possessing and being at one with an undivided world: 'When you name a thing you really lose it'. It became clear to her that using a symbol meant an acceptance of the separateness of her object from herself, the acknowledgement of her

own aggressiveness, 'chopping up', 'cutting', and finally losing the object.[70]

As in Woolf's bath-time scene in 'Sketch', meaning here is perceived as an act of violence. Note how Segal invests words themselves with aggressive drives; as if the writer's aggression can only be located for her in the space where words appear. Language is imbricated with a lack of being, a negative lining of aggressivity, which Kristeva, for example, later recognizes as a paradigm in modernist writing.[71] Sexual difference is not an explicit issue in Segal's paper; yet if, following Klein, separation from the mother is invariably a more fraught and anxious process for the little girl, it follows that for women language, the deployment of metaphor, will also carry the weight of persecutory anxiety.

It is for this reason that Segal sees this drive-invested language not as a form of sublimation, but as an inhibition, a failure to accede to the law of depressive relations. Full sublimation, in the form of 'aesthetic value', by contrast, is the outcome of an avowal of destructiveness and loss. For Segal, the true artist must 'acknowledge the death instinct, both in its aggressive and sub-destructive aspects, and accept the reality of death for the object and the self'.[72] In what looks like a possible solution to Heimann's dilemmas, Segal inscribes a masochistic logic of self-destruction within the aesthetic itself. Good art, for Segal, we could say, paraphrasing Bernheimer's reading of Woolf, is a moment of 'ontological revelation' whereby the subject makes manifest her own desire for death, not as a pathology, but as a form of art.

Two years after the war, when the deadly discontents of civilization that concerned Freud had reached their apocalyptic conclusion, Segal makes art the privileged site through which we can avow our own sadism; as if the aesthetic can contain and redeem what history could not. Bersani's claim that Kleinism offers a theory of sublimation 'disguised as transcendence' seems particularly apposite in Segal's case. Art, for Segal as for Fry, is not only the repetition, but the valorized de-realization of the ego's vexed and anxiety-ridden entrance into culture. When Segal concludes her essay by drawing on Dilthey's concept of *nach-erleben* ('living in retrospect') to explain aesthetic pleasure, then, it might seem that Kleinian psychoanalysis joins with that philosophical tradition which Benjamin associates with the attempt to find a 'true experience' as a response to the alienated experience of modernity.

Refocused through a psychoanalytic prism, Dilthey's *nach-erleben*, which Segal interprets here as a way of understanding others by reconstructing their lives, literally as 'after-living them', becomes equivalent to the unconscious identification the reader, listener or viewer makes with the work of art as a whole:

> The author has, in his hatred, destroyed all his loved objects just as I have done, and like me he has felt death and desolation inside him. Yet he can face it and he can make me face it, and despite the ruin and devastation we and the world around us survive. What is more, his objects, which have become evil and were destroyed, have been made alive again and have become immortal by his art. Out of all the chaos and destruction he has created a world which is whole, complete and unified.[73]

As persuasive a description of reparation as this is, Segal's claims for art also carry intimations of a post-war fantasy: who wouldn't, in 1947, wish for an experience which could create a unified world out of all the chaos and destruction?

'It is only by putting it into words', wrote Woolf in a similar wartime fantasy, 'that I can make it whole.' This wholeness is no merely redemptive fantasy; nor is it some personal deathly mysticism. Woolf's drive for formal unity is also a drive towards death. Hanna Segal reminds us of this and, in so doing, also reminds us that whatever is creative about this drive is also historical. At the same time as her formalism aestheticizes the destructive element, Segal changes the terms of formalism itself. In a footnote to 'A Psycho-Analytical Approach to Aesthetics', half-concealed and presented almost as an afterthought, Segal begins to take apart what she sees as the paradox which lies behind Fry's claims to aesthetic autonomy. 'What the formalists ignore', she argues, 'is that form as much as content is itself an expression of unconscious emotion. What Fry, following Clive Bell, calls significant form, is form expressing unconscious emotional experience'.[74] 'Cutting-up', 'chopping-up things': Segal's description of persecutory anxiety is perhaps the nearest we can get to an example of 'form expressing unconscious experience' in her own writing. In a much later essay, Segal elaborates her criticism of formalism, and draws on Picasso's *Guernica* to demonstrate that the socially associative significations of art cannot be separated from aesthetic form: social associations are also unconscious associations and these cannot be separated from art. In Picasso's painting, she argues, 'there is a path leading from the immediate associative emotion: the Spanish war to all war ... the path leads not only from the current war to war in general, but also to what such wars represent in our unconscious'.[75] To identify unconsciously with this work of art, thus, would not be to repair a world fraught with destruction, but to arrive at a question: what does war represent in the unconscious? Fry, as I suggested earlier, arrives at a position where his theory begins to sound like a form of psychoanalysis, in so far as the aesthetic is a way of making conscious what everyday experience keeps unconscious. Segal provides Fry with his apotheosis: aesthetic experience is superior to everyday experience, not because of the intrinsic value of purely formal relations, but because it brings to light what culture would have us repress. A far cry from Fry's attempts to immunize art from history, for Segal, aesthetic significance is a way of asking what contemporary history means in psychic terms.[76]

The work of British Kleinians does not so much provide the grounds for an understanding of Woolf's work, but is involved in a series of questions which echo Woolf's project in the 1930s and 1940s. Instead of laying down a universalizing ontology, Klein, Heimann and Segal are working through the question of what kind of ontology is appropriate with their own theoretical terms. Kleinian attempts to fold the destructive element within an aesthetic are not only an effort to foreclose a set of theoretical dilemmas but, like Woolf, these analysts are endeavouring to discover what kind of aesthetic is appropriate to contemporary experience. If, according to the Kleinian account, women are particularly exposed to guilt and aggression, how can a woman 'be'? What type of aesthetic is appropriate to this existence? It is with these questions in mind that I want to return to Woolf's 'A Sketch of the Past'.

* * *

For Benjamin the 'shock experience' in Proust and Baudelaire is both a symptom of their alienation from modern life and the basis of a new poetics – a poetics of shock. In Benjamin's esoteric reading of *Beyond the Pleasure Principle*, Freud's theory of the death drive is read, along with Proust's *mémoire involuntaire*, as offering a theory of the response of consciousness to the increasing reification of experience within modernity. Only what has *not* been experienced consciously can become the basis for memory or recollection. Modern consciousness, by contrast, serves the function of immunizing itself against experience: consciousness, in Freud's famous formulation, is foremost 'a protection against stimuli'. This is a formulation which we have already seen in Woolf's 'The Mark on the Wall'. As for Woolf in 'Sketch', for Benjamin too, experience in its atrophied state can only appear as a series of 'shocks'. The repetition of the shock experience, as for Freud's war-time patients who repeatedly replay their traumas through dreams, works retroactively in order to produce the anxiety necessary to counter those shocks. The result, for Benjamin, is the 'disintegration of *aura* in the experience of shock';[77] the disintegration, in other words, of the mystificatory appeal of the aesthetic. 'Perhaps the special achievement of the shock defence', notes Benjamin, 'may be seen in its function of assigning to an incident a precise point in time in consciousness at the cost of the integrity of its contents. This would be a peak achievement of the intellect; it would turn the incident into a moment that has been lived (*Erlebnis*)'.[78] Gone, then, is the valorizing appeal to perceptual integrity (beloved of Fry); in its place is an uncanny twist whereby *through* shock (and not, for example, as the result of a process of trying to repair damage done), there lies the potential for the devalorization of phenomena and a negative reacquaintance with specificity. Far from laying the ground for an eventual scenario of aesthetic transcendence, 'shock' for Benjamin changes the terms of the aesthetic itself. This is the poetics of the fragment, the constellatory encounter which Benjamin both teases out of Baudelaire and practises in his own writing.

Woolf's practice lags behind Benjamin's. Although Woolf frequently calls upon the aesthetic as a negation of socially lived consciousness, for her it is still a superior form of lived experience (this is also an indication of the immense and obvious political and autobiographical differences between Woolf and Benjamin). From opposite directions, however both writers respond to the same problem: how to produce art in a world where its claims to transcendence are continually under question. Woolf's final acts mark the beginning of a new, if belated, intensity in her questioning not only of the doctrine of aesthetic autonomy, but of her own poetic practice (her last three works, *Roger Fry*, 'A Sketch' and *Between the Acts* can all be described as acts of mourning). It is as if irony is no longer enough.

Read this way, those moments of self-negation in 'Sketch' can be re-figured not only as inscriptions of a masochistic self-shattering, or as one woman's 'inevitable' transition to self-negation under the burden of psychic and cultural laws, but also as the beginning of an important realignment of the relation between art and experience in Woolf's thinking. Woolf does not embrace the 'shock experience' as a means of making productive modernity's alienation of experience. 'Sketch' does, however, express an anxiety about recollecting experience in a world which no longer provides contemplative distance. 'The past', Woolf writes,

> only comes back when the present runs so smoothly that it is like the sliding surface of a deep river. Then one sees through the surface to the depths. In these moments I find one of the greatest satisfactions, not that I am thinking of the past; but that it is then that I am living most fully in the present. For the present when backed by the past is a thousand times deeper than the present when it presses so close you can feel nothing else, when the film on the camera reaches only the eye.[79]

As for Benjamin, so too for Woolf, the only past worth recollecting is a past which one does not experience consciously ('not that I am thinking of the past'). This kind of consciousness potentially redeems the immediacy of an age of reproduction, of a present which 'presses so close you can feel nothing else, when the film on the camera reaches only the eye'. But for Woolf in 1940 the shocks of the present can no longer be parried. 'But to feel the present sliding over the past, peace is necessary. The present must be smooth, habitual.'[80] In 1940 there is no peace and so the past is no longer a moment to be transmuted into an aesthetically lived experience. Rather, as in Woolf's bath-time scene, once the past is recollected it returns to shatter the subject of her memoir in scenes which uncannily recall and repeat the very fragmentation of history, meaning and authority that Woolf was witnessing all around her. In Kleinian terms, the internalization of violence that is played out in the *mise-en-scènes* of 'Sketch', points to a return of an early persecutory anxiety whereby the frontiers which separate the psyche from the real are at their most precarious: 'cutting-up', 'chopping-up', form as unconscious emotional experience. The message here seems to be that, in war-time, the 'shock defence' breaks down. If, then, Woolf's room is a tomb, it does not contain the corpse of a self-defeating feminine aesthetic any more than it simply presents her desire for death; rather, her war-time writing encrypts the defeat of an aestheticization of the destructive element.

By continually marking the failure of aesthetic transcendence, Woolf's poetics not only offer an aesthetics of negation; she also questions the autonomy and the mystificatory appeal of the aesthetic itself. Witness this appeal made in her 1940 essay 'Thoughts of Peace in an Air Raid': 'Let us drag into consciousness the subconscious Hitlerism that holds us down. It is the desire for aggression; the desire to dominate and enslave. Even in the darkness we can see that made visible'.[81] It is this aggression which, for Hanna Segal, art has to avow if it is to redeem the psychic negativity out of which it is born. But where Segal in the post-war 1940s verges on turning this requirement into a moral imperative, in 1940 Woolf can be read as offering a tentative answer to Segal's later question: what can art tell us about what war represents in the unconscious?

In part, I want to examine Woolf's response to this question in the next chapter. One final description of a 'shock experience', however, provides a clue to the direction Woolf eventually takes:

> At any moment a bomb may fall on this very room. One, two, three, four, five, six ... the seconds pass. The bomb did not fall. But during those seconds of suspense all thinking stopped. All feeling, save one dull dread, ceased. A nail fixed the whole being to one hard board. The emotion of fear and of hate is therefore sterile, unfertile. Directly that fear passes, the mind reaches out and instinctively revives itself by trying to create. Since the room is dark it can create only from memory. It reaches out to the memory of other Augusts – in Bayreuth, listening to Wagner .... Scraps of poetry return.[82]

Woolf never gives up on the idea that Eros can win over Thanatos. In *Between the Acts*, those 'scraps of poetry' return to demonstrate how her own poetics are thoroughly bound up with both an articulation of and resistance to the dreadful negativity of her age. In her biography of Roger Fry, Woolf notes: '"Art and life are two rhythms" he says ... "and in the main the two rhythms are distinct, and as often as not play against each other"'. Of the two rhythms, it is not difficult to guess which is superior for Fry. Woolf is more interested in the interplay between these two rhythms in the context of Fry's response to World War One. 'If he survived the war, it was perhaps that he kept the two rhythms in being simultaneously. But it is tempting to ask', Woolf adds, 'were they distinct?'[83] It is these rhythms that I want to turn to next.

3

Rhythm: Breaking the Illusion

> Science, they say, has made poetry impossible; there is no poetry in motor cars and wirelesses. And we have no religion. All is tumultuous and transitional. Therefore, so people say, there can be no relation between the poet and the present age. But surely that is nonsense. These accidents are superficial; they do not go nearly deep enough to destroy the most profound and primitive of instincts, the instinct of rhythm. All you need now is to stand at the window and let your rhythmic sense open and shut, boldly and freely, until one thing melts into another, until the taxis are dancing with daffodils, until a whole has been made from all these separate fragments. I am talking nonsense I know .... I do not know what I mean by rhythm nor what I mean by life.
>
> Virginia Woolf, 'Letter to a Young Poet'[1]

> The rhythm seemed to rock and the unintelligible words ran themselves together almost into a shriek ... There was something horrible in the noise they made. It was so shrill, so discordant, and so meaningless.
>
> Virginia Woolf, *The Years*[2]

Where Fry distinguishes the rhythms of life from those of art, in Woolf's writing the ebb and flow of rhythm seems to pull life into the order of art. In her 'Letter to a Young Poet' Woolf champions an elegiac and lyrical rhythmical instinct that has the power to transcend disunity, to make a 'whole' out of the 'separate fragments' of contemporary experience. Woolf had given a voice to such a young poet in the character of Bernard in *The Waves*:

> But it is a mistake, this extreme precision, this orderly and military progress; a convenience, a lie. There is always deep below it,

> even when we arrive punctually at the appointed time with our white waistcoats and polite formalities, a rushing stream of broken dreams, nursery rhymes, street cries, half-finished sentences and sights – elm trees, willow trees, gardeners sweeping, women writing – that rise and sink even as we hand a lady down to dinner.[3]

Beyond everyday illusions, Bernard hears the rhythms of another experience, anterior to linear temporality and the convenient lies of society. In *The Waves* itself Woolf bears out Bernard's observation and gives the lie to the illusions of the development and progress of human individuality by continually dashing her characters' monologues against an intricate web of 'broken dreams', 'nursery rhymes', 'half-finished sentences and sights'. The voices that haunt *The Waves* are not so much those of individual characters with stories to tell, but those of subjects kept buoyant on the rhythms of perception; dispersed only to reassemble in the form of what Jane Marcus has called a 'collective sublime'.[4] If rhythm in Woolf is a call to arms against modern alienation, this elaborate defence is at the same time a form of counter-poetics and, some have argued (awkwardly), politics.

The gloss I have just given on rhythm in Woolf's writing is a familiar one. Many recent approaches to modernist writing have sprung from an interest in the place of the subject within poetic language. From this perspective, rhythm is an index of an enunciative process which subverts conventional language patternings and literary forms to reveal a subjectivity founded on an alterity; be it that of a 'collective sublime', as in Marcus' case, or a psychoanalytically defined sublimity of the drives and unconscious processes. The subversive power of rhythm, from this angle, is frequently assumed to lie in the challenge that it presents to the myth of the sovereignty of the subject and the supporting illusion that language's prime function is to represent. Rhythm, so often a handservant to representation, in the modernist text becomes an agent of its partial demolition and in this way, it is argued, throws the authority both of language and of the subject into question.

In Woolf studies this interest in rhythm can be traced back to the influence of Julia Kristeva's *Revolution in Poetic Language* in the 1970s and 1980s. 'The song … the call to our primitive instincts. Rhythm – Sound, Sight', notes Woolf in a marginal comment in her unfinished work, 'Anon'.[5] Compare this with Kristeva's well-known description of the 'semiotic' in Mallarmé's 'Le Mystère dans les lettres'. 'Indifferent to language, enigmatic, and feminine, this space underlying the written is rhythmic, unfettered, irreducible to its intelligible verbal translation; it is musical, anterior to judgment but restrained by a single guarantee: syntax'.[6] Rhythm facilitates a non-semantic revolution by privileging what is in excess of representation and meaning (the enigmatic, the feminine) which, because it is articulated in poetry ('restrained by syntax'), can be written without a fall into madness or psychosis. Substitute Woolf for Mallarmé, and that textual revolution, apparently, becomes a sexual/textual comment on women, writing and gender politics.[7]

Feminist readings inspired by Kristeva have been important in bringing into view Woolf's difference, in particular her sexual difference, from her modernist contemporaries. Yet the critical privileging of the role that rhythm plays in Woolf's presentation of subjectivity also prompts a set of troubling questions for feminist readings of modernism. How thin, for example, is the dividing line between a liminal, rhythmic space 'beyond the subject' and the demand that this space reconstitutes a specifically feminine voice? If Echo, in Woolf's writing, usurps Narcissus, then what images of femininity, gender and writing does this produce? It is salutary to remember that it was precisely on the grounds of a too lyrical femininity that Woolf was once not only criticized, but rejected. One of the most phobic of these repudiations can be found in Wyndham Lewis' portrayal of Woolf as an all-powerful Venus 'introverted matriarch' presiding over the promulgation of a distinctly feminine 'subterraneous' stream-of-consciousness style – 'grabbing the cow' of the 'feminine principle' by the horns is how Lewis describes his essay on Woolf.[8] It is necessary, of course, to dismiss Lewis' anti-feminism. Yet it is just as important to be aware of those moments when feminism's attempt to describe an image of women's writing risks repeating less welcome cultural and historical stereotypes of femininity. The collapse of the 'feminine' into a generalized concept of rhythmic writing (or the even more enigmatic 'poetic language'), it seems to me, risks shoe-horning Woolf's work into a set of gender binaries that do as much harm as good. (By wilfully and vengefully quoting him out of context, a word of warning from Lewis himself, from the same essay, might suffice:

> 'Is it necessary for us to repeat here for the thousand and first time how illusory this division ['classification by gender'] is

found to be, upon inspection … that veneer of habit, and a little bit of hair on the chin and chest, is about all that fundamentally separates one sex from the other?'.)

In this chapter, I want to approach rhythm in Woolf's work with the suggestion that it was precisely a collision between the attempt to articulate a counter-poetics of being and writing, and a dominant and oppressive cultural and historical iconography, that interested and perturbed Woolf in her last writing. 'I do not know what I mean by rhythm', Woolf concludes her letter to the young poet, 'nor what I mean by life'. Woolf's doubts about rhythm in 1932 can be read as a symptom of the way in which she, along with other writers of the 1930s, was compelled to reassess her own modernist practice in the light of the unremitting political spectacles, illusions and rhetorical displays that were being played out all around her. With reference to both the early and later drafts of *Between the Acts* it is possible to trace the final realignments made in Woolf's writing by concentrating on the way that rhythm, for so long an established part of Woolf's poetics, is called into account in her last novel. Rhythm in *Between the Acts*, as in her earlier novels, provides Woolf with a poetic form with which to experiment with the limits of subjectivity, language and culture. What Woolf also begins to explore in her last novel is the extent to which rhythm can also support the most regressive of political fantasies.

This concern about the proximity between what starts as a potentially liberating articulation of the hidden, repressed and primitive underside of culture, and its uneasy return into the culture as a whole is also central to Kristeva's later writing. In *Powers of Horror*, Kristeva's study of psychic and political abjection, rhythm sings to a tune that is very different from the chorus of sexual/textual emancipation with which it has come to be associated. In this account the politics of writing do not inhere solely within a critique of the subject, but also in the troubling relation between the psyche, literature and ideological fantasy. Of Céline's rhythms, for example, Kristeva writes:

> Against the ternary economy of a Transcendence, Céline proclaims the immanence of substance and meaning, of the natural/racial/familial and the spiritual, of the feminine and the masculine, of life and death – a glorification of the Phallus that

does not speak its name but is communicated to the senses as Rhythm.[9]

Like the earlier rhythms of Mallarmé, Céline's music can be read as an attack on the symbolic. Unlike Mallarmé's revolution, however, this 'Rhythm' attempts to substitute a counter-law in its place: a full and reassuring order dedicated to nature, race and family – phallic rather than heterogeneous. Far from articulating an alterity which would liberate the subject from the tyranny of meaning and unity, 'Rhythm' falls straight into the arms of the mysticism of fascist ideology.

Kristeva's renegotiation of the psycho-politics of rhythm has an important precedent in British psychoanalysis. At exactly the same moment that the politics and poetics of rhythm became an issue for Woolf, psychoanalysis too was concerned with the political and poetic potential of the rhythms of the unconscious. One analyst who made rhythm central to the theory of sublimation was Ella Freeman Sharpe. Sharpe had been involved in English psychoanalysis since its beginnings. A member (alongside May Sinclair) of the Medico-Psychological Clinic, she was analyzed by Hanns Sachs (like H.D); Sharpe became a full member the British Psycho-Analytic Association in 1923. She was also analyst to Adrian Stephen (Woolf's brother). Some of Woolf's hostility to psychoanalysis, critics have suggested, stemmed from what she perceived to be its pernicious influence on Adrian and Karin Stephen's marriage. Sharpe's theoretical writings, in turn, occasionally offer tantalizing clues as to the role that Virginia Woolf herself played in her brother's analysis.[10] Sharpe's interest in the psychic rhythms of the unconscious in part reflect her interest in literature and art: she was trained as a literature teacher and, at the time of her death in 1947, was writing a full-length study of Shakespeare. Like many psychoanalysts in the 1930s, Sharpe was attempting to find an adequate account of sublimation amidst the rise of fascism and a political culture obsessed by its own destructive elements. Sharpe, in all senses of the word, was an 'independent' psychoanalyst. As her measured and impassioned appeals for generosity and moderation during the Controversial Discussions attest, although she became increasingly critical of Klein, she was genuinely appalled by the bad behaviour of both the Anna Freudians and the Kleinians. Back in the 1930s Sharpe's work can be read as an attempt to respond to and, to an extent, to rewrite Klein's theory of reparation. She does not, as we will see, shed the psyche of the destructive element, but neither does she valorize it. Rather, like Woolf, Sharpe renegotiates the frontier between the psyche and culture and, as importantly, between art and ideology.

* * *

While concepts of fictionality, temporality and the question of origins have, to a large extent, directed comparative studies of modernism and psychoanalysis, as I discussed in the last chapter, of equal significance to the relation between British psychoanalysis and modernism is their shared interest in formal concerns.[11] The title of Ella Freeman Sharpe's 1934 paper, 'Similar and Divergent Unconscious Determinants Underlying the Sublimations of *Pure* Art and Pure Science' (emphasis mine), for example, echoes Fry's claims for the purity of high art. Following her contemporaries' formal concerns and in a move which also resonates with some of Woolf's poetic principles, in this paper Sharpe gives rhythm a new priority in the psychoanalytic account of sublimation. As in other psychoanalytic accounts, Sharpe begins by taking us back to 'the childhood of art'. The origins of the artwork, she says, can be traced to the origins of the infantile ego; to early phantasies, identifications, introjections and projections. What is so original about Sharpe's version of sublimation is the way she refuses to relegate art to the status of a symptom or substitute formation. Rather, what the artist keeps from childhood are the first perceptions which mark and characterize the early and fragile coming into being of an ego: 'He retains and maintains the vivid sense-perception of infancy associated with good and bad things'.[12] Art then does not, as in other accounts of sublimation, *stand in* for a missing object. Far from being vicarious in respect of something lacking, art is essentially an *affirmative* space. Just as the primary processes know no negation, so too for Sharpe pure perception belongs to a period in psychic life in which 'anxiety is absent'. The figure that marks the absence of anxiety is rhythm. Art is thus produced 'not by repression or reaction-formation, but by making a control by rhythm, which means ultimately the rise and fall of tensions that are rhythmical and pleasurable'. Early perceptions, signs that signify nothing beyond themselves, are engraved upon the work of art; rhythm, the specific patterning of these perceptions, marks the presence of what Sharpe calls 'the libidinal unfoldment' of the drives. Sublimation repeats these rhythms. Disorder and 'un-rhythm', by contrast, 'mean for the unconscious mind menace and destruction'.[13] Unlike its characterization within Klein, Heimann and Segal, art here is not a stage upon which the subject repairs a world attacked by anxious desire with vicarious cultural symbolizations, but is rather a space in which pre-social and libidinalized rhythmic tensions are played out.

Already we can see similarities here between Sharpe's psycho-aesthetics and Woolf's poetics. For both, rhythm signals an affirmative and unifying act of creation which seems pointedly set against the drives toward negativity and destruction. Sharpe's emphasis on immediacy and perception also echoes Woolf's pursuit of the phantoms of consciousness. Compare Sharpe's description of the genesis of the psyche, with Woolf's famous appeal for modern fiction to become true to human subjectivity by placing perceptions and impressions over and above realist conventions of plot and narration: 'Look within and life, it seems it is very far from being "like this" ... the mind receives a myriad of impressions – trivial, fantastic, evanescent or engraved with the sharpness of steel'.[14] When Sharpe, almost ten years after the publication of Woolf's 'Modern Fiction', looks 'within' and behind, to the history of human subjectivity, and discovers the determinants of art in pure perception, she is, like Woolf, also reaffirming Post-Impressionist doctrine. Just as Ford Madox Ford's writing produced, in Michael Levenson's apt phrase, a 'subjectivity in which the subject has disappeared', in this paper Sharpe sketches out a vision of human identity in art in which the attitudes or preferences of the artistic self are obfuscated by the rhythms to which the artist is subject.[15] An ego which is barely coming into being forms the core of Sharpe's version of sublimation and, while rhythm in her account is also a sign of the work of the 'self-preservative' instincts, there is no sense in which this 'self' is reflexive, determining or sovereign. Like Woolf's famous description in *A Room of One's Own* of Mary Carmichael's writing, which she contrasts with the insistence of the 'I' ego of the male writer, Sharpe's artists too seem to match Woolf's evocation of an art produced 'unconsciously, merely giving things their natural order'.[16]

What is also particular to the comparison between Woolf and Sharpe is their joint insistence on the unifying power that rhythm can bestow on the chaotic perceptions which make up psychic life.

By the 1930s, for both writers this affirmation begins to take on cultural and political as well as aesthetic connotations. 'If we are to compensate the young man for the loss of his glory and his gun', writes Woolf in 1940, 'we must give him access to his creative feelings'.[17] Similarly, for Ella Sharpe in 1934; 'Applied arts and ordered civilization are only possible upon an initial achievement of the artist. I suppose it represents the first massive successful achievement of controlling aggression from within the immature psyche'.[18] This inflation of the power of art, of course, was a common symptom of an anxiety in the period about the life-redeeming potential of art in the face of the death-driven spectacles of fascism and war. But it is far too easy to read such insistence on unity and creativity simply as an unreconstructed nostalgia for the creative powers of the imagination – unity itself, for both Woolf and psychoanalysis, is also a back-handed testimony to the power of destructive drives. Contrary to their more vapid pronouncements, rhythm in the work of both Sharpe and Woolf increasingly comes to signify not only an affirmation of life, but also that 'menace and destruction' that both wish to counter and redeem.

Alongside her affirmation of the rhythmic powers of the unconscious, Sharpe sketches out another scenario between rhythm and the psyche which harbours a more deathly potential. Where the artist might achieve order by returning to primordial rhythms, for 'the melancholic and the suicide' this backward path is a dangerous one to tread; 'losing reality sense', the melancholic, 'attempts this preservation by death, which is very often the phantasy of re-union and starting a new life, beginning, that is, at the breast a refinding of this rhythm, an escape from intolerable tension'.[19] As much as rhythm is a life-giving form of sublimatory progression, in other words, it is also, and by the same logic of return, a death-driven regression. Rhythm ceases to affirm a life beyond consciousness, and instead reveals itself as a figure of death. Neither is the deathly aspect of rhythm confined to pathological states. The same failed attempt at triumphing over aggression can be traced in the formal properties of the work of art itself: 'Frustration and anxiety caused the hostile phantasies of using destructively, of spoiling and draining and exhausting the good imago. The picture, the statue, the poem, make a moment immortal, fixed for ever at rhythmic perfection, unspoiled and unused and unusable'.[20] In contrast to Sharpe's earlier stress on creative affirmation, 'rhythmic perfection' stands here as a memorial to the culture of the death drive; a redundant, useless icon to a hostility which it can barely conceal. A precursor to the rhythms which Kristeva will later discover in Céline, it is with this passage that we can begin to see how Sharpe's evocation of the affirmative power of rhythm is underpinned by a more troubling psychic economy.

A similar moment of pure rhythmic perfection also appears in Sharpe's 1930 paper 'Certain Aspects of Sublimation and Delusion', in the following extraordinary description of an analysis which removed an inhibition in dancing:

> To see new steps, a new dance, was to receive a picture through her eyes. She could then practice 'in her head'. Like a negative she had taken the image. Then it could be reproduced as a picture taken from a negative. She was negative and she reproduced the picture. The sounds of music suggested dance. Sound and movement went together naturally. The body bent this way and that, swayed and moved as though it were one thing – all one thing – as a bird in flying is one thing. She was like a bird, was a bird. She was it and it was herself. That is, she was the magical phallus. The dancing was in her. She had become the thing she once saw through eyes of desire, love and hate. She had incorporated it and after the manner of cannibalistic beliefs she had become endued [sic] with the power of the thing incorporated.[21]

With these short repetitive sentences it is as if the analyst's pen too, in some form of rhythmic counter-transference, is endowed with the power of the sublimation she is describing. The passage also enacts a crucial shift of emphasis in Sharpe's theory of artistic representation. It begins with an appeal to the same immediacy of perception which we saw earlier. As if heeding Woolf's advice to the young poet, Sharpe's patient lets 'her rhythmic sense open and shut', here like a camera shutter. Halfway through the passage however, the idea of a kind of rhythmic perception is disrupted by a growing emphasis on a new figure; metaphor or, more precisely, simile. The patient's body moved 'as *though it were* one thing ... *as* a bird in flying is all one thing. She was *like* a bird ...'. No sooner than the figure of metaphor is introduced, however, it too seems to efface itself. 'She was ... a bird. She was it and it was herself. That is, she was the magical phallus'.

Rhythm, then, ceases to signify a continuity between the primary processes and art, and instead becomes caught up in a chain of metaphoric substitutions. In other words, as an image, picture and metaphor, the rhythmic dance itself comes precisely to *stand in* for something which is lacking – the phallus. This is a move away from the emphasis on pure perception in the psyche and art, and towards a theory of psychic production which presupposes neither immediacy nor primacy, but negativity and representation. The key to this shift lies within the concept of incorporation. The dancer does not so much retain and maintain her early rhythmic rise and fall of tensions, she *incorporates* an image of rhythmic perfection. Elsewhere Sharpe describes the relation between incorporation and art as follows:

> At the oral level the ego must magically control the seemingly hostile parent, because of the infant's inadequate knowledge of reality. Then everything depends upon the ability of the ego to eject this hostile incorporation from itself. This means in effect an ego control, in the outer world, of *something* which can represent the primarily introjected hostile imago. The artist externalizes that hostility into a work of art.[22]

The *gap* in the infant's relation to the outside world produces the imaginary incorporation of the hostile parents; it is then necessary that 'something' material comes to represent this image. As we saw in the rhythmic dancer passage, that introjected 'something' is a metaphor ('she was like a bird') which, once established, is quick to reproduce a sense of imaginary illusion ('she *was* a bird'): I know the object is lacking, yet I continue to believe in its existence – that I am it. Or, in the words of one of Sharpe's patients in her description of a slightly different scenario in her 1940 paper 'Psycho-Physical Problems Revealed in Language: An Examination of Metaphor', 'I see these things, but they are not real, I feel like this, but I mustn't feel like this, not really'.[23]

In this later paper Sharpe pursues the analysis of the relationship between incorporation and metaphor by opening up what she calls an 'avenue of "outer-ance"' between the body and language. According to this theory, metaphor evolves in both language and the arts once the bodily orifices become controlled. Although the idea that metaphor simply expresses the body is still dominant here, at the same time Sharpe opens up a new space in which to explore the relation between art and phantasy The thesis that Sharpe rehearses in some senses anticipates Nicolas Abraham's and

Maria Torok's later work on incorporation and introjection. According to them, the psychic process of introjection marks the loss of an object through the acceptance of figurative language. This is a process which begins with the empty mouth waiting to incorporate the object: 'First the empty mouth, then the absence of objects become words, and finally experiences with words themselves are converted into other words'.[24] Although this suggests a developmental narrative – first the phantasy of incorporation and then the introjection of substitutes – this process, as Abraham and Torok theorize it, actually takes place the other way around. The phantasy of incorporation, of maintaining and retaining the vivid sense-perceptions of early infancy in Sharpe's terms, is a nullification of figurative language, a retroactive 'making literal' of the object set up to deny loss and preserve the status-quo. There is no phantasy of incorporation, in other words, without the metaphor which first produces a sense of the object *as* lost. This movement between metaphor and incorporation is subtly exemplified in the words of one of Sharpe's patients: 'When I get what I want it turns to dust and ashes in my mouth'. Sharpe interprets: 'The mechanisms of melancholia are explicit in this last metaphor. "Dust to dust, ashes to ashes" – the object is dead within the mouth'.[25] The melancholic phantasy of preserving the object thus can be read *through* a metaphor which, by effacing itself, reproduces the deadly illusion of an original, and now death-ridden, incorporation.

If we return now to Sharpe's earlier melancholic who, in an attempt at preservation by death desires to 're-find' the peristaltic rhythms of incorporation at the breast, we can begin to unravel a new relation between rhythms, the psyche and art. As a figure, type or metaphor, rhythm can reproduce the illusion of an originary incorporation. No longer merely a libidinal formation which gives things 'their natural order', rhythm in Sharpe's second account emerges as the figure or model of a phantasy of non-separation. From the point of view of linguistics Benveniste has echoed this last point. He argues that although historically it is through rhythm that a seemingly 'natural' relation between the body, the cycles of the seasons and, we might add, the psyche and artistic practice is established, there is, in fact, nothing 'natural' about rhythm at all. Rather, for Benveniste, rhythm is the figure through which we have come to naturalize the relation between the body, psyche, nature and writing. The Greek ϡυθμος does not, as Benveniste's painstaking analysis of its etymology attests, connote a natural flowing rhythm of the waves, but rather, a 'configuration of movements organized in time'. Far from a 'simplistic picture that a superficial etymology used to suggest', notes Benveniste, 'it was not in contemplating the play of waves on the shore that the primitive Hellene discovered "rhythm"; it is, on the contrary, we who are making metaphors today when we speak of the rhythm of the waves'.[26] It is this aspect of 'making metaphors' out of rhythm that is important here. It is surely for this reason that while rhythm can seem to represent the very margins of semantic and cultural signification, at the same time it is also closely aligned with cultural *mythologies* of the natural and primordial. In the case of Sharpe, it also follows that as much as the rhythms of art can affirm the creative impulse to triumph over the forces of aggression, fragmentation and disunity, they can also come to support a regressive phantasy of preservation. Through recent approaches to modernist poetics that I evoked at the beginning of this chapter, we become accustomed to reading rhythm as a property of poetic language which opens itself up to a critical analysis of enunciative shifts in the literary text. In this way, the critic can observe the means by which rhythm bridges the frontier between the sayable and the unsayable, and so vouchsafe for the destabilizing effects of rhythm upon the work of art. If, however, following Sharpe, we read rhythm as figure, or metaphor which supports the production of illusion, the stakes in this reading are changed. The issue is no longer how rhythm is a liminal process of *signifiance*, but one of what kind of illusions rhythm can support and maintain.[27]

Where, then, does this leave Sharpe's claim for the redemptive power of art? Under the shadow of fascism, many English analysts in this period began to explore the social and political significance of the phantasies and illusions they heard from the couch and uncovered in art and literature. Sharpe, for example, hints at an affinity between literary and political spectacles in her last work, an unfinished study of rhythms of Shakespeare's plays. Instead 'of taking the stage for a world', she remarks, Shakespeare might have 'taken the world for his stage, as Hitler did' – a comparison which implies that the only qualitative difference between Shakespeare's rhythms and those of Hitler is that the latter's lead to 'bloody instead of bloodless revolution'.[28] Sharpe's artists and analysands appear to exist in a political and cultural vacuum in which their sublimations seem to speak to no-one but themselves. Lacan's point about Sharpe's and the Kleinian's lack of interest in the dimension of the social in their theories of sublimation is rather blatantly borne out here ('Completely left out is something that must always be emphasized in artistic production ... namely, social recognition').[29] But as war breaks out and as the British psychoanalytic community finds itself torn apart by internal divisions, Sharpe begins to hint at a different kind of political premium that underpins phantasies of incorporation. Compare, for example, her earlier evocation of an art sustained by vivid sense perceptions of what is good and bad, with the following two impassioned statements made during the Controversial Discussions:

> The entire belief in the good concrete object within, or the bad object without, preserves the illusion of non-bodily separation .... Our troubles start with reality, with separation, and a mother who was sexual and bore other children by a father, the recognition of which realities is the blow to narcissism and idealism.
> ... For a belief in the actual good object the actual bad one results in world affairs with a Hitler-ridden Germany and pipe-smoking optimists elsewhere who say 'God's in His Heaven, all's right in the world'.
>
> Freud showed us the way to individuality out of mass-psychology, the way of emergence from the matrix, called by some "the racial unconscious". It is by shedding illusions about ourselves and others, and the deepest illusion is in the belief in the actual incorporated object.[30]

This plea for the preservation of the individual was echoed by many in this period. Roger Fry, as Woolf points out in her 1940 biography, makes much the same point as does Leonard Woolf.[31] There is, however, another more immediate context to Sharpe's remarks. They follow the presentation of Susan Isaac's important paper, 'The Nature and Function of Phantasy'. Treading a characteristically diplomatic path between the Kleinians and Anna Freudians, Sharpe concurs with Isaacs in so far as she too is interested in psychosis underlying phantasies of incorporation. What particularly interests Sharpe is the extent to which this 'wish psychosis' that is embodied in the belief of the incorporated object supports a dangerous political mysticism; a regressive mysticism which, she hints, is as apparent in the Discussions themselves as it is in the 'Hitler-ridden Germany'. 'I do not believe in the omnipotence of the analyst or psychoanalysis', she concludes, 'The *psychical* delivery of the patient is only brought about by the patient: relinquishing the belief in the incorporated analyst'. Is that analyst Anna Freud or Melanie Klein? Many at the Controversial Discussions did indeed behave as if they believed in the incorporated analyst (compare Sharpe's measured tone with Melitta Schmideberg's tart dismissal of Isaac's paper, on the grounds that Isaacs implies too close a relation between Schmideberg and her by then estranged mother, Melanie Klein). If Sharpe objects to Kleinism here, it is to charge British psychoanalysis more generally for its failure to recognize its own complicity with the nature and function of the phantasies it is supposed to be debating. This, in Sharpe's terms, is both a psychic and a political failure. Yet Sharpe also presents us with something of an impasse in this, practically her last published statement. The rhythmic perfection of Sharpe's dancer also reproduces the same 'belief in the actual incorporated object'. 'She was like a bird, was a bird. She was it and it was herself ... She was the magical phallus'. She was perhaps, as Kristeva puts it in relation to Céline, 'a glorification of the Phallus that does not speak its name but is communicated to the senses as Rhythm'. By the 1940s, the phantasies that underpin the production of art, by Sharpe's own analysis, are very similar to the psychopathology of mass-fantasy.

* * *

Woolf did not begin to read Freud until 1939, and it is highly unlikely that she read any of her brother's analyst's work. Sharpe, however, certainly read Woolf. In an analysis of a case of conversion hysteria, Woolf's *A Room of One's Own* is cited as part of a series of associations which unravel an original scenario of infantile desire and hostility:

> 'My heart is like a singing bird
> Whose nest is in a water'd shoot'.
> You remember Christina Rossetti's poem? That's a nice book of Virginia Woolf's – you remember that, don't you? (I do, I remember that the quotation above is in the book mentioned, and that Virginia Woolf sees a Manx cat in the middle of the lawn without a tail, and thinks: 'Was he born so, or had he lost his tail in an accident?').[32]

The patient's symptom, her angina, disappears once the analysis has replaced the pain back in the context of the anxiety produced by a desire for the father's phallus: a desire which, once more, does not speak its name but is 'communicated to the senses by rhythm' inscribed upon the body. 'Her pain is in her heart. But her heart is like a singing bird whose nest is in a water'd shoot', interprets Sharpe, both echoing the image of the phallic dancer (singing bird – water'd shoot) and producing an original interpretation of the relation between the unconscious and the rhythms of poetry. For the point here is not that the rhythms of the patient's discourse unproblematically take us back to unconscious ('wave-like') libidinal rhythms, but that the *figure* of rhythm, here in the form of a literary citation or poetic fragment, stands in for 'the wish to possess the father, to have his penis'.[33] What emerges is not a sense of continuity between the unconscious and poetic language, but a demonstration of how the figure of rhythm, the lines from Rossetti, circulates within an economy of fantasy.

Turning to Woolf's own interpretation of the significance of the Rossetti lines, we find a similar analysis of the power of poetic citation to evoke deep-seated fantasies. For Woolf, Rossetti's rhythms are a historical index of a general human register which resonated before World War One. Before the war, she observes 'people would have said the same things but they sounded different, because in those days they were accompanied by a sort of humming noise, not articulate, but musical [sic] exciting which changed the values of the words themselves'. In contrast to Rossetti and Tennyson, Woolf continues,

> the living poets express a feeling that is actually being made and torn out of us at the moment. One does not recognise it in the first place; often for some reason one fears it; one watches it with keenness and compares it jealously and suspiciously with the old feeling one knew. Hence the difficulty of modern poetry.[34]

It is not difficult to identify Woolf's own poetics here. 'The rhythmical ... is completely opposed to the tradition of fiction, and I am casting about all the time for some rope to throw the reader'.[35] As many critics have argued, rhythm in Woolf's work is both what makes it modern, makes it 'difficult', and the figure which endows her texts with a unity or continuity (throwing the reader a rope). As with Sharpe, the question Woolf begins to broach in the 1930s and

1940s is that of the power of rhythm to reproduce illusion and, in so doing, support not only individual but collective fantasies. The liminal qualities of rhythm, its alterity – for so long a figure of liberation in Woolf's literary carpet – is the very thing that she begins to find suspect. Woolf, however, engages more directly with the questions that Sharpe could not engage with: *who* does rhythm speak to? What part does *social recognition* play in the fantasies that rhythm is able to reproduce?

Reading rhythm in terms of its cultural signification is a difficult project, not least because its liminal qualities seem to empty out all semantic content. Yet this is the wager which Woolf appears to set herself in the war years. This is a move which entails a crucial shift away from an alignment of rhythm with the margins of representation and towards a consideration of what rhythm, in fact, *represents*. If, in her earlier work, rhythm was used to expose the 'lie' of a unitary subjectivity, by the end of the 1930s, Woolf's concern lies less with the phantoms that pursue the individualist subject than with the ideological and social effects of rhythmic perfection upon the community as a whole.

In the essay 'Anon', for example, which Woolf began in 1940, she analyses the effects of rhythm on the listener or reader throughout literary history. 'Anon', the androgynous nameless voice of early English songs and ballads, beats out a rhythm which cannot be differentiated from the voice of the audience. 'The audience itself was the singer. "Terly, Terlow", they sang; and "By, by lullay" filling in the pause and helping out with a chorus. Every body shared in the emotion of Anons [sic] song, and supplied the story'.[36] Murmuring beneath the conventional ideological tropes of English literature, here rhythm provides Woolf with a model for a site of collective identification. Although the patronage and court systems, the rise of the printing press and, above all, the growing self-consciousness of the writer, have gradually severed the poet from the audience, Woolf finds faith in the ways that the rhythm that evokes this collective spirit has been preserved.

> The song has the same power over the reader in the twentieth century as over the hearer in the eleventh. To enjoy singing, to enjoy hearing the song, must be the most deep rooted, the toughest of human instincts comparable for persistency with the instinct of self-preservation. Only when we put two and two together – two pencil strokes, two written words, two bricks ...

> do we overcome dissolution and set up some strokes against oblivion. The passion with which we seek out these creations and attempt endlessly, perpetually, to make them is of a piece with the instinct that sets up preserving our bodies, with clothes, food, roofs, from destruction.[37]

Once again Woolf presents rhythm as an essentially affirmative force which, just as for Sharpe, appears to guard against destruction. In the same stroke, Woolf also naturalizes rhythm. Two rhythmic beats, two bricks ... from instinct to song to house-building, rhythm in this passage is the trope which unites the collective spirit and poetic practice.

The ground is laid here for Marcus' claim that Woolf's poetics appeal to a kind of 'collective sublime'. Anon's audience is not so much a social or cultural community, but a timeless collective of people 'like ourselves, stripped of the encumbrances that time has wrapped about us'.[38] Well within the bounds of the conventions she is at the same time attacking, the imagery in Woolf's essay draws upon the traditional motifs of pastoral as home-spun locals, for instance, sing out a timeless song which reveals 'the ages of toil and love'.[39] Barely five years earlier, William Empson had defined pastoral as a process which puts the 'complex into the simple'.[40] As Woolf interpolates her own poetics into a tableau of 'Englishness', rhythm in 'Anon' is more than just a means of affirming a deep-rooted continuity between instinct and art. It also works as a kind of myth-making figure which stands in for a pastoral ideal that, by 1940, is perceived both as lacking and offering the potential for redemption. Is Woolf's essay, perhaps, another example of what Empson might have seen as English pastoral's capacity to domesticate the destructive element?

It certainly looks as if Woolf is using rhythm to construct a kind of organic myth of the natural, timeless and communal. Yet there is an increasing tension in her writing between this largely mythologized view of a poetics from the margins and Woolf's own difficult engagement with the complexities of a community at war. In 'The Leaning Tower', her 1940 lecture given to the Brighton Worker's Educational Association, Woolf rehearses the themes of 'Anon' in terms of a more overtly political and cultural agenda. The privileged class of 'leaning tower' poets of the 1930s, Woolf argues (unfairly), are ultimately locked within their own political self-dramatization; despite their socialist protestations, they are prisoners of class, tradition and privilege. Through their introspection, however, 'with help from Dr Freud', these writers have opened up a space for the unconscious, a force which, according to Woolf's own understanding of the term, holds the key to a new inclusive, collective form of literature.[41] The stage is set for a politics of 'Anon' as an 'unconscious' poetics from the margins promises a form of collective redemption. Woolf's solidarity with the Brighton WEA audience compares well with the role of a 'sympathetic observer' of working-class life which she outlined in her Introductory Letter to *Life as We Have Known It* (allowing that the Brighton WEA would probably have been more *petit-bourgeois* than working-class) but, as John Mepham points out, it contrasts abruptly with the diary entry in which she describes her contribution to the war-time community as having her mind 'smeared by the village and WEA mind: & having to endure it, & simper'.[42] From this perspective, Woolf's evocation of the collective rhythms of pastoral might begin to read as little more than an attempt to throw an ideological rug over her own sense of cultural unease. But this unease goes further than a familiar contradictory schism in Woolf's poetics and politics. If there is a tension here, it lies less with the fact that 'real' people fail to match up to Woolf's aesthetic ideals, and more with the sense that a form of pastoral poetics is indeed beginning to manifest itself within the political and cultural formations of the late 1930s and early 1940s – but not in the way Woolf imagined or wanted. The community *is* beginning to match up to the ideal and this, precisely, is the problem.

'Began reading Freud last night; to enlarge the circumference ... Always take on new things. Break the rhythm &C'.[43] In 1939 The Hogarth Press published *Civilisation, War and Death*, a selection from Freud's 'Thoughts for the Times on War and Death' (1915), *Civilization and Its Discontents* and *Why War?* (1933), edited by John Rickman (an ex-analysand of Klein's and an army psychiatrist during World War Two). In the same year Woolf began to read Freud's *Group Psychology and the Analysis of the Ego* (1921). In what looks like a straightforward commentary on the theories of Le Bon and Trotter, Freud opens *Group Psychology* by pointing to the ambivalence that inheres in any collective identification. From an 'expression of tenderness' to a 'wish for someone's removal', the unconscious identification that binds a group together can as easily result in a regression to the most primitive of destructive instincts

(Le Bon) as it can to the crowning monuments of cultural sublimation; art, literature, music (Trotter).[44] In her diaries, Woolf talks in similar terms about her own dread of the 'herd impulse' which contaminates a community at war.[45] This interest in group psychology is, in a sense, the social correlative to the masochism at work in her autobiographical 'Sketch'. If that text is concerned with a violence directed towards the self, the public Woolf, as in *Three Guineas,* is concerned with the violence that inheres, not only in Italy and Germany, but in England as the ambivalent ties of identification that bind the community at war threaten to turn Woolf's pastoral community of 'Anon' into a sinister homogeneous whole. 'I dislike this excitement, yet enjoy it', Woolf notes of her own experience of war-time London, 'Ambivalence as Freud calls it. (I'm gulping up Freud)'.[46] Leaving aside this suggestively incorporative metaphor for Woolf's relation to psychoanalysis, I want to argue that it is this ambivalence which cuts across Woolf's last novel *Between the Acts*. At stake in this text is the ability of rhythm to construct a fictional illusion for collective identification. As war breaks out, the question is what kind of illusion can rhythm give voice to. Is it the pastoral rhythms of 'Anon'? or is something more ambivalent being worked through? Sharpe's affirmation of the libidinal power of rhythm was undercut by a theory in which rhythm comes to stand in for a lost phantasy of a deathly preservation. In *Between the Acts* Woolf gives rhythm a political twist. As in her previous work, she gives voice to a rhythm which is culturally repressed. This articulation, however, is far from a straightforward celebration or affirmation of a form of counter-poetics. Rather, Woolf asks the more difficult question of what happens when the primitive rhythms of the repressed do indeed stage their return within the tableaux of cultural formations. What happens when the hidden underside of culture lyricized in 'Anon', does in fact receive social recognition?

* * *

Rhythm, rhyme and poetry are foregrounded in *Between the Acts*, as are the fragments, citations and genres of literary history which make up both Woolf's dramatization of one summer's day in the English countryside and the local pageant which forms the central stage of the novel. With its self-conscious intertextual play, its cunning and punning literary allusions, *Between the Acts* is renowned for its manipulation of illusion. A text which quotes itself as much as the 'scraps, orts and fragments' of literary history, the structure of the novel has been compared to a Möbius strip.[47] The fictional drama of Miss La Trobe's pageant has no non-fictional 'outside' in the drama which is simultaneously being played among the audience. Rather, the play and audience, inside and outside, reflect one another in a ceaseless sequence of repetition and difference. Rhythm is central to this illusory *mise-en-abîme*. It's clear from an earlier draft of the novel Woolf intended her audience to read rhythm as a silent thread which weaves through the text creating and preserving illusion:

> And yet we who have named other presences equally impalpable – and called them God, for instance, or again The Holy Ghost – have no name but novelist, or poet, or sculptor, or musician, for this greatest of all preservers and creators. But this spirit, this haunter and joiner, who makes one where there are two, three, six or seven, and preserves what without it would perish, is nameless. Nameless it is, yet partakes of all things named; is rhyme and rhythm ...[48]

As in Ella Freeman Sharpe's earlier formulations, rhythm here bestows a covert continuity without a sense of authority ('no name but novelist, or poet, or sculptor ...'). But even as Woolf presents it as 'nameless', rhythm is actually frequently 'named' in *Between the Acts*. Poetic citations from literary history, irruptions of metrically regular lines and phrases and self-consciously foregrounded conceits loudly punctuate the text. Rhythm forms the central topos of the novel which very markedly 'joins' characters, tropes and themes. In so far as it is a silent 'haunter and joiner', rhythm is a self-conscious figure or metaphor in *Between the Acts*. As each 'type' of rhythm folds back upon the other, it becomes increasingly difficult to sustain the idea that rhythm is the 'natural' link between alterity and art.

To an extent, *Between the Acts* returns to familiar ground. As in Woolf's earlier novels, rhythm signifies a potentially liberatory space beyond the illusions of everyday life and social repression. The unhappily married Isa, for instance, is a closet poet who scribbles down her rhymes in a book disguised as an account book. Her 'unacted part' lies between the covers of her oppressive cultural and social identity as the wife of Giles, the unfaithful stockbroker, the epitome of the kind of patriotic brutish masculinity that Woolf mocked in *Three Guineas*, and whose behaviour, as Alex Zwerdling points out, is 'very close to the Fascist threat he fears'.[49] As in 'Anon', Woolf's concern here is with the ability of rhythm to construct a spectacle for collective identification. Most obviously this is dramatized by the conventional English rhythms of the pageant to which Miss La Trobe's audience taps its feet with an identificatory beat as the tableau of English literary history is played out before them. 'For I hear music, they were saying. Music wakes us. Music makes us see the hidden, join the broken'.[50] Rhythm, we are invited to conclude, 'joins' the audience together by providing a common emotion for a play in which the 'plot did not matter'. Another rhythm, however, more sinister and harder to grasp, lies beyond those of traditional literary history: 'Chuff, chuff, chuff went the machine. Could they talk? Could they move? No, for the play was going on. Yet the stage was empty; only the cows moved in the meadows; only the tick of the gramophone needle was heard. The tick, tick, tick seemed to hold them together, tranced'.[51] Although like the rhythms of 'Anon' this rhythm is anterior to tradition and convention, it is by no means affirmative. On the contrary, the deadly 'tick, tick, tick' of pure repetition between intervals gestures to a darker set of ties which bind the audience together. Rhythm holds the audience paralysed, prisoners not even of a spectacle, but of the bare promise of an illusion signified by the empty stage and the 'chuff, chuff, chuff' of a music yet to come. It is as if the rhythmic perfection, much noted by readers of *The Waves*, returns in *Between the Acts* to reveal a more sinister underside.

Part of Miss La Trobe's task, as Woolf dramatizes it, is to keep this ominous repetition of intervals at bay, and to produce in its stead an illusion which, while fragmentary, can nevertheless be sustained. This is a challenge, as many commentators have noted, that Woolf herself confronted as she struggled to write within the turmoil of war. But dramatic illusion in *Between the Acts* is constantly shown to fail: or, more precisely, if not to fail then to turn back upon itself, as in the following, frequently quoted passage:

> The words died away. Only a few great names – Babylon, Nineveh, Clytemnestra, Agamemnon, Troy – floated across the open space. Then the wind rose, and in the rustle of the leaves

> even the great words became inaudible; and the audience sat staring at the villagers, whose mouths opened, but no sound came. And the stage was empty. Miss La Trobe leant against the tree, paralysed. Her power had left her. Beads of perspiration broke upon her forehead. Illusion had failed. 'This is death', she murmured, 'death'. Then suddenly, as the illusion petered out, the cows took up the burden. One had lost her calf. In the very nick of time she lifted her great moon-eyed head and bellowed. All the great moon-eyed heads laid themselves back. From cow after cow came the same yearning bellow. The whole world was filled with dumb yearning. It was the primeval voice sounding loud in the ear of the present moment. Then the whole herd caught the infection. Lashing their tails, blobbed like pokers, they tossed their heads high, plunged and bellowed, as if Eros had planted his dart in their flanks and goaded them to fury. The cows annihilated the gap; bridged the distance; filled the emptiness and continued the emotion.[52]

Many critics have read this passage as a testament to Woolf's redemptive drive in *Between the Acts*.[53] The rhythms of nature take over from the point where the rhythms of art fail; Eros triumphs over Thanatos and the illusion is preserved. Makiko Minow Pinkney has described the passage as inscribing an archaic return of the 'semiotic drives'; hence, for her, the cow signifies a return of the maternal which, she argues, contributes to a 'certain libertarian euphoria in the novel' (adding a different slant, perhaps, to Lewis' idea of grabbing the cow of the 'feminine principle' by the horns).[54] But if a 'primeval voice' can redeem the failure of a fictional illusion, within the self-reflexive logic of the text itself, it follows that its rhythms are yet another fiction and a repetition of the illusion they supplement. Far from calling on the rhythms of nature as a redemptive force, Woolf can be read as displacing the opposition between nature and culture. The passage demonstrates how the rhythms of nature are called upon to supply a kind of 'mythification' of illusion in which the cow's primeval yearning works as a metaphor, a substitute, which produces the *effect* of a homogeneous illusion of completion. Read this way, Woolf's pastoral evocation begins to take on a somewhat less euphoric or liberating significance. There is indeed more than a little of the 'herd instinct' in this witty reminder of the extent to which crowds need their illusions, however cod-pastoral they are in content.[55]

The final version of *Between the Acts* is not, of course, without its genuine redemptive moments (such as, for example, the moment when a sudden downpour similarly rescues La Trobe's pageant from failure).[56] A more sinister, bitter and ambivalent tone, however, pervades Woolf's first draft of the novel, *Pointz Hall*. 'Love, hate, peace', for example, is the three-fold ply which provides the thematic principle both for Miss La Trobe's pageant and the sexual drama being played out among the audience in the novel's final draft.[57] 'Love, hate, *fear*' (emphasis mine), is the three-fold ply in the novel's original version.[58] In keeping with this less pacific tone, *Pointz Hall* reveals an even more pointed critique of the scene with the cows and the redemptive potential of the rhythms of nature. In the first draft, the cows' rhythms do not just supply an image of wholeness, Woolf also uncovers an even more difficult subtext lurking behind the pastoral appeals of nature. In the first draft, homophobia is the motivation for the appeal to archaic rhythms. Here is how Woolf concludes the passage quoted above in *Pointz Hall*:

> The cows stopped; lowered their heads; once more browsed statelily [sic] <as if content.> 'That's done it', said Miss La Trobe, hurrying on the scene changers. 'Pish', she said, fixing her bold dark eyes upon William Dodge <whose head jutted out.> 'You couldn't have done that, Mr. Whatsyourname: Billy loves Buddy; Buddy has a smut – Oh bless me it's a pimple – on the end of his nose – that's your universal common feeling, Mr. Whatsyourname'. Why make him responsible for the failure of modern poetry to provide a common human feeling? She had only one second to register the fact that human beings have failed each other; we need scapegoats not heroes; <are> without reverence; him for me, I for him; <so> there's no hope for us. We have recourse to cows ... So in one second she reasoned out her choice of Dodge for scapegoat; her discontent with poetry; her gratitude to cows; before she turned to the next item in the programme.[59]

At the very least this passage makes it difficult to sustain the suggestion that the plaintive rhythms of the calfless cow are some kind of liberating textual inscription of the maternal or 'semiotic'. The price to be paid for the solace of the rhythms of nature is, as Miss La Trobe diagnoses it, the scapegoating of the figure of the homosexual, William Dodge. In this version, Woolf reveals how on the other side of preservation of illusion by 'recourse' to the imagery of natural rhythms lies a denial of difference and, in particular, of sexuality. The return of the 'primeval' into the pageant here is neither a celebration of the repressed or marginalized, nor an example of the redemptive powers of nature, but a troubling return of a primitive and defensive psychopathology.

Only a form of mysticism, of the type that dismayed Ella Freeman Sharpe, could read such evocations to primitive rhythms as a call to redemption. The character of Mrs Swithin, a Christian and 'unifier', offers one such interpretation. For her, rhythm means harmony and unity

> Sheep, cows, grass, trees, ourselves – all are one. If discordant, producing harmony – if not to us, to a gigantic ear attached to a gigantic head. And thus – she was smiling benignly – the agony of the particular sheep, cow or human being is necessary; and so ... we reach the conclusion that *all* is harmony, could we hear it.[60]

In the novel's original draft, it is the 'torture' of each sheep, cow or human being which is necessary to the preservation of an illusion of harmony. 'Harmony' comes to figure the preservation of an illusion that carries with it a deathly legacy. For Ella Freeman Sharpe, it was the preservation of such illusions of homogeneity which supported mass-psychology. For Freud also in the 1930s, it was not only repression, but regression to the most primitive of psychic mechanisms that upheld the psychopathology of fascism.[61] Most recently for Julia Kristeva, it is the thwarted return of early fantasies, culturally connoted through the maternal body, which advents both the psychic and political violence of texts such as Céline's.[62] To go back to the first quotation from Kristeva with which I began, it also possible to argue that the very tropes which are often read as testaments to Woolf's writing – the enigmatic, the 'feminine' and, most especially, the 'rhythmic' – are called into question in her last novel through her engagement with the role that rhythm has in supporting the duplicitous nature of illusion.

'But to amuse myself', notes Woolf in an early diary entry about the novel,

> let me note: why not Poyntzet Hall: a centre: all lit. discussed in connection with real little incongruous living humour; & any-

> thing that comes into my head; but 'I' rejected: 'We' substituted: to whom at the end there shall be an invocation? 'We' ... composed of many different things ... we all life, all art, all waifs and strays – a rambling capricious but somehow unified whole – the present state of my mind?[63]

The oscillation from 'I' to 'We' and then back to the 'present state of *my* mind' here, as in so much of Woolf's work, might suggest that identity belongs to the shifting positions of subjectivity within language. But in so far as *Between the Acts* can be read, like *The Waves*, as a text which channels identity through the ebb and flow of rhythm, by the end of the novel that 'we', that rhythmic 'capricious whole' which seems to index not just a collective identity but also Woolf's own poetics, has become an insistent and ambivalent figure. 'To whom at the end there shall be an invocation?' The rhythmic 'we' can indeed be read as the muse which, in accordance with poetic convention and her own argument in 'Anon', Woolf once more calls upon for assistance in *Between the Acts*. But if we actually turn to the novel's final 'invocation', Woolf's question mark here can be read as retrospectively taking on a new urgency. The pageant's dénouement takes place in the scene where Miss La Trobe turns the tables on her audience in her experiment 'Present Time – Ourselves'. Rhythm in this scene does not secure the continuity of illusion, but irreverently breaks it up:

> The tune changed; snapped; broke; jagged. Fox-trot was it? Jazz? Anyhow the rhythm kicked, reared, snapped short. What a jangle and jingle! ... What a cackle, a cacophony! Nothing ended. So abrupt. And corrupt. Such an outrage; such an insult; And not plain. Very up to date all the same. What is her game? To disrupt? Jog and trot? Jerk and smirk? Put the finger to the nose? Squint and pry? Peak and spy?[64]

These jazz rhythms are in keeping with the rest of the pageant. Bearing in mind the way Woolf parodies the conventional rhythms of English literary history from its pre-history through the Victorians, it is perfectly fitting that Woolf should try to use modern rhythms to signal the present age. And, in keeping with their moment, these rhythms are accompanied by a savage exposure of the investment of the spectator within the work in art. In 'Present time – Ourselves' La Trobe sends her cast onto the stage with a collection of mirrors which reflect the desires of the audience back to them; reflecting not the security of illusion, but disunity:

> Ourselves! Ourselves!
> Out they leapt, jerked, skipped. Flashing, dazzling, dancing, jumping. Now old Bart ... he was caught. Now Manresa. Here a nose ... There a skirt ... Then trousers only ... Now perhaps a face... Ourselves? But that's cruel. To snap us as we are, before we've had time to assume ... And only, too, in parts ... That's what's so distorting and upsetting and utterly unfair.

In 1936 Lacan, in one of his more pro-Kleinian moments, had argued that there can be no identification, no illusion of identity, without aggressivity; Woolf, it seems, agrees.[65] But while the effects of this identificatory *mise-en-abîme* are threatening, this dismantling of illusion itself also provides the occasion for yet another spectacle. In her reading of the novel, Elizabeth Abel observes that in this same scene Mrs Manresa, the novel's voluptuous 'wild child of nature', turns to face the chaos of the splintering mirrors and proceeds to powder her nose. 'Magnificent! cried old Bartholomew. Alone she preserved unashamed her identity, and faced without blinking herself. Calmly she reddened her lips'.[66] Throughout the novel, Abel suggests, Mrs Manresa 'exploits her chosen role as body and nature, as source of the nurturant sensuality a desiccated culture needs.' The mirrors reflect back a collusion of femininity and nature, a hideous stereotype of the sensual woman which, Abel argues, was one of the ideological mainstays of fascism. For Abel, the scene demonstrates how the figure of the maternal in the novel reveals an 'incarnation of nature to be profoundly interior to culture'.[67] The iconography of maternity, like the figuring of rhythm, turns culture into nature and nature into culture; hence its ideological dangers. Something, perhaps, of 'magical phallus', Manresa's narcissism serves as a reminder that accompanying the heterogeneity implied by the breaking rhythms of jazz lies the potential for a further dedication to homogeneity, substance, heterosexuality and nature.

Woolf's jazz rhythms, it seems, are no more immune from the trappings of an ideologically suspect form of mysticism than the rhythms of nature. It is not surprising, therefore, that when Woolf makes her final 'invocation' in *Between the Acts* it is to plea for a suspension of the identificatory lures of rhythm. In the final act, the voice of Anon calls the audience from behind the bushes not, as previously, to identify with the rhythms of a collective sublime, but, on the contrary,

> *Before we part, ladies and gentlemen, before we go ... let's talk in words of one syllable, without larding, stuffing or cant. Let's break the rhythm and forget the rhyme. And calmly consider ourselves. Some bony. Some fat. ... Liars most of us. Thieves too. ... The poor are as bad as the rich are. Perhaps worse. Don't hide among rags. Or let our cloth protect us. Or for that matter of that book learning; or skilful practice on pianos; or laying on of paint. Or presume there's innocence in childhood. Consider the sheep. Or faithful in love. Consider the dogs. Or virtue in those that have grown white hairs. Consider the gun slayers, bomb droppers here and there. They do openly what we do slyly.* (emphasis in original)[68]

But it is not possible to break the rhythm or forget the rhyme. With its repetitive sequences and incantatory phrasing, Anon's voice, even as it appeals to a investigation of our own psychic and political culpability, persists as a silent invocation to rhythm. Within Woolf's poetics, representation without rhythm would be unthinkable. 'Unrhythm', as for Sharpe's artists, would mean death. Even as the pageant closes, another rhythm starts up again. 'The tune began; the first note meant a second; the second a third. Then down beneath a force was born in opposition; then another. On different levels they diverged'. In this final invocation, Woolf makes clear rhythm's ambivalent legacy:

> from chaos and cacophony [rose] measure; but not the melody of surface sound alone controlled it; but also the warring battle-plumed warriors straining asunder: To part? No. Compelled from the ends of the horizon; recalled from the edge of appalling crevasses; they crashed; solved; united.[69]

An admission of ambivalence, a plea to Eros as much as Thanatos, this invocation to the power of rhythm is one of the novel's most enduring images. Just as in the novel's last scene where Giles and Isa open a new act ('Before they slept they must fight; after they had fought, they would embrace. From that embrace another life might be born'), this ambivalence is articulated in a highly sublimated form; tragedy is about to be born. Perhaps part of the passage's power lies in its promise of an aesthetic solution to a text which, in the last analysis, raises more questions about collective identification, the power of illusion and, most importantly, the duplicitous nature of rhythm, than it can fully account for.

John Mepham has noted that all of Woolf's three final works, *Roger Fry*, 'Sketch of the Past' and *Between the Acts* are about sublimation.[70] I would add that *Between the Acts* is also a text about the failure of sublimation in the face of a world at war. Sharpe began her work on sublimation by affirming rhythm in a work of art as the mark of an eroticized repetition of the 'libidinal unfoldment of the drives', but ended with an analysis of the power of the same rhythm to reproduce a deathly illusion of phallic splendour. The move from a poetics of the unconscious towards the politics of psychoanalytic theory could not be clearer here. In her last novel Woolf, in a sense, crosses and perhaps falters on the same terrain. In an earlier draft of the novel Owen Felkin, a misanthropic character who was written out of the final version, offers another perspective on the collective sublime which points toward an ambivalence that goes beyond the Wagnerian appeal of 'battle-plumed warriors'. Like all of the characters in *Between the Acts*, Owen Felkin is a spectator. But he is spectator to a scene that could not finally be assimilated into the novel as a whole.

> He stayed on, noting that the human body, perpetually oozing at various orifices, smells; when those bodies are confined in an enclosed space, the smell ... he raised his head the better to appreciate (if that word is not too strong) the odour that now filled the Barn.[71]

In this chilling scene, Woolf presents us with an image of disgust and the primordial which cannot finally be sublimated – either by rhythm or by any other means.

* * *

'"In the destructive element immerse"'. In Chapter 1, I argued that Richards' version of the destructive element fed into a dominant modernist mythology whereby epistemological and cultural violence was avowed and, thereby, transcended through art. This is a paradigm which also runs across the Kleinian account of human identity and art, and is one which thwarts itself at every turn. No more than Richards, Fry and Woolf can British psychoanalysis be said simply to valorize aesthetic experience over the contingency of historical life, as some of Klein's critics suppose. Rather, and more compromisingly, Klein, like the later Freud, sees the origins of psychic life as determined by an essentially hostile relation with culture – an anti-cultural cultural destructiveness (in Bersani's terms) or a 'Kismet' (in Trilling's) – which proves difficult for both Klein and her followers either to redeem or contain. Ella Freeman Sharpe's and Virginia Woolf's engagement with the duplicity of primordial rhythm marks a shift in the history of this dilemma. Both attempt to escape from the decrees of a brutal psychic and political world into a notion of the aesthetic. And for both this is a journey that takes them from Bokhara to Samarra – to a knowledge that the rhythms of art and the psyche are no escape route from the destructive element. More than a matter of psychic or theoretical vertigo, for Sharpe and Woolf writing in war-time England this 'Kismet' is an irredeemably ideological and political matter.

In the next two chapters, I pursue this conflation of the psychic, the aesthetic and the ideological by looking at the work of Adrian Stokes and Marion Milner. Their work needs to be approached in the light of two corresponding historical developments. First, their writing is testimony to the extent to which the unfolding history of fascism and World War Two provoked a reassessment both for modernist aesthetics and for psychoanalytic accounts of psychic life and creativity. Second, as representatives of a later generation of psychoanalytic thinkers Stokes and Milner re-draft Klein's version of the destructive element. What emerges from their work is both an attempt to temper the violence of Klein's account of the entrance into culture and the development of new models of subjectivity and art. If Klein is the theorist who muddies the frontiers between inside and outside, who, far from taking us 'beyond culture', as in Trilling's account, reveals how tenaciously we remain within its grasp, Stokes and Milner provide a lucid and compelling account of what this impasse means for modernist war-time and post-war aesthetics.

4

Stone Love: Adrian Stokes and the Inside Out

> Some sort of *rigor mortis*. I am frozen in this moment. Perhaps I held it all my life, it is what they called my 'imagery'; even now, they speak of 'verse so chiselled as to seem lapidary', and they say, 'She crystallizes – that is the right word'. They say, 'that is the right word'. This moment must wait 50 years for the right word.
>
> H.D. *End to Torment*[1]

> Down are the arches, and burnt are the walls
> Of the secret bed of the divine Ixotta …
>
> Ezra Pound, Canto LXXII[2]

When H.D. begins her 1958 memoir of Ezra Pound 'frozen' at the moment of their first meeting, we might expect that, faithful to the doctrine of her long-time lapidary friend, what will follow is a memoir of stone-cut precision, a recollection carved into the 'right word'. But H.D. never arrives at the 'right word' for Pound, not least because her memories of him are the results of her sessions with the analyst Eric Heydt, prompted, in part, by the traumas of Pound's Rome broadcasts, his post-war incarceration and now, in 1958, his imminent release. The 'right word', the word to crystallize the relation between H.D. and Pound, or the word, as H.D. puts it, to make Pound 'manifest', is suspended and deferred through the threads of the psychoanalytic transference – the very 'pig sty' Pound once admonished H.D. to crawl out of.[3] Just as her earlier *Tribute to Freud* is notable for the way it troubles the frontiers between modernism and psychoanalysis, *End to Torment*, once again, shifts the relation between the two; not by arriving at the right word but, one might say, by asking the right questions.

For many recent reappraisals of modernism, the significance of H.D.'s affinity to both psychoanalysis and modernism lies in the way she forces the question of sex back into the debate.[4] In this chapter, I want to pursue the complex intertwining of modernist aesthetics and ideologies by re-casting the relation between psychoanalysis and modernism through the work of another writer who was also uniquely poised between the two; the writer, art critic and painter, Adrian Stokes. Short-term friend of Pound and long-term analysand of Melanie Klein, Stokes, like H.D., occupies a shifting middle ground between modernism and psychoanalysis. Unlike H.D., whose writing offers a frequently combative dialogue with both psychoanalysis and modernism, Stokes, at first glance, might seem to promise little in the way of an alternative aesthetics of modernism. One reading might suggest that his work simply extrapolates high modernist precepts, sheds them of their troubling political legacy and, with the aid of psychoanalysis, transforms modernist prescriptions into ontologizing universals. What I want to suggest here, however, is that Stokes' writing disturbs the frontiers between modernism and psychoanalysis and, crucially, between the ideology of modernism and the psycho-politics and aesthetics of British psychoanalysis.

Adrian Stokes made many transitions, many journeys, intellectual and geographical, in his life. The late 1920s and early 1930s found him in Italy, friends with the Sitwells and Pound. When Stokes arrived on the South side of the Mont Cenis tunnel in the 1920s, it was as if, he later wrote, he had been reborn into a dazzling and enlarged existence. In contrast to the ugliness of Edwardian London, dramatized by the horrors of childhood days in Hyde Park, Italy offered Stokes a new land and the model of a new aesthetic. There was nothing particularly unusual about Stokes' geographical and cultural itinerary, or indeed about the conjunction between a certain version of modernism and elite tourism. What distinguishes Stokes from some of his contemporaries is the vocabulary he later uses to describe that journey: 'Of course', he says, 'it is basic human relationships, above all, that my two landscapes describe. Hyde Park is especially a destroyed and contaminated mother, Italy the rapid attempt to restore.'[5] This is the language of Kleinian psychoanalysis. In place of the modernist myth of masculine anti-heroic escape, Stokes' version of 'abroad' is ultimately an account of a journey home.[6] Stokes' flight from the motherland turns out to be a return to, or fantastic re-making of, the mother's damaged body. While Stokes' Italian excursion speaks in the register of a certain strand of masculine modernism, it is the voice of psychoanalysis that has the last word here. But if Stokes troubles the geographical and conceptual frontiers of modernist aesthetics, it does not follow that his work produces a straightforward account of psychoanalysis as a discourse of aesthetic emancipation. A further reason for returning to Stokes' writing lies in its continuing theoretical proximity to modernist precepts at a moment when, in the case of Pound especially, modernism was most blatantly called into political account.

* * *

Where H.D.'s equivocation over the lapidary values of Imagism signals a difficulty in ending the torment of her relation to Pound, the relation between Pound and Stokes is cemented by their joint love of sculpture. In Pound's favourable review of his contemporary's 1932 study of 'Quattro Cento' art, Stokes' appreciation of Italian sculpture is compared to a Gaudier-Brzeska bas-relief. 'He has loved this mixed product of literature and stone', Pound writes, 'and has felt constrained to justify it against the incult, the squalid, the half-baked flux which in our day obscures the work of the few really first-rate makers'.[7] This reference to an admixture of sculptural and literary values was anticipated two years earlier by Stokes in an article in *The Criterion*. If 'Quattro Cento' art 'has an alliance with one of the non-visual arts', he says, pressing his version of the Quattro Cento into an identity with modernist poetics with more than a nod to Pound, 'it is ... to the immediacy of the poet's image'.[8] Note here the debt to Pater's insistence on immediacy and, indeed, to his alliance between the medium of the sculptor and that of the writer.[9] As Donald Davie points out, it is not merely stone, but more precisely, a fascination with the permeability of limestone that binds Pound and Stokes at this point.[10] In his second work of art history, *The Stones of Rimini* (1935), Stokes traces the play of an 'imaginary identification between water and stone' in Italian bas reliefs back to limestone's geological origins: 'Limestone is concreted ocean, a concretion of sea-life: marble is a compressed form of limestone'.[11] In Italian sculpture, limestone betrays its watery origins, and so figuratively dissolves the difference between the natural and the cultural. Compare Pound's 'Canto XVII' in which, similarly, Venice emerges through an oscillation between the tropes of stone and water that culminates in the permutation of one into the other: 'the stone trees – out of water –/ the arbours of stone'. Just as water is transmuted into stone, so too – as in H.D.'s 'Oread' – are the distinctions between nature and art similarly marked and then suspended: marble leaves overlay organic leaves and, by the end of the Canto, the carved 'stone trees' are indistinguishable from the 'Cypress there by the tower'.[12]

For both Pound and Stokes, this attraction to stone signals more than a shifting, indeterminate poesis: stone, for both, is also a synecdoche for a particular cultural and ideological epistemology. For Stokes, limestone is the trope that both unleashes an affirmation of the primacy of the sensual and immediate *and* forms the basis of an entire geographical, historical and cultural aesthetic:

> If we remember the glow of light upon pure limestone, like the glow of flesh; if we remember the ease of its fracture, if we have gathered the impression of such a ratio obtaining between man and Mediterranean nature as will influence the artist to represent natural forces as idealized human forms: then we may understand how mere marble men and women could be works of art and could be deities ... why fountains of limestone, colonnades of limestone, baths of pillared hues and crystalline cooling depths, porticoes of deep shadows reverberating like wells, are common in classical art ... why, in effect, in all stonework typically Mediterranean there is somewhere expressed water made solid, permanent, glowing instead of glassy, set in space and brightened by the dripping rains.[13]

This passage can be read in two directions at once. On the one hand, the 'glow of light' evoking 'the glow of flesh' is characteristic of Stokes' devotion to the sensual impressions of life made manifest in the form of an aesthetics of pure immediacy; an aesthetic which he describes as 'a dream where time is suspended by pure sensuousness'. As in Conrad's 'Preface' to *The Nigger of Narcissus*, the 'permanently enduring' in art, for Stokes, is grasped by an appeal to the sensory and immediate. Likewise, the qualities of Stokes' own writing practice seem to meet Conrad's demand that the writer should 'strenuously aspire to the plasticity of sculpture'.[14] But at the same moment, this aesthetic is the triumph of 'Quattro Cento' Humanism and the 'emblem' of a new, virile self-expressive culture. As the phrase 'idealized human forms' suggests, this is an aesthetic with a mythological dimension. Just as limestone tropes the dissolution of differences, so 'Quattro Cento' art replays this metamorphic merging and similarly allows for the imaginary representation of a new kind of self-reflecting humanism.

As for Pound in the 'Malatesta Cantos', for Stokes too there is a contemporary cultural and historiographic lesson to be learnt from Italian 'Quattro Cento' sculpture. Both conceptually and figuratively, limestone encrypts and repeats an enduring pre-historical fantasy that permits the past to fold into the present:

> Limestone exhibits in mummified state the life no longer found in the Silurian and other distant ages, just as the Istrian palaces of Venice present to us in terms of space, the hoard of ancient Venetian enterprise. The very substance of limestone suggests concreted time, suggests that purely spatial and objective world which limestone architecture has organized for us. Though they have lacked the knowledge of limestone's origin, yet the unconscious fantasies of races have directed artists to obtain spatial completeness in their use of this stone.[15]

Just as in Freud's analogy between the way different historical moments are simultaneously preserved in the architecture of Rome and the preservation of the past in the psyche in *Civilization*, here concreted limestone transforms time into space.[16] Similarly, just as Freud pursues his analogy in an attempt to account for the persistence of the 'oceanic feeling', a state where the boundaries between the ego and the world are not constant, Stokes' spatial aesthetics of limestone imply a relinquishing of controlled aesthetic consciousness. But this passage also reveals the cultural and ideological underpinnings of Stokes' aesthetics. Limestone not only transforms diachrony into synchrony, it also works as an analogy which *naturalizes* the relation between the past and present, its geological origins and the development of humanism and, in turn, between 'the hoard of Venetian enterprise' and the 'unconscious fantasies of races'. Accordingly, humanism appears as natural as limestone's geology and, likewise, the origins of mercantile capitalism as inevitable as a phylogenetic fantasy. As a naturalizing analogy, limestone not only provides the basis for a daring metamorphic poetics; in so far as it spatializes time, it also puts history on hold to produce a homogeneous set of identities between past and present, 'enterprise' and 'fantasy'. While the permeability of limestone depicts the discontinuity of fragmented surfaces, it is also a figure for the mastering of aesthetic, cultural and historical discontinuity. Adding a hard edge to Ruskin, Stokes' stones of Italy are no watery dream: stone is, rather, 'the greatest instrument of mass-effect, of instant revelation: non-rhythmic for the flux of life has passed into objective forms'.[17] Because they imply temporality and so mediation, music and rhythm obscure this desired manifestation of the material and sensual and are thus 'banished' from Stokes' aesthetic. As for Pound, so too for Stokes, turning the 'flux of life' into an 'objective form' promises to transmute disorder into identity; to stave off 'the incult, the squalid, the half-baked flux'.

Limestone, then, is a trope which dissolves differences in order to propose a new unity; or, more precisely, it is the catalyst for an awesome proliferation of identities with a specific cultural and ideological import. The way in which limestone naturalizes the differences between the political, the psychic and the aesthetic to give the impression of a timeless 'mass-effect' already signals that part of its tropic function is to produce a coherent, if illusory, representation of the world. Moreover 'Quattro Cento' carving, for Stokes, also epitomizes the development of a particular model of artistic subjectivity, by providing the ideal medium for a process akin to what Nietzsche (who by his own account was first inspired to write *Thus Spoke Zarathustra* in Rapallo, the same town in which Stokes met Pound) calls the 'will to begetting' or the 'creative will'. In Stokes' terms, this is an exuberant drive towards self-expression which signals the dawning of the new humanist individualism. 'Objects perceived simply as related in space', he says, 'encourage the ambition of everyman for complete self-expression; for an existence completely externalized. Our love of space is our love of expression'.[18] 'Quattro Cento' 'fantasies connected with stone' permit the illusion that the world expresses, contains and holds the subject's desires. Limestone carving embodies a dream of self-completion which, Stokes concludes, for the 'Quattro Cento' artist was 'a desire fulfilled'.[19] 'Quattro Cento' carving not only proffers a totalizing image of the human subject, but reflects too a powerful iconography of bodily solidity and virility: 'Into the solidity of stone, a solidity yet capable of suffused light, the fantasies of bodily vigour, of energy in every form, can be projected, set out and made permanent'.[20] The bodily vigour of the new humanist subject is projected into stone, while stone, in its very form, reflects back – like to like – an image of this solidity. Compare Nietzsche's description of a similar outcome of the exercise of creative will: 'thus', he writes in *Ecce Homo*, 'it drives the hammer to stone ... I see an image sleeping in the stone, the image of my vision! Ah, that it must sleep in the hardest, ugliest stone! *Now my hammer rages fiercely against its prison.* Fragments fly from the stone .... I will complete it, for a shadow came to me .... The beauty of the superman came to me as shadow.'[21]

Stokes' 'Quattro Cento' individualist is, then, a sculptor of the self – not quite a superman, more a kind of self-made new man. Just as limestone connotes the transformation of permeability into objective forms, so too does the artist achieve a 'cutting away'; an objectivization of the object which enables the subject to manifest itself. 'Death', says Stokes, 'is the name for complete objectivization; the subject to be converted has been eliminated'. Stokes himself, however, circumvents this potentially solipsistic model of artistic subjectivity in an appeal to a dialectic whereby the death of the other inaugurates the integrity of the 'Quattro Cento' subject in the name of an affirmation of life:

> Revelation of life made possible by that of death, gives us consciousness; we feel living: and revelation of death made possible by that of life leads us to conceive the world, objects, to make ourselves manifest, to objectify, to concrete the flow of living into personality so that there be passions and passionate intellect to the purpose of their expression.[22]

Implicit here is Stokes' opposition between 'carving' and 'modelling' art. The value of stone-carving, as in Italian bas-relief, lies in the way it illuminates stone. Such respect for stone signifies a separation of subject and object; an individuation which marks the self's integrity and which is recognized – and mirrored as a fitting emblem for that self – by the autonomy of stone. 'Whatever its plastic value, a figure carved in stone is fine carving when one feels that not the figure, but the stone through the medium of the figure, has come to life'. Modelling art, on the other hand, implies a merging of the subject into the object; it is, says Stokes 'a more facile process of homogenous soft materials' which lacks the desired separation of self from other.[23]

As Peter Nicholls has argued with reference to the 'Men of 1914', this kind of logic, whereby the other – be it the past, desire or, we could add here, the medium itself – is objectified in order better to erect the frontiers of the self, is intrinsic to certain strands of modernism.[24] Similarly, Tony Pinkney has suggested that Stokes' early version of the distinction between 'carving' and 'modelling' corresponds with, among others, Hulme, Eliot and Pound's stress on a classic 'objectivization' of the other as opposed to what they all see as the dangerous, decadent, effeminate, 'modelling' merging of heterogeneous identities which characterizes, for Hulme for example, Romanticism and, for Eliot, as Nicholls points out, the decadence of Swinburne.[25] For these modernists, one form of narcissistic merging is continually denigrated in order to erect and protect an aesthetics of a higher (perhaps secondarily narcissistic) form of self-identity. In this respect, the solidity and integrity that Stokes' subject recognizes in stone carving also points to the gendered dimension of this kind of modernism. Just as the other can be sculpted into some form of self-identity, so too, for Stokes, can that other threat to self-identity, woman. 'Man', concludes Stokes, 'in his male aspect, is the cultivator or carver of woman, who in her female aspect, moulds her products as does the earth'.[26] Man is then to carving, as woman is to modelling. Not only does modelling art connote a dangerous merging of identities and, by dint of association, femininity, it also signals the dangerous proliferation of art in an age of mechanical reproduction: 'should the growth of plasticity, of manufacture, in labour and in art, overpower carving activities altogether', Stokes warns, 'there is then no future for visual art as hitherto conceived by the European races'.[27]

For Stokes, as for Pound, the epitome of such an aesthetic 'conceived by the European races' is to be found in the Tempio at Rimini built under the patronage of Sigismondo Malatesta. 'In the Tempio reliefs', writes Stokes, 'Mediterranean life has complete expression: water is stone'.[28] The Tempio had long been (and still is) an object of avid art-historical inquiry. First built in the thirteenth century, and reconstructed by Sigismondo in the mid-fifteenth as a monument to his love for the divine Isotta, the Tempio is the work of an inspired tyrant. Mythologized for his prowess as a warrior, his love of art and his opposition to the Pope, in Sigismondo Pound and Stokes discover not only a model of aesthetic living, but the blueprint for a form of cultural and historical transcendence. This church which is not in fact a church but a monument to pagan love, this incomplete monument to, as Stokes puts it 'a primitive fury', is a testament to one outstanding individual creative will. For Pound, Lawrence Rainey argues, Sigismondo represents 'the historical exemplar of an ahistorical form of life.'[29] This lesson in ahistory has its own history. As a key exemplum of a successful merging of political economy and aesthetic production, for Pound, the triumph of Sigismondo's Tempio lies in the way it 'registers a concept' out of an architectural palimpsest and generic 'jumble'.[30] Pound's praise of Sigismondo's constructive skills, as Peter Brooker points out, compares with his equally idolatrous assessment of Mussolini, 'the *artifex*' who, similarly promises the creation of a 'live nation' out of a 'junkshop'.[31] Pound's key source for Sigismondo (as Rainey has shown) was Beltramelli, who also wrote the first biography of Mussolini, *The New Man*. Add to these analogies the fact that, as New Critical commentaries have been at pains to point out, the *Cantos* can be read as a poem which continually attempts to create a permanent pattern out of its own textual fluidity, 'to shape stone out of water', and the seemingly benign literary trope – 'water is stone' – finally reads as uneasily dovetailing into Pound's self-conscious dissolution of a latent cultural and political order into aesthetic practice.[32] 'In delivering Sigismondo from lies', Stokes once noted in a distinctly Poundian vein, 'we deliver ourselves from the primary mistakes of our condition'.[33] 'Our condition' for Stokes in the late 1920s and early 1930s was one that lacked the drive for a will to art. 'Today we cry out for emblem. The aesthetic sense cries out for emblem.'[34]

In the case of *The Cantos*, this desire for aesthetic and cultural homogeneity defeats itself under the weight of its own demand.[35] *The Cantos* do not so much 'register a concept' out of a textual jumble, as brilliantly adumbrate a pained diffusion of their own historiographic and aesthetic fragments. In a characteristic modernist irony, the final self-dislocation of *The Cantos* is both the necessary correlate and invariable symptom of the desire for aesthetic totalization. The case with Stokes, however, is somewhat different. Both *The Quattro Cento* and *The Stones of Rimini* are littered with acknowledgments to Pound's vision and scholarship. But Stokes stops short of an explicit engagement with the 'Malatesta Cantos'. More accurately, such an engagement is continually promised and then deferred. In *The Quattro Cento*, for example, Stokes quotes an extant letter of Sigismondo's to Giovanni de' Medici from Pound's poem. He footnotes the 1923 appearance of the 'Malatesta Cantos' in *The Criterion*, the Three Mountains Press edition and *XXX Cantos*, published by the Hours Press, and promises: 'In the next volume I will be referring constantly to the great poem'.[36] In the next volume, however, what we find is a further deferral:

> The present volume does not fulfill the promise made in *The Quattro Cento* to give a complete account of the Tempio .... Agostino's sculpture, the themes of stone, and of stone and water, demand a book to themselves. And so, in the present volume there has not been embodied to any large extent my researches into the history of the Tempio's construction, of its artists and of its founder, Sigismondo Malatesta, tyrant of Rimini. Matteo de' Pasti, Pisanello, Sigismondo and Isotta, Alberti, will, I hope appear again in a subsequent volume to whose compilation the *Sigismondo Cantos* of Ezra Pound have long inspired me.[37]

That inspiration is writ large across *The Quattro Cento* and *The Stones of Rimini*. But just as H.D. cannot find the 'right word' for Pound in 1958, neither can Stokes in the late 1920s and 1930s.[38]

Stokes' eventual turn away from Pound in the 1930s has been read as a refusal to collapse the aesthetic into the political and an attempt, amid the unfolding history of fascism, to re-think modernist aesthetics. Paul Smith, for example, describes the break with Pound in the following terms:

> Stokes's abandonment of the sequel to *Stones of Rimini*, in which Pound and Sigismondo were to figure so firmly, basically marks his refusal to be drawn into the way of the forces which took Pound along with them. Compared to Pound's call for large scale action, for the monumental no less, Stokes's position might profitably be described in terms of his own image of the perfect form created by 'the authentic Humanism', namely the involucrum: the whorls and hidden depths of the psyche produces a concrete and stable edifice against the brash energy of the invader. His retreat into that shell belongs to the years of rising fascism and of the second world war, and has its rubric in *Inside Out*, a text given over (to adjust Stokes's own pun) to 'working out' – working out the problems of the relation of psyche to creative activity.[39]

One significant event that marks this shift is Stokes' analysis with Melanie Klein between 1931 and 1936. Stokes' own analysis of sublimated masculine rivalry in his 1956 paper, 'Psycho-Analytic Reflections on the Development of Ball Games, Particularly Cricket', might go some way towards explaining this transferential shift away from the man he met at tennis match in Rapallo in 1926 (the father of Modernist aesthetics), to the more maternal embrace of seven years analysis with Klein (the mother of child analysis) and his subsequent career as a Kleinian art critic.[40] In Smith's terms, this displacement from paternal to maternal desire effectively extrapolates the aesthetic from the grip of ideology through a 'retreat' inwards. Stokes refuses Pound's politics by removing 'his reparative activities to the level of the psyche'. Pound, in the meantime, continues his project of manic reparation on a cultural scale and hence remains, says Smith, 'in the paranoid-schizoid position, having split the world into good and bad and drawing sensations of persecution from bad objects thus created'.[41] While a retreat inwards certainly characterizes Stokes' wartime work, the Kleinian narrative by which Smith explains this transition is also open to a different reading. In a later dialogue with Stokes in 1965 which accompanies the text of *Painting and the Inner World*, Donald Meltzer points out that the transition from the paranoid-schizoid position to the depressive position is 'never complete': 'progress from the paranoid-schizoid to the depressive position (or regressions in the opposite direction) fluctuate throughout the course of life'.[42] It follows that an attempt to insulate reparative activity within the psyche would carry with it, as a necessity within the Kleinian account, those gestures of splitting, denial and disavowal which, in Smith's terms, constitute Poundian megalomania. To retreat *from* the poetics of a modernism that has gone to the ideological, to continue Smith's analogy, would be to discover that, in some senses, you were still there. As well as carrying therapeutic connotations, 'inside out' for Kleinian psychoanalysis, as we saw in Chapter 1, also means 'outside in'. Accordingly, we should not be surprised to find that the 'brash energy' of modernist poetics and politics is also secreted within the apparent safety of 'whorls and hidden depths' of its potential redeemer, psychoanalysis.[43]

What happens if Stokes' engagement with Klein is read not only as a retreat inwards, but as a *continuing* dialogue with the questions that his earlier form of modernism provoke? If inside-out also means outside-in, to what extent does his engagement with Kleinian psychoanalysis challenge the poetics and inherent ideology of the subject of the 'self-same' that Stokes discovered in the

'Quattro Cento'? Stokes' work can be read, like Virginia Woolf's, as an example of a modernism which, by the late 1930s, was beginning to call itself into account. His later commitment to psychoanalysis is not just a run for cover, but an attempt to renegotiate the frontiers between art and politics. Before examining this renegotiation, I want, first, to take a detour into an alternative thesis on limestone as a prelude to some more contemporary speculations on aesthetics and ideology.

* * *

> What the present controversy demonstrates is that the category of the aesthetic is not the primary one for human life, and the attitude which holds aesthetic considerations to be primary is far from primary itself, but is produced by very many historical, social and moral conditions.
>
> William Barrett[44]

> [L]et us at least ask ourselves whether fascism is or is not one of the 'myths' of *The Cantos*. Who will deny that it is?
>
> Karl Shapiro[45]

The controversy referred to by William Barrett here was the decision of the Fellows in American Letters of the Library of Congress to award the first annual Bollingen Prize for poetry to Ezra Pound's *The Pisan Cantos* in 1949. Seen by some as a testament to the liberalism of the West as the ideological parameters of the Cold War began to establish themselves ('this could never happen in Russia' rejoiced one radio commentator),[46] and by others as evidence of the extent to which the anti-semitism of Maurras and Eliot had inflected New Criticism (Eliot was one of the Bollingen judges), the award caused nothing less than a scandal. W.H. Auden was also one of the Bollingen judges. His defence of the judges' decision published in *Partisan Review* reflects some of the unease which characterized debates about art and politics in the 1940s. 'An art which does not accurately reflect evil would not be good art', he notes. Art is a 'mirror in which the spectator sees reflected himself and the world, and becomes conscious of his feelings good and bad, and what their relations to each other are in fact'. Auden then qualifies this by adding that those Gentiles who are not properly ashamed of their anti-semitism – who cannot tell good from bad – 'must be regarded as children who have not yet reached the age of consent in this matter and from whom, therefore, all books ... which reflect feeling about Jews ... must be withheld'. Fortunately, *The Pisan Cantos* are unlikely to be read by such people. Were this the case, Auden would gladly withdraw the book, but not the prize.[47] This is a familiar, if self-cancelling argument (if good art prompts such self-consciousness, then surely the 'children' should be encouraged to read it?), and it hardly answers the case against awarding Pound the prize.

By comparison Auden's 'In Praise of Limestone', written in Italy in May 1948, reads as a critical elegy for Pound's and Stokes' pre-war enthusiasm for limestone's poetic and totalizing aesthetic potential and, as Jean-Michel Rabaté hints in a suggestive footnote in his essay on Pound and Stokes, offers itself as a dialogue with Stokes' thesis on limestone.[48] Auden had earlier praised Stokes' work. 'The poetry in *The Quattro Cento*', he wrote to Stokes in June 1932, 'is quite devastating. You are one of the three contemporary writers who I can read with genuine admiration' (alas, there is no mention of the other two).[49] A poem which is as alert to the dangers of the coalescence of identities within the aesthetic as it is anxious to somehow hold onto the radical potential of art, 'In Praise of Limestone' can be read as a 'poetry lesson' (to adapt the phrase which Auden uses to describe Freud's work)[50] which teases out the tension we have seen so far in Stokes between a potentially radical appeal to an aesthetics of the sensual and immediate and its permutation into gestures of cultural and ideological mastery.

'If it form the one landscape that we the inconstant ones/Are consistently homesick for, this is chiefly/Because it dissolves in water'. For Auden, as for Stokes, Italian limestone tropes the sensual dissolution of separate identities. Unlike Stokes', however, Auden's praise of limestone is equivocal. Just as Freud's 'poetry lesson', in Auden's words, uses the 'unhappy present to recite the past', in this poem the permeability of limestone signifies a pre-historical merging of identities which captures a powerful, idyllic homoerotic fantasy of non-individuation and non-separation:

> What could be more like Mother or a fitter background
> For her son, for the nude young male who lounges
> Against a rock displaying his dildo, never doubting

> That for all his faults he is loved, whose works are but
> Extensions of his power to charm?

Auden's limestone landscape is a fitting backdrop to a primary narcissism which is all the more compelling because of its apparent limitlessness. But where for early Stokes such stone fantasies embody the self-expressive power of 'Quattro Cento' humanism, for Auden such omnipotence is, more bathetically, a fantasy for which we are homesick – a simile for Mother ('I hadn't realized how like Italy is to my "Mutterland", the Pennines', Auden wrote to Elizabeth Mayer in 1948.)[51] If limestone is a synecdoche for an aesthetic here it is one which, as in Freud's theory of creativity, seduces on account of its infantile and regressive appeal.[52] For Auden in 1948, such a recapturing of narcissism bodes not so much the promise of a powerful aesthetic, but an artistic culture which, while it seduces, is ultimately stultified by the gratification of its own desire. While 'the young male' may desire 'to receive more attention than his brothers', in this early-oedipal limestone landscape, Auden's group of young rivals/artists are too locked in an aesthetic torpor to awake the violence necessary for either separation or a new kind of art:

> ... engaged
> On the shady side of a square in midday in
> Voluble discourse, knowing each other too well to think
> There are any important secrets, unable
> To conceive of a god whose temper-tantrums are moral
> And not to be pacified by a clever line
> Or a good lay: for, accustomed to a stone that responds
> They have never had to veil their faces in awe
> Of a crater whose blazing fury could not be fixed;

Limestone's permeability responds too readily to pleasurable free-play. What is lacking is not only the paternal figure of 'a god whose temper-tantrums are moral', but a landscape which would check such omnipotent auto-affectation with a sure dose of ungraspable differentiation: 'Their eyes have never looked into infinite space/Through the lattice-work of a nomad's comb. Their legs have never encountered ... the monstrous forms and lives'. Wrapped in the untroubled embrace of a limestone landscape, the brothers/artists go 'to the bad', become pimps or 'deal in fake jewelry'.

Aesthetic pleasure, limestone's playful and sensual indeterminacy, degenerates into the decadent desires of a marketplace of the senses.

The aesthetics of limestone, then, for Auden, produce an imaginary topos that tricks its subjects into the lure of an imagined totality which, here, screens them from history. Auden does not 'praise' or, as does the early Stokes, exult in this myth, he unmasks it: 'this land is not the sweet home that it looks/Nor its peace the historical calm of a site/Where something was settled once and for all'. In the third stanza, which formally enacts a separation from the non-individuation proposed by limestone with the introduction of a dialogue of differing voices, history, by contrast, is located as taking place on more 'immoderate soils where the beauty is less external': on the plains of clay and gravel, for example, where 'there is room for armies to drill; rivers/wait to be tamed', and where imperialist, rather than aesthetic, desire is given licence (clay is 'soft as the earth is mankind and both/Need to be altered'). 'In Praise of Limestone', then, draws on the psychoanalytic narrative of the child's progress from indiscretion to discretion, from pre-history to history, to make a point about the duplicity of aesthetic beauty. For all its seductive appeal, the permeability of limestone, its coalescence of identities, can result in a indolent aesthetic which, tricking us into believing that it responds to our desires alone, captures us in the embrace of an imaginary reserve. It is as if, in response to Pound and Stokes, Auden is replying that the aesthetic which promised to shore up modernist identity against the heterogeneous merging of identities implied in 'modelling art', is as narcissistic, as dangerously permeable, as the aesthetic they once vilified. 'Like Mother', limestone tropes a dissolution of identity which, in Auden's poem, is presented as both desirable *and* decadent and duplicitous.

While the first three stanzas suggest the ambivalence of limestone, by the fourth Auden points again to its subversive qualities. (In fact, we've already had a whisper, an 'oceanic whisper', of this in the third stanza.) '[I]n spite of itself', limestone retains a 'worldly duty', and a potential to call 'into question/All the Great Powers assume'. Limestone, with its uncanny as well as indolent poetics, 'disturbs our rights'. It disturbs, in part, through the power of its mythical sensory appeal that the poem itself has done so much to unmask. The poet, for example, 'is made uneasy/By these solid statues which so obviously doubt/His antimythological myth'.

Similarly the 'gamins' who pursue the scientist down the colonnade with their lively offers rebuke cold science by retrieving the sense of a playful homoeroticism that the poem evoked earlier. The agitation provoked by limestone's seductive and mystificatory appeal, however, does not provide the grounds for its straightforward rehabilitation as an aesthetic form. The value of limestone's reproach, rather, lies in its power to provoke a resistance to its own narcissistic collapse of identities and, hence, to precipitate a subsequent mediation, or sublimation, of its sensual poetics of the self-same. An interjection in the poem's final stanza suggests just such a mediation and, at the same time, allegorizes the poem's own aesthetic preference:

> ... I, too, am reproached, for what
> And how much you know. Not to lose time, not to get caught,
> Not to be left behind, not, please! to resemble
> The beasts who repeat themselves, or a thing like water
> Or stone whose conduct can be predicted, these
> Are our Common Prayer, whose greatest comfort is music
> Which can be made anywhere, is invisible,
> And does not smell.

In response to limestone's feared yet predictable repetition of identities ('like water/Or stone'), music, once banished by Stokes, emerges as an alternative aesthetic. Less corporeal, less transgressive of permeable boundaries (it does not smell, but – more self-consciously – is heard), music, in the 'invisible' spaces of the rhythms and repetitions of the poem itself, has in fact mediated limestone all along. Seen in this light, Auden's praise of limestone, in effect, reads as a eulogy not for limestone, but for poetry itself (in a poem which is one of Auden's least metrically complex). Limestone's both desired and reviled promiscuous permutation of boundaries shores up the hermetic self-identity of the poem as one form of narcissistic self-identity is transcended in order be exchanged, invisibly, for another. This mediation can be heard in the poem's closing celebration of the disturbing ebullience of Italian limestone:

> These modifications of matter into
> Innocent athletes and gesticulating fountains,
> Made solely for pleasure, make a further point:

The blessed will not care what angle they are regarded from,
Having nothing to hide. Dear, I know nothing of
Either, but when I try to imagine a faultless love
Or the life to come, what I hear is the murmur
Of underground streams, what I see is a limestone landscape.

While limestone retains its unashamed appeal, Auden's marble men and women cannot, as they could for the early Stokes, become deities or cultural monuments; the aesthetic they connote is simply too historically tarnished, too 'seedy' and suspect: a 'faultless love' of limestone, as Auden's pun suggests, cannot be without fault. Yet, mediated through the ears and eyes ('what I hear'/'what I see') of the poet, and hence interceded by reflexive self-consciousness, its beauty can to an extent be redeemed. Within the parabolic structure of 'In Praise of Limestone', the regressive 'homesickness' for a limestone landscape, its indolent illusory wholeness, is tempered – and hence granted back a measure of its aesthetic appeal – by a poetic consciousness that both requires and contains it.

If we read Stokes' early aesthetics of limestone alongside Auden's later, double-edged, praise, something like the following narrative emerges. Where for early Stokes limestone tropes both sensual immediacy and the self-identity of the 'Quattro Cento' subject, Auden's poem establishes a relation of mediation to Stokesian immediacy which acknowledges the beauty of limestone whilst resisting its mythical import. In this way, these two theses on limestone exemplify the transition between an earlier modernist appeal to mythological structures and an attendant drive towards monumentalism, and a post-war suspicion and working through of the potential ideological duplicity of such an aesthetic. What, however, remains common to both these writers is an association of the aesthetics of limestone with a powerful appeal to the sensual and indeterminate, which is tempered and contained by an equally strong appeal to the identity of one. Where in Stokes carving is to modelling as self-identity is to narcissistic merging, in Auden's poem, one aesthetic is represented as too permeable, too indolent, in order to privilege the identity of its own, preferred medium. In 'In Praise of Limestone' the final appeal to poetry is both sustained and produced by an aesthetic which appears to be its opposite but which, within the poem's self-reflexive structure, it also mimics. The struggle 'not to resemble' conceals, at least in its manner of operation, a kind of uncanny semblance; just as, if we read Stokes' aesthetics of limestone through Auden, the carving of the 'Quattro Cento' autonomous subject is shadowed by the collapse of desire into a medium associated with 'modelling' art.

In so far as the encounter I have staged between Stokes and Auden turns on strategies of mystification and demystification of the ideological dimension of one strand of modernist aesthetics, these two theses on limestone offer themselves as part of a historically located narrative. We return here to the same tension between the aesthetic, cultural and political fantasy which characterized the work of Ella Freeman Sharpe and Virginia Woolf. In their case, rhythm began as gesturing towards a potentially emancipatory space beyond the illusions of everyday life and the supposed authority of the subject of representational art, only to cross over into a risky psychic and cultural appeal to homogeneity and completeness. This tension is, of course, not only particular to debates in the 1930s and 1940s but is also rehearsed in contemporary arguments about what has come to be known today as the ideology of the aesthetic – the same ideology that, for William Barrett, condoned the Bollingen Prize in 1948 because it refused to recognize the historical, social and moral determinations of claims to aesthetic autonomy.

For Terry Eagleton, aesthetic autonomy, the idea that art exists apart from social practice, both provides a certain 'ideological model of subjectivity', that is, of a self-regulating, self-determining human being – precisely as in Stokes' myth of the 'Quattro Cento' aesthetic subject – and, in the same move and more radically, offers the basis for an unleashing of human energies towards revolutionary practice. In his reading, the Kantian subject is split: it is precariously situated between the demands of the moral law and the evidence of felt experience, and categorically fissured between practical and pure reason, the phenomenal and the noumenal, materiality and intelligibility. Kant's aesthetic subject of the Third Critique is, hence, the 'heuristic fiction' that comes in to plug this gap.

> The Kantian subject of aesthetic judgement who misperceives as a quality of the object what is in fact a pleasurable co-ordination of its own powers, and who constitutes in a mechanistic world a figure of idealized unity, resembles the infant narcissist of the Lacanian mirror stage, whose misperception Louis Althusser has taught us to regard as an indispensable structure of ideology.[53]

One of the essential functions of ideology, says Eagleton, is to achieve a balance between this centring of the subject, granting it an illusory autonomy, and simultaneously maintaining the subject's submissiveness. This is where the sublime and a second analogy with psychoanalysis comes in. The Kantian sublime, for Eagleton, is like the Freudian unconscious, in so far as both threaten to engulf the subject with an ungraspable excess. Like the subject of the unconscious, the subject of the sublime is 'decentred, plunged into loss and pain, undergoes a crisis and fading of identity'. Yet, adds Eagleton, 'without this unwelcome violence we would never be stirred out of ourselves, never prodded into enterprise and achievement'.[54] The passage through the beautiful is therefore, to paraphrase Eagleton, only a temporary rest on the journey back to pure reason. In this way, the relation between the beautiful and the sublime re-enacts the hegemonic trick of centring the subject by allowing it to believe that, unlike the commodity, the object can, for once, be blissfully apprehended, while simultaneously tempering such gratification by pushing the subject up against the limits of the imagination through the reintroduction of the moral law, underwritten here with all the unrelenting demands of the id-bound Freudian super-ego.[55]

I am less interested in what Eagleton has to say about Kant here than I am in what his argument suggests about psychoanalytic readings of the aesthetic.[56] For Isobel Armstrong, Eagleton's tinkering with the ideology of the aesthetic using psychoanalytic analogies has, in the case of Kant at least, quite simply got out of hand. Not only does such *bricolage* ontologize 'psychoanalytic structures as universals' but, and more seriously, this generalization risks carrying over – and masking – the historical role that the category of gender has played in aesthetic thought. The beautiful is not only one side of the structure of ideology; by bestowing it with an imaginary dimension, Eagleton also returns us to the mother's body and, by dint of this, to the historical association between the aesthetic and femininity. Take, for example, the following passage from Eagleton with which Armstrong begins her critique:

> What else, psychoanalytically speaking, is this beautiful object which is unique yet universal? ... The beautiful representation, like the body of the mother, is an idealized material form ... with which, in the free play of its faculties, the subject can happily sport. The bliss of the aesthetic subject is the felicity of the small

> child playing in the bosom of its mother, enthralled by an utterly indivisible object which is at once intimate and indeterminate, brimming with purposive life yet plastic enough to put up no resistance to the subject's own ends.[57]

Accustomed to an object that responds too readily, the Kantian subject of the beautiful is, as in Auden's poem, locked in imaginary torpor. 'Like Mother', the imaginary domain of the beautiful grants the illusion of subjective autonomy which, for Eagleton, is one side of the ideological structure of the aesthetic. For Eagleton to imbue the aesthetic with a founding narcissistic permeability, then, says too little about Kant and too much about the persistence of the association between femininity, narcissism and the aesthetic. 'Only a Kleinian anger, the infant's resentment of the mother's withholding', Armstrong remarks, 'could find this explanation plausible'.[58] Added to this anger is an anxiety which, perhaps, is as common to the structure of modernist poetics that I identified earlier as it is, for Armstrong, to contemporary theoretical characterizations of the aesthetic in the work of not only Eagleton but, from a differing perspective, Derrida and De Man. As Armstrong argues:

> The aesthetic is feared as the collapse and elision of categories, as a permeable meltdown of difference in the law of the same: the threat of metaphor. Phallic self-identity is at one and the same time shored up and undermined by the aesthetic figuring as metaphor.[59]

At issue here is not the aesthetic *per se* but the production of the aesthetic based on a particular reading of metaphor as a trope whose activity is to produce likeness out of difference. Compare how for Stokes the aesthetics of limestone rests on a carving of water into stone ('water is stone'), which is shadowed – 'shored up and undermined' – by a homogenous 'more facile' modelling-type collapse of difference into identity; just as for Auden, the poetic task is *not* to resemble a thing 'like stone/Or water'.

Changing the terms through which we see metaphor provides the basis for Armstrong's answer to what she sees as Eagleton's 'worst-case' reading of the ideological dimension of the aesthetic. Stressing, with Ricoeur, that it is the play of unlikeness, the transformation of categories, which is crucial to metaphor, Armstrong attempts to extract the aesthetic from its inevitable ideological fate through a transition from Kleinian anger to Winnicott's 'play'. Drawing from Vygotsky's materialist and cognitive account of play, in place of a theory of metaphor as semblance Armstrong posits his 'pivotal object'; the object by which the infant makes the cognitive leap between the immediacy of the visual world and the world of meaning. To Vygotsky, Armstrong adds Winnicott, whose 'transitional space' similarly opens up a site of 'play' which promotes the transformation of categories. Winnicott's transitional object (the famous blanket or teddy) is both me and not-me; an object which sets up an intra-subjective arena (which is not, Winnicott stresses, that of narcissism) and thus a 'potential space' between the individual and culture – a place where meanings are negotiated and constantly remade. 'Play' then provides Armstrong with the basis of an alternative, potentially emancipatory aesthetic. Play, she says, 'is part of a continuum in which madness subsists at one end and ideology at the other – and only becomes art, perhaps, when we *choose* to call it so'.[60] Is such play, however, an alternative aesthetic? How is it possible to 'choose' when play becomes art and when it becomes ideology? *Who* chooses? Madness, Winnicott teaches, erupts when the absence of the loved object blocks the child's toleration of ambivalence and anxiety and produces fetishization and persecution fantasies in their stead. Is ideology too, perhaps, the regression of the transitional object to the fetish? Is ideology madness? The acceptance of anxiety, the recognition that the object is both me and not me which Armstrong places at the centre of her alternative aesthetic, after all, carries a faint shadow of the dialectic between autonomy ('me') and subjection ('not-me') which Eagleton recognizes in ideological consciousness. 'Play', in other words, can still be ideology.

Psychoanalysis is not an aesthetic, any more than it is simply an ideology. It does, however, for both Armstrong and Eagleton at least, allow us to imagine an alternative mode of being, and hence a new aesthetic which can both undo and challenge the constraints of ideological consciousness. Whatever the reasons for the theoretical turn to psychoanalysis now, this move towards the founding of a new aesthetic echoes Stokes' similar project fifty years earlier. A writer for whom the dangers of an aestheticization of politics were all too clear (as the break with Pound over Sigismondo dramatically illustrates) Stokes' later work was also an implicit retheorization of the aesthetic object through psychoanalysis, which, as we will see, anticipates, traverses and, I want to suggest, finally refigures contemporary and current debates over the ideology of the aesthetic.

* * *

In 1934 Pound reviews Stokes' second work on the 'Quattro Cento', *The Stones of Rimini*. While he again extols Stokes' lapidary values ('Stokes has found at least one basic unity or antithesis: Water and Stone. For that alone the book is worth printing'),[61] Pound now seems to distance himself from Stokes. Stokes, says Pound, 'has quite astutely refused to be entangled by a set of axioms which my decade, or the period from Brancusi to Gaudier-Brzeska, had erected for the totally different problem of SCULPTURE'.[62] Pound's distancing compares with Stokes' own retrospective account of his earlier years in Italy in *Inside Out* (1947). This book is the product of Stokes' war-time meditations. World War Two finds Stokes in English modernism's home from home, St Ives, Cornwall, doing his bit with the home guard, friends with Barbara Hepworth and Ben Nicholson and other more temporary exiles. Stokes' war years were a time of anxiety, the threat of invasion was ever-present and his personal life was complicated (he separated from Margaret Mellis whom he married in 1938, and married her sister, Ann, in 1947). But Cornwall also provided a landscape and a space which, one senses, allowed Stokes to recover after his heady days in Italy and to reformulate his aesthetics in the light of his analysis with Klein. Consequently, *Inside Out* is at once a psycho-biography, a piece of art criticism and a work of intense lyricism. Where Pound seems to want to take sculpture to a higher level of modernist abstraction, Stokes now interprets his Italian fascination with stone in terms of phantasy:

> Existence was enlarged by the miracle of the neat defining light. Here was an open and naked world. I could not then fear for the hidden, for what might be hidden inside me and those I loved. I had, in fact incorporated this objective seeming world and proved myself constructed by the general refulgence. Nothing, for the time, lurked, nothing bit, nothing lurched.[63]

Where 'Quattro Cento' carving was once the epitome of the self-identical subject, Stokes now suggests that the objectivity of stone only *seemed* so and that, correspondingly, his model of artistic subjectivity was an act of illusory self-construction. Anticipating Auden's poem by one year, Stokes here demystifies the very imaginary structure he had once so painstakingly erected. The parallel with Auden's reassessment of limestone gains pace when Stokes completes this passage with a retrospective 'musical' view of Italian landscape:

> As I think now of that valley at Rapallo ... I have the sensation of a sound which contains every note, prolonged, entirely sustained, as good beneath as above, a sound that provides every aural want; at the same time it is itself the epitome of complete self-realization.[64]

Sound, music, now comes to mediate the seeming ebullience of Italian landscape. Moreover, as again with Auden, as it mediates, sound now promises a new form of self-identity: in place of emblem, sound is now 'itself the epitome of complete self-realization'.

As with H.D.'s similar retrospective account of an earlier modernist moment, the sounds by which Stokes now mediates his earlier aesthetics are resonant with the 'sounds', or exchange of signs, of the psychoanalytic transference (*Inside Out* is presented explicitly as the product of Stokes' seven-year analysis with Klein). In this sense, when Stokes looks back to an earlier form of modernism, he too is involved in a process of writing a new narrative; not of 'emblems' and 'monuments' but of phantasy and desire. On the one hand, this results in a remarkable piece of self-analysis. The analyzed Stokes now pictures the young Stokes as journeying through Italy, an interpretation of Kant's *Critique of Pure Reason* tucked under one arm, in a desperate search for the absolute: 'I was engrossed entirely in the absolute ... the problem had always been "how to bring the distant things near"'.[65] The problem was to bridge the gap between the noumenal and the phenomenal. Seen in this context, Stokes' earlier aesthetics of limestone, as with Eagleton's reading of Kant, might seem to be part of the production of a 'heuristic fiction' designed to plug that gap. Just as Eagleton uses Freudian psychoanalysis to undo the seeming autonomy of such a fiction, Stokes now reinterprets this search for the absolute in terms of his own desire. The hypothesized autonomy of the 'Quattro Cento' subject now emerges as a *symptom* of his response to the fragmentation and destruction which characterized Italy in the 1920s and 1930s. 'Over and over again', writes Stokes in a passage in which one can hear the footfalls of his anxieties about fascism and, perhaps, intimations of Pound's betrayal, 'everything of value was taken away, ruthlessly, sadistically; even the Rapallo experience'. The response to which, Stokes now says, was an attempted reparation of a chaotic and splintered world: 'bit by bit I was reconstructing the good mother amid conscientious ruins'. The self-identity of 'Quattro Cento' aesthetics is, then, newly interpreted as the product of an imaginary maternal suturing; an act of reparation which, in this context, has undertones of manic protestation. From this angle, it looks as if Stokes' later commitment to psychoanalysis will thwart any attempt to reproduce his earlier aesthetics of the self-same, and, indeed, to an extent it does just that. Yet if Kleinian psychoanalysis does reinscribe Stokes' earlier writing, this is not simply because it decodes or explains modernist aesthetics. Rather, the shift in Stokes' thinking is the outcome of a critical discourse that is frequently at odds with itself. Stokes' search for the absolute is still pursued in his later work, and is interpreted and, to an extent, normalized through Klein. But it is in that very attempt at normalization that the ideological dimension to Stokes' aesthetics is finally re-figured.

Such attempted normalization is most famously apparent in Stokes' mapping of the opposition between 'modelling' and 'carving' art onto Klein's paranoid-schizoid and depressive positions. Modelling art is now associated with the psychic mechanisms of splitting, projective identification and idealization. Carving, on the other hand, represents an integration of the ego through which respect for medium – stone love – is now associated with a working through of guilt and anxiety. Carving then comes to embody a recognition of the whole object in an act of tender reparation, whereas modelling marks a form of regression. In what perhaps is in itself a depressive gesture, the former split between 'bad' modelling and 'good' carving is now attenuated. Stokes now sees art as the dramatization of both 'positionalities', although the moral emphasis continues to be laid on the maturity of the 'carver'. On the one hand, this reinscription seems to exacerbate the ideological dimension of Stokes' aesthetic. 'Beauty' is now the product of an idealized 'good object' tempered by the 'sublime' demarcation of the object's unassailable otherness resulting from the depressive position. 'Beauty', Stokes remarks at one point,

> is a sense of wholeness. From the opposing elements that can fuse in the sublime, we may sense at peace the impulse of life and the impulse of death or inertia, so well symbolized by the inanimate nature of the material through which the artist conveys his fantasies and achieves an occasion for outward thrusting Eros the perfection of arrest. By means of aesthetic pleasure we appropriate the external world without disturbing it.[66]

Kleinian concepts are welded together with the aesthetic in order to produce a similar 'hegemonic trick' to that identified by Eagleton in Kant. To rephrase Eagleton in a Kleinian idiom, the fetish of the idealized good object of the paranoid-schizoid position is exchanged for the 'fetish' of the law of the depressive position: one form of absolute self identity is traded, yet again, for another.

This elision of the structure of the psyche and the structure of ideology is, however, by no means as seamless as it first appears. In other moments in his writing, Stokes produces a more troubling and challenging account of what lies behind the construction of his own 'heuristic fiction'. The same tension between a sense of wholeness and an apprehension of difference, for example, can be found in a question which Stokes first poses to himself in 'Form in Art', his challenging work on psycho-aesthetics. Here this tension reveals a far more complex view of the relation between early psychic states and the aesthetic:

> How can it be that the homogeneity associated with idealization (the inexhaustible breast), is harnessed by the work of art to an acute sense of otherness and of actuality? (Thus, space is a homogeneous 'state' into which we are drawn and freely plunged by the representations of visual art; concurrently it figures there as the mode of order and distinctiveness for 'pre-existent' objects).[67]

How can it be, in other words, that the subject can both merge into the object and yet recognize its difference? This homogeneous state into which one is 'plunged' does not (as it does for Eagleton) belong to any feminized narcissistic merging, but to the Kleinian account of the fragile constitution of the ego in the paranoid-schizoid position. Although Stokes talks of 'oceanic merging', his emphasis lies not on a narcissistic collapse of identities, but on the way art 'invites' us to repeat those structures of projective identification which characterize the intrusion into and constitution of the premature ego by the super-ego. For Klein, as we saw in the first chapter, this moment inaugurates the primal splitting of the ego, produced and fissured by an anxiety which will henceforth be repeated in perverse set of cultural interdicts (the super-ego) whereby the desire to make good is as tyrannical as that to make bad – hence the infant's drive towards an often manic idealization of its objects. If this is 'Beauty as wholeness' it is so, as Stokes suggests, at a price. In this respect, Stokes' question can perhaps be rephrased: How is it that a subject originally hollowed out and divided by a super-ego which both forbids and induces its desire can possibly reach a position whereby the world is disinvested of that desire? How can it be that *that* subject can approach anything like the disinterested desire, that subjectively impersonal pleasure of aesthetic taste, which Stokes simultaneously wants to maintain?

Stokes' answer to this question in 'Form in Art' in some ways prefigures Armstrong's later relocation of 'Kleinian anger'. In an account like Hanna Segal's, as we saw in Chapter 2, such 'anger' is translated into aesthetic value by an avowal of the destructive element and its transmutation into pure form. Stokes has high praise for Segal in this paper, yet he resists aestheticizing the destructive element. Instead he affirms the concrete corporeality of early projective identification; that is, the processes by which the early ego is constituted by the vicissitudes of a drive-affected semiosis; 'upheld by qualities of "id-language" such as interchangeability from which poetic identifications flow'.[68] While the paranoid-schizoid position inaugurates both the constitution and the estrangement of the ego, for Stokes, more optimistically, such mechanisms of splitting and the incorporation and expulsion of the other also mark the point of a first communion; a first love whereby the premature ego goes 'to meet, as if for the first time, the phenomenal world and the emotions it carries'. In an attempt to temper both the manic protestations and idealizations of the paranoid-schizoid position, and their potential repetition in the 'vicious circle' which characterizes the Kleinian account of ascension to the depressive position, Stokes finally invents a new positionality:

> the aesthetic position perhaps deserves a category of its own, between the predominant manic defence and a normal outcome; a position, however, not without relevance to an analysis of

> integration, since it uncovers a more creative role than usual for the manic defence mechanism: one that is potentially non-stultifying.[69]

As Tony Pinkney has argued, Stokes' 'aesthetic position' is, in some senses, a precursor to Winnicott's 'potential space'.[70] As in Winnicott's account, Stokes' emphasis is on the ability to tolerate the ambivalence of the relation between a subject who is not yet a subject and an object which is not yet individuated. The subject, says Stokes, 'cathects a medium'; the object is both the medium for projective desire and yet has a meaning, an autonomy, outside of the ego's phantasies: the object, hence, is both 'me' and 'not-me' in a partial negotiation between the symbolic and imaginary where meanings are at 'play'. While this suggests a transition from 'Kleinian anger' to 'Winnicott's play', Stokes' direct reference here is to Marion Milner's 1952 paper 'Aspects of Symbolism in Comprehension of the Not-Self', in which she constructs an imaginary space whereby '"the basic identifications which make it possible to find new objects, to find the familiar in the unfamiliar, requires a temporary loss of self, a temporary giving up of the discriminating Ego"'.[71] Like Milner, Stokes constructs a paradoxical site for both art and early phantasy whereby the subject can *at once* be at one with its objects and yet recognize their distinctiveness. As we shall see in the next chapter, Milner's surrender of the self through phantasy carries with it its own ideological dimension. What then, of the ideology of Stokes' renegotiated aesthetic?

Tenaciously, Stokes continues to hold on to the ideal of aesthetic autonomy. Indeed, the 'aesthetic position', with its bipartite stress on a blissful apprehension of the object, coupled with a presentiment of its ungraspable difference, could be seen as simply a mellowed version of Stokes' earlier Poundian aesthetics of limestone. However, whereas that aesthetic relied on the trading of one, reviled, self-identity, for another, Stokes' new stress on projective identification uncovers the ground for an aesthetics based on the *non*-identity of the subject to itself. In a much later paper, for example, Stokes, always the anti-Romantic, goes out of his way to resist the kind of Ericksonian argument which would posit a psycho-aesthetic ground for the reconstitution of the self, and dismisses what he calls 'delirious romantic talk about primary processes where it serves as a magical *deus ex machina* for explaining aesthetic super-dynamism'.[72] By contrast, Stokes' own interest lies in Freud's paper 'Negation' (1925) with its emphasis on the constitution of the ego out of the psychic processes of expulsion. It is the way in which this negating process, and not a romanticization of the primary processes, is repeated in the aesthetic that concerns Stokes.

Corresponding with this emphasis on a founding non-identity in artistic subjectivity, Stokes' former stress on the self-identity of the 'Quattro Cento' subject is superseded in his later work, by a growing emphasis on the figure of the 'stranger'. Whereas the young Stokes constructed an aesthetic out of his identification with the 'refulgence' of Italian limestone, in his account of war-time Cornwall (the place which, in some ways, the post-Pound Stokes substitutes for Italy), it is the 'element of being abroad' at home, that now concerns Stokes. 'The stranger', he says, 'brings another aspect, "the outside-in"'.[73] In his 1967 study of the nude, Stokes charts the fate that can befall the figure of the stranger under the sway of phantasy:

> We may … translate [the stranger] into a part-object, the possessor of some trait or function, the over-riding emphasis of which becomes almost a fetish. It is as if we had entered a party, joined a conglomeration of heads and straining faces, ours among them, a succession of presences and absences with which we are compounded … this merging with an object is often the tritest form of intimacy though at other times the mode of deepest sympathy and of capitulation of control.[74]

It is to the precarious frontier between the 'tritest form of intimacy', an 'as-if' identification where the subject merely uses the stranger for its own desires, and the more genuinely empathetic 'capitulation of control', that Stokes' work on aesthetic value is now directed. 'Good art', accordingly, neither expels nor incorporates heterogeneity, but refuses the fetishization of the stranger by dramatizing the ambivalence of projective identification. In this account the best art is, therefore, 'anti-ideological' in so far as it unveils this 'psychic structure difficult to grasp and little known'. In so doing, art resists cultural hegemony by revealing a fundamental disquiet 'over the cultural veils by which sublimation has dulled the ache for psychic actuality, for psychic truth as far as repression allows us to entertain it'.[75] Given Stokes' allegiance to Klein's account in which an object can only be 'restored' through phantasy to some kind of *phantasized* distinctiveness, what 'psychic actuality' might actually consist of remains unclear. Nonetheless, the point remains that in a striking reversal of his simultaneous claim that the aesthetic can reconcile the subject to the world, at moments such as this Stokes' aesthetics are, in fact, profoundly 'anti-aesthetic':

> Art and popular culture, of course, seek to join the split, to reconcile us, to make us elated with our urban environment, or to devise other attitudes by which we may 'take it'. There would be an even stronger spur to art were the deeper causes understood of restlessness, refusal, dissatisfaction with this home we cannot leave.[76]

Not, then, a triumphant construction of self-identity, but 'restlessness, refusal, dissatisfaction' and the uncanny are now the terms through which Stokes construes artistic subjectivity. In place of the illusion of 'bodily solidity', here it is an aesthetic that incorporates the strangeness of the other without fetishizing it that can potentially 'reconcile' us to the world. Arguably, such an aesthetic can be no more an ideological palliative than a discourse of liberation: rather, it admits the projective violence and negativity at the core of identity, in order to prevent the violence which Stokes sees as characterizing those more manic projections which culture 'veils' over psychic actuality.

In an unpublished, undated paper delivered to the Imago group, Stokes finds a new object to define his kind of psycho-aesthetics. In a critique of Freud's *Civilization and its Discontents*, Stokes returns to the 'oceanic feeling' he outlined in 'Form and Art'. What he wants is a cultural location for 'pleasurable immersion, contemplation'. He continues:

> I am employing the word 'immersion' not wholly in a figurative sense. Maybe the recreation representative of civilized needs today is diving and swimming ... there are no better methods of partaking in, of joining up with, a vast expanse of space or of merging with a substance. We talk of things going swimmingly and of being in the swim. Matters of dress, of social position particularly slang and so on are concerns that invite a facile in-the-swim stroke. These are small examples. It seems to me that swimming in a wider sense which includes keeping one's head above water, is an important factor in most civilized activities,

> and the satisfactions of modern life, by and large, are those of a Lido, uncontrolled [sic] only in size.[77]

This – libido/lido – is a wonderful example of what Stokes means by 'id-language': his 'oceanic whispers' are not only puns, they testify to a breaching of the barrier between inside and outside ('Above all', as Stokes puts it in *Inside-Out*, 'as we regard what is external, ourselves speak there'.)[78] The Venetian lido beloved of the elite tourists from a former generation of male modernists resurfaces in the form of, to borrow Orwell's phrase, 'the naked democracy of the swimming pools' (at the same time note how Stokes' 'pleasurable immersion' replaces the call for an immersion in the destructive element; released from treading the watery depths of the destructive element, the post-war Stokes, 'head above water', comes up for air).[79] From the Tempio at Rimini to the public lido, from an ahistorical appeal to primitive monumentalism, to the phantasies that support the collective monuments of the post-war consensus – far from being a privatization of desire (outside-in) Stokes' shift to psychoanalysis is part of a concerted and timely attempt to make phantasy public (inside-out).

If the terms of Stokes' aesthetics have changed, what then of the gendered structure of his modernism that I identified earlier? Lisa Tickner is correct to suggest that Stokes' use of Klein's positionalities genders them and that, at times, Stokes is perilously close to simply perpetuating an equation whereby woman is identified with 'matter, modelling and the paranoid-schizoid position and men with the depressive'.[80] But at other moments in his writing, Stokes seems to suggest something more radical. Far from inhering in psychoanalytic categories, he implies, gendered determinations belong to the psychic inability to tolerate ambiguity and result in the manic fetishizations which follow in its wake. Gender is one of those 'cultural veils' which, he argues, evidence 'a manic counteraction of vulnerability, of the existence of the flesh'. Fixations on gender point to a denial of sexuality, and so support the reification and alienation of the body that pervades cultural iconographies such as the advertising system.

> Drink, perfume, girl, cigarette are not allied only: there is an attempt to identify them; or perhaps the girl is processed for the evening meal: her clothes make the packaging; we are commanded to taste her as an aspect of the food that is advertised.

> Consider also the over-riding male genital symbols of our time, the engines, rockets, guns: they too are clean, gleaming, unpocked but, in contrast, unyielding, like the spaces they occupy such as the stripped bareness of the barrack-room. Are they symbols of the male?[81]

This passage is notable for the way it foreshadows contemporary discussions of the means by which ideology offers an imaginary and alienating representation of sexual identity in relation to real conditions of existence. The difference is that whereas in those accounts the task is to reveal a body determined and fissured by class and gender relations, for Stokes the task is to reveal a body hollowed out by desire and, crucially, to *restore* it.

Restore it to what? In spite of the internal strain that Stokes' encounter with psychoanalysis puts on his former aesthetics, his writing frequently comes full circle, back to the dream of aesthetic autonomy. While the 'aesthetic position' offers a potentially 'non-stultifying' idealization of the other, Stokes never gives up the dream of aesthetic disinterestedness represented, for him, by the authority of the depressive position. The cultural imperative to restore the Kleinian good object (a body, perhaps, free from fetishization) is manifest throughout his work: it is as if its restoration, coupled with the development of a fully integrated ego, promises an aesthetic solution to Stokes' discovery of a more psychotic structure at the heart of identity. 'If the depressive position itself implies humanist attitudes for the adult who has embraced it well', he remarks at one point, 'the paranoid-schizoid position, to which the enveloping mechanisms and disconnecting noise of limitless cities pay court, certainly does not'.[82] We return here (although it is difficult to envisage what else he could have done) to Stokes' earlier cultural nostalgia for the power of an art 'conceived by the European races' to redeem modernity's excesses, underwritten here with all the authority of a claim to psychic health. To this extent, the 'brash energy' of modernist politics is, indeed, to be found secreted in the hidden whorls and depths of the human psyche.

* * *

> Yes, it is absolute hell ... I am thankful that we have your book about Rimini .... One can't look at anything now without feeling sad and even guilty.

> I've been putting off telling you – what perhaps you already know – that the Malatesta Temple is roofless .... It really is too horrible for words.
>
> Osbert Sitwell to Adrian Stokes[83]

Christian Metz has written, in relation to film criticism, of the way in which the critic's love of her or his object can produce a discourse which is 'a kind of advanced structure of the phobic (and also counter-phobic) type, a proleptic reparation of any harm which might come to the object ... an unconscious protection against a possible change in taste of the lover himself'.[84] Something similar could be said of Adrian Stokes' writing. It is as if his love of art, and in particular his commitment to the aesthetic as a meaningful category, is caught up in a discourse which in the very attempt at protecting that object, continually turns back upon itself: indeed, it is the effort to repair the aesthetic, to make it whole, that finally cuts it loose from its former ideological underpinnings. For Metz, the task of the critic is to slip one's imaginary moorings and 'win' the object for the symbolic. By contrast, Stokes is a writer who, one could say, remains stubbornly in the field of the imaginary. This is not, I think, because he failed as a psychoanalytic critic but because for Stokes psychoanalysis was never a critical hermeneutic. This is perhaps why his later aesthetics continue to embody an ideological dimension, that balancing act between autonomy and subjection which Eagleton identifies in the aesthetic. But this is also why, when the cracks begin to show in that structure, Stokes does not, like Armstrong, promise to theorize a 'flagrantly emancipatory aesthetic'. Rather, that negative core to identity which Stokes uncovers in his 'aesthetic position' is born from *within* the internal stresses of an ideology of the aesthetic. The 'aesthetic position' thus does not become art when we 'choose to call it so': for Stokes it *has* to become art as a counter (a counter-phobic?) to that end of the continuum where ideology and madness co-exist – not least, in Stokes' own writing.

There can be little doubt that Stokes read psychoanalysis as a discourse which had the potential to redeem the aesthetic and humanism from the psychic, cultural and historical devastation that he witnessed in the 1930s and, in particular, in the war. Pound's response to the bombing of the Tempio by the allies in the winter of 1943–4 was captured in Cantos 72 and 73, in which the bombing of the Tempio is avenged by the story of the young girl who led

Canadian troops into a minefield: ('What a young woman!/In the north the fatherland is being reborn/Yet what a young woman!/what young women/what young men/are wearing the black [uniform]').[85] These Cantos were excluded from the 1948 edition of *The Cantos* (and did not appear until the 1989 edition). If for Pound the Tempio continued, in Rainey's words, to be 'a privileged site that is essentially autonomous, private, and opposed to the illegitimate constraints of the public sphere', Stokes' response to its bombing was to re-figure an aesthetics in which the psyche goes out to meet the public sphere.[86] The fact that his reading cannot, in the last analysis, sustain itself in the face of Stokes' more radical observations, reveals a splintering at the heart both of a certain strand of modernism and, indeed, of British psychoanalysis. The fact that, in the face of his theory's own internal incoherence, Stokes will continue to attempt to secure the aesthetic as a 'good object', perhaps says less, in the end, about any conservatism than about the psychic and historical situation to which Stokes was responding.

'The prison actually of the Self', H.D. notes in her memoir of Pound, 'was dramatized or materialized for our generation by Ezra's incarceration'.[87] Stokes' response to what he saw as an increasingly recalcitrant and violent psycho-political reality, took a strikingly different course from Pound's, yet was no less concerned with the prison of the self. In a much later experiment in short-story writing, 'Face and Anti-Face: A Fable', Stokes suggests a form of self-imprisonment as an antidote to psycho-political ills. In this curious post-war allegory, a vaccine has been invented to cure all human disease. The vaccine's unfortunate, or in the case of Stokes' propagandist narrator, fortunate side-effect is the growth of quills which form a trellis of spines around the human face, particularly the mouth. Stokes' narrator looks out from behind his cage of quills and sees not a world of ugliness, but a world redeemed. For the quills are not just a cumbersome and unpleasant side-effect of the vaccine, but a psychosomatic representation of aggressive oral projective identification: 'much destructiveness or negation ... much of the power behind the blatancy of self-contradiction or denial has been converted into the psychosomatic symptom of the quills, of their growth and continuous sharpness'.[88] The beneficial consequences of this dramatization of self-abnegation include a lowering of the crime rate, a greater respect for the stranger and a 'decrease in social stupefaction: we are less hungry for the group or the leader'.[89] In this peculiar imaginary social world, Stokes can envisage the aesthetic he constantly longs for: 'Art has abandoned the vogue of enveloping the spectator: artists perfect masks of otherness; their works hold their distance; in this too they have quills'.[90] This is another example of Stokes' id-language: these quills are not only porcupiny, they are also instruments of writing. The ink they spill carves an image of otherness without manic protestation. But is this psychic and aesthetic utopia not also an example of the Kleinian vicious circle at its bleakest? The integrity of the ego can only be imagined at the cost of the punishment of the body; the symptom, impossibly, is championed as the cure. Stokes' fable looks like a phobic response to a perceived threat to a loved object that risks exacerbating the violence it sets out to check. Yet if there is a lesson in Stokes' final work it lies in the same willingness to 'face' the 'anti-face'; to risk an aesthetic which would expose and explore the cruelty inside in order to attempt to prevent the violence which risks exploding on the outside. Such an aesthetic is no more simply ideological than it is emancipatory: it is both. At the very least it reveals the precariousness of the frontier, not only between modernism and psychoanalysis, but between the 'outside' and 'inside' of the psyche, the aesthetic and the political.

5

Frames, Frontiers and Fantasies: 'Nasty Ladies Within' – Marion Milner and Stevie Smith

In the nursery, that is where to find the themes of human nature: the rest is 'working-out', though it be also the real music. But if we want the heart of the matter we must go back to the themes, however bare, to the matchless mental suffering, for instance, of seventeen-months-old Christine, who said: 'Mum, mum, mum, mum, mum …' continually in a deep voice for at least three days.

Adrian Stokes[1]

There is no existence of a private peace: you fight for your country or, refusing to fight, you yet fight, and directly for the enemy. That is perhaps the ultimate most horrible demand of war; the State must have your conscience.

Stevie Smith[2]

Seventeen-months-old Christine, whose poignant 'mums' open Stokes' 1947 *Inside Out* is in fact a child named Carol (temporarily separated from her mother in war-time) whose suffering is described in Anna Freud's and Dorothy Burlingham's *Young Children In War-Time.*[3] Stokes was not alone in thinking that the themes of human nature could be found in the war nurseries. But where he finds a disquieting eloquence in Christine's/Carol's monotonous monologue, others were more nervous about the apparent frailty of the frontier between inside and outside: inside the head, outside in the world, inside the nursery, outside in the war. In *War in the Nursery*, Denise Riley quotes a leader (entitled 'War in the Nursery') for the *British Medical Journal* in 1944. The editorial notes, with due foreboding, that 'in the years from two to five the battle between love and primitive impulse is at its height ... Winnicott, Bühler, Isaacs, Bowlby and others all note the turbulent characteristics of the age ... Destructive impulses let loose in the war may serve to fan the flame of aggression natural to the nursery age'.[4] The *British Medical Journal*'s argument has a familiar circularity: if the war 'lets loose' destructive impulses that 'fan' infantile aggression, from where do those impulses first arise? Where does the destructive element come from? 'Infantile unconscious phantasies' is the Kleinian answer to this question, and it is an answer which, as I have been arguing, provokes as many questions as it resolves. Psychoanalytic discussions of phantasy, as Laplanche and Pontalis point out, always evoke the opposition between the imagination (*Phantasie*) and reality.[5] In the psychoanalytic texts of war-time Britain, this opposition is by turns, rigidified, called into question and exacerbated.[6] Readers of Melanie Klein's *Narrative of a Child Analysis*, her retrospective account of her war-time analysis with Richard, the articulate and gifted evacuee, for example, cannot fail to be struck by the extent to which the events, images and rhetoric of the war 'fan' Richard's phantasy life. Where other analysts of the period protest that reality can check the destructive elements that the war sets loose, Klein inverts this opposition: for her, and by implication for Richard, the events of war (reality) are only made intelligible once they are couched in the language of infantile phantasy. As Mary Jacobus has argued, while Klein's interpretative heavy-handedness comes close to making infantile phantasy the sole referent for Richard's pre-occupation with the war, her narrative of Richard's analysis is also a compelling exploration of the psychic meanings of war – of what it might mean to have a Hitler inside your head.[7]

Frontiers and phantasy, frontiers of phantasy and phantasies of frontiers, are common tropes in psychoanalytic writing and in literary texts of the late 1930s and early 1940s. One way of reading the Controversial Discussions is as protracted debate about the legitimate frontiers of phantasy. The Kleinians, as far as the Anna Freudians were concerned, knew no bounds when it came to phantasy. The Anna Freudians, by contrast, for the Kleinians, were too quick to erect pedagogical fences around the transference. In literature too, numerous border-crossings were undertaken. Edward Upward's *Journey to the Border* (1938), 'Murray Constantine's' (Katherine Burdekin's) *Swastika Night* (1937), Auden's and

Isherwood's *On the Frontier* (1936), Aldous Huxley's *Eyeless in Gaza* (1936) and Stevie Smith's *Over the Frontier* (1938), are all frequently cited as texts that deal with the 'fantastic realities' of the political culture of the late 1930s.[8] 'Awash with the destructive element', is one way of describing English intellectual culture of the late 1930s, as if I.A. Richards' footnote has bled out of his discussion of Eliot into the culture as a whole. 'Theatricals of cruelty' is the phrase that Cunningham uses to describe the content of works by Smith, Huxley and Lewis.[9] The phrase is apposite (even though the echo of Artaud is less so). But if these are 'theatricals' who is watching and producing them? How, and where, does the spectator position herself? What kind of self is it that tells these tales of psychic-frontier crossing?

In this chapter I address these questions by looking at the work of two very different writers, Stevie Smith, and the psychoanalyst and autobiographer, Marion Milner. Phantasy, as has frequently been argued in recent years, is the privileged field for the staging of both the psyche and the political. In the 1930s and 1940s, Smith and Milner traverse a similar theoretical and political terrain. Both are concerned with the relation between the destructive element within and those theatricals of cruelty which dominated contemporary cultural politics. Marion Milner (Joanna Field) is best known for her first two works of autobiography, *A Life of One's Own* (1934), with its obvious allusion to Woolf's essay, and *An Experiment in Leisure* (1937), and her 'self-help' book on art, *On Not Being Able to Paint* (1950). She went into analysis with Sylvia Payne after the publication of *Experiment in Leisure*, and in 1939, after the evacuation ended her psychological research in girls' schools, began her analytic training and started work on *On Not Being Able to Paint*. Given that her training took place during World War Two (Milner gave her membership paper in the basement of 116 Gloucester Place on the day that the V1 bombing began) and therefore coincided with the Controversial Discussions, it is not surprising that from very early on in her work Milner is preoccupied with the frontiers of phantasy. Where the Kleinians seem to engulf the child in a phantasy world, Milner, in both her autobiographies and her psychoanalytic work, attempts to construct a 'frame' for phantasy and illusion: a space where the inside can traffic with the outside, where the self can meet the not-self. But how does one construct such a frame for the self (and the not-self) in a time when, as Stevie Smith puts it 'there is no private peace'. Am I outside or inside my phantasy? Do I produce the phantasy or it me? Indeed, is this my phantasy in the first place, or does the prospect of my subjection to the power of mass phantasy subtend any polarization of insides and outsides? These are the questions that Smith's second novel, *Over the Frontier*, provokes. *Over the Frontier* is a powerful allegory of the extent to which war (to borrow Anna Freud's phrase) provokes an identification with the aggressor.[10] Pompey Casmilus, secretary to Sir Phoebus, a newspaper magnate, leaves England for a rest cure in Schloss Tilssen on the German border. There she becomes entangled in a bizarre set of events which eventually propel her 'over the frontier', as Pompey is transformed from a melancholic and eccentric Englishwoman who is an unwitting but witty spectator of the perverse cynicism of British imperialism, the rising tide of fascism and the forthcoming war, to a soldier and spy who is an assured and willing participant in the cruelty of war. For Smith the State does not only have your conscience; more troubling, perhaps, it also has your phantasies. As for Milner, for Smith too, the destructive element is, foremost, a question of agency (or double-agency).

* * *

> There is then this division between the laborious cruelty-fan and the artist also with his artist's soul creating and brooding upon the darkness of pain? Why yes certainly there is this division. But where is the line of severance? Ah yes where is it? This is already getting dangerous.
>
> Stevie Smith, *Over the Frontier*[11]

The history of the concept of phantasy in psychoanalysis is marked not only by theoretical differences between separate schools, but also by national and cultural differences between the Anglo-American concept of the 'self' as agent and producer of its phantasies, and the French 'le soi' which, as the word denotes, seems to be positioned or placed in respect of its phantasies rather than the author of them. Note, says Pontalis, the way in which the English 'self' seems to connote the idea of a personal space, or the experience of psychic space. The French 'soi', by contrast he says, 'evokes being tied to a fixed landmark, signalled by *"quant à soi"*, *"for(t) intérieur"*'. How, Pontalis asks, can we reconcile what appears to be an Anglo-American attachment to the concept of a unified experiential self with Freud's irreducible splitting of the subject *(Ichspaltung)*? Is it enough, he adds, to dismiss it as pre-analytic nostalgia for a worn-out concept?[12] Marion Milner's work is not only part of this history (appearing, at first glance, to be exemplary of the first tendency), but also provides a starting point with which to re-examine this difference. In her appendix to *On Not Being Able to Paint*, Milner proposes to relieve the word phantasy of the 'heavy burden of meaning' that it has to carry in psychoanalytic thought by a return to the term 'reverie'. By 'reverie' Milner means both day-dreaming and absent-mindedness, but the term also carries distinctly romantic connotations of the visionary and the fanciful. What Milner wants is a 'setting in which it is safe to indulge in reverie, safe to permit a con-fusion of "me" and "not-me"'; a space she finds in both art and analysis.[13] In demarcating this space Milner develops her trope of the 'frame'; an arbitrary mark of difference which separates reality from phantasy, the literal from the figural and the outside from the inside. In Milner's later work there is no 'frontier' between the phantasies of the 'mad' and those of the artist: rather, art and phantasy are 'framed' as part of the same process.[14] Milner's analytic artworks (such as her famous drawings in *On Not Being Able to Paint*), produce something quite different from the stereotypical 'family romance' that appears so frequently in novels, films and other cultural productions of desire. In her writings Milner and her analysands partake in scenarios in which the *dramatis personae* do not matter as much to the protagonist of the phantasy, as his or her relation to artistic media. Paint, ink, line and contour replace mummy and daddy as Milner, like Stokes, concentrates on the formal structuring, and not the content, of unconscious phantasy.

This is a marked departure from other psychoanalytic models of phantasy of the time. It differs, in particular, from the Kleinian theatre of phantasy and its presentation of the ego's relation to its objects. For Milner, art and phantasy are not, as they are for Klein, vicarious in respect of either the drives or their objects. Art and phantasy are 'frames' for what she calls the 'illusion' of an originary discovery of the object: a necessarily mythical moment of 'primal creativity' in which 'to open one's mouth was to create the nipple that filled it'.[15] Crucially, this model means that it is difficult to sustain an idea of phantasy within the order of representation (in which art and phantasy, like the semiotic sign, stand in for the absence of an object) through which it is traditionally perceived. At the same time, in so far as she emphasizes a primary fusion and merging with the object, as opposed to the guilty phantasies which accompany its loss in Kleinian thought, Milner, like Winnicott, also attempts to bypass the aggression and negativity, the destructive elements, which are so central to the Kleinian vision.

With hindsight, it may look as if Milner's 'framing' of phantasy, whatever its radical potential, carries with it the problem of what Laplanche and Pontalis, in relation to Susan Isaac's work, term 'subjective intentionality', in that the theory seems to collapse back onto a pre-given notion of a biological human self whose drives and instincts phantasy is presumed to express.[16] For Milner, as for Isaacs, unconscious phantasy is not so much another scene expressing a wish which is inaccessible to consciousness, as a stage for 'self-discovery'. 'Ultimately', she writes, 'it is ourselves that the artist in us is trying to create'. By submission to what Milner terms 'the integrative influence of reflective thinking', it is through phantasy that the self is recognized.[17] We are back, or so it seems, to the supposedly normative, unified and recoverable self of Anglo-American psychoanalysis. Rather than dismiss Milner on the grounds of a theoretically unfashionable nostalgia for the self, however, perhaps it is more interesting to ask what it is in psychoanalytic theory and, in particular, in thinking about the concept of phantasy in relation to the self, that should leave a space for the return of such a concept.

In contemporary psychoanalytic readings, phantasy emerges as nothing less than *the* question of the subject. From this perspective, as I/ego or author/actor or again self/subject, the 'agent' of phantasy wears a variety of different, frequently deceptive, guises. Such duplicity testifies to Freud's insistence that phantasy is the medium *par excellence* for the staging of the desires of the ego. The artist, says Freud, by 'making use of special gifts to mould his phantasies into truths of a new kind', has privileged access to the enactment of the fulfillment of his egocentric desires: by the public presentation of his crafted phantasies 'in a certain fashion he actually becomes the hero, the king, the creator or the favourite he desired to be'.[18] Crossing the frontier from the phantasies of the neurotic to those of the artist here carries a certain egocentric pleasure premium for the artist. Elsewhere Freud replaces this frontier with a more general metaphor; not a frame but, famously, a theatrical model underpins Freud's thinking about phantasy. Comparing the scenarios which children construct in play to poetic creation, Freud observes:

> Language has preserved this relationship between children's play and poetic creation. It gives the name of *'Spiel'* ['play'] to those forms of imaginative writing which require to be linked to tangible objects and which are capable of representation. It speaks of a *'Lustspiel'* or *'Trauerspiel'* ['comedy' or 'tragedy': literally, 'pleasure play' or 'mourning play'] and describes those who carry out the representation as *'Schauspieler'* ['players': literally 'show players'].[19]

From unconscious phantasies, children's play, day-dreams, through to reveries and cultural productions of phantasy such as novels, romances, short stories and myths, legends and fairy tales, phantasy, for Freud, as for many of his commentators, is figured as a theatrical staging or spectacle in which the protagonist of the phantasy is represented. In this way phantasy becomes the stage upon which the subject can be assigned a fixed position, as romantic hero or heroine, for example; its ego fragmented into many parts, as in the modern novel; or disguised, apparently 'desubjectivized', at first glance seemingly not in the phantasy at all, as in the famous case history 'A Child is Being Beaten'.

In contrast to Milner's discovery of a hidden self, here phantasy poses the question of the subject's *division* within representation (*Vorstellung*, 'that which one represents to oneself').[20] Phantasy is a form of exteriority, an 'other scene': as Lacan puts it, the 'subject situates himself as determined by the phantasy'.[21] Such determinism appears most emphatically in the case of 'primal phantasies' (of parental intercourse, castration and seduction), whereby retroactively (*Nachträglich*) the respective origins of subjectivity, gender and sexuality are represented and hence determined. In answer to the question 'do I produce this phantasy or is it me?', from this perspective, it places 'me' (or, at least, how I am unconsciously represented). Laplanche's and Pontalis' summary of this position is well-known:

> In fantasy the subject does not pursue the object or its sign: he appears caught up himself in the sequence of images. He forms no representation of the desired object, but is himself represented as participating in the scene although, in the earliest forms of fantasy, he cannot be assigned any fixed place in it (hence the danger, in treatment, of interpretations which claim to do so). As a result, the subject, although always present in the fantasy, may

> be so in a desubjectivized form, that is to say, in the very syntax in question.

Amid this generalized metaphorics of 'theatricality' and 'fictionality' the question of aggressivity and cruelty, the negativity, for instance, that Milner's 'frame' seems to circumvent, persists. Laplanche and Pontalis continue:

> On the other hand, to the extent that desire is not purely an upsurge of the drives, but is articulated into the fantasy, the latter is the favoured spot for the most primitive defensive reactions, such as turning against oneself, or into an opposite, projection, negation: these defences are even indissolubly linked with the primary function of fantasy to be a setting for desire, in so far as desire originates as prohibition, and the conflict may be an original conflict.[22]

What is important here is the suggestion that in such theatricals of cruelty, phantasy not only stages desire, but also its prohibition; in other words, it is not only the return of the repressed that is figured, but also repression itself.

This is exemplified for Laplanche and Pontalis in the phantasies of the predominantly female patients in Freud's 1919 paper, 'A Child is Being Beaten'. For Freud, these phantasies present the unconscious Oedipal desires of his women patients as little girls. Freud presents three, structurally uniform, scenes of phantasy from his patients' different narratives. Out of the three scenes, the first and third pre-conscious phantasies, which portray the child beaten by a powerful father figure, are staged as something of a sadistic disguise ('A child is being beaten', 'I am probably looking on'). The second scene, by contrast, presents the little girl herself being beaten. This second unconscious scene is a 'construction of analysis', and is hence, for Freud as well as for Laplanche and Pontalis, the most significant, for it reveals through the little girl's 'masculinity complex', both her desire (for the father) and its repression (the beating).[23] Through this vacillation of disguises and repressions, Freud's patient discovers not her self through this phantasy, but its displacement. Phantasy reveals a subject fundamentally estranged from itself.

While the beating phantasy could in no straightforward sense be said to *express* the desires of the little girl (as in Isaacs' and Milner's models), nonetheless Freud presents us with the spectacle of a subject in representation. Does renaming the self as the 'subject of representation' (as has become customary) necessarily get us out of the self-reflexive logic that Milner left us with? The prospect of a return of the specular self within psychoanalysis is Mikkel Borch-Jacobsen's point of departure in his reading of Freud's essay. Central to Freud's account is not for him, as it is for Laplanche and Pontalis, the axis of repression and desire, but the difference between a theatrical 'specularization' of the phantasy and what Borch-Jacobsen calls a *'lexis'* of mimesis which underpins it; a difference which corresponds to the psychoanalytic distinction between desire (wanting to *have* an object) and identification (*being* the object).[24] For Borch-Jacobsen, to narrate the phantasy (to tell it like an autobiography – which is precisely what Freud gets his patients to do) is simultaneously to designate it to the order of the specular (the visible, the theoretical), whereby the subject is represented to the subject in the *mise-en-scène* of the phantasy. In the same twist, the self-appropriating, self-mastering subject which psychoanalysis claims to have displaced, in effect, returns. What both escapes and precipitates this specular appropriation of the subject is the more persistent and, to an extent, primary logic of identification or mimesis. In this second mode, the desire of the little girl is not so much to *have* the object, but to *be* the protagonist of the phantasy: 'the subject's place in phantasy is always the place of another'.[25] This is revealed most strikingly in Freud's second, unconscious scene which is neither recollected nor narrated by the analysand (it is a construction of analysis). In this scene the subject does not observe the scene, she enters into it ('I am being beaten'); as such she 'is' the mimetic double of the phantasy and thus cannot represent the scene to herself. This 'impossible' position is what Borch-Jacobsen refers to as the 'blind-spot' of the phantasy; an irreducible 'point of otherness' at which the traditional model of representation breaks down. The emphasis here, then, is on the way that the possibility of representing and so either recognizing or mis-recognizing the self as other in phantasy is precipitated by the impossibility of a self-other relation. As Borch-Jacobsen puts it: 'The lack of distinction between self and other – the mimesis – has to be acted out; yet no sooner is it represented to the subject in the specular mode than it is betrayed'.[26]

The strength of Borch-Jacobsen's reading, for my purposes, lies in its analysis of the way that the vertigo induced by the problem of the self's production of, and the subject's relation to, her or his phantasies, is arrested by structures of representation, of narration and diegesis which, at the same time, reveal their failure as strategies of containment. This kind of double-difficulty emerges repeatedly in Marion Milner's work. Her 1945 essay, 'Some Aspects of Phantasy in Relation to General Psychology', for instance, begins with the idea that it is through phantasy that we discover the 'hypothetical structures of ourselves', and yet centres upon the following, dizzying, proposition: 'it is my problem here to try and consider psychoanalytic theory of the way in which these psychic realities are experienced by the self that owns or disowns them.'[27] The abyssal relation that Milner opens here between a psychic reality that constructs the 'self', and a 'self' which can at the same time be in a position to own or disown its 'phantasy world' or psychic reality, can perhaps now be seen as less a symptom of a theoretical nostalgia for an unfashionable concept, or the last vestiges of Romanticism, than a measure of the difficulty for psychoanalysis in catching hold of this relation between self and other in phantasy.

When Anna Freud returns to 'A Child is Being Beaten' in her 1922 paper 'Beating Fantasies and Day-Dreams', she too turns phantasy into a space for self-creation. In her more 'up-beat' version these sado-masochistic phantasies are eventually sublimated into writing ('We could say: she has found the road that leads from her fantasy life back to reality'): the little masochist turns creative writer.[28] If we remember that Freud's case-history is assumed to be based on his analysis of his daughter, it is not surprising that when Anna Freud writes the Foreword to Milner's *On Not Being Able to Paint*, she praises Milner's affirmation of the creative aspects of phantasy, and singles out the extent to which Milner's work departs from Klein's reparative hypothesis. It is as if Milner restores an element of creative agency to the sadism and masochism of phantasy which was unveiled by Freud the father, and legitimated and exacerbated in the theories of Klein, the opponent. Milner herself later commented that much of her earlier psychoanalytic work bore traces of her 'struggles to find [her] bearings in the controversies then raging within the British Psycho-Analytic Society'.[29] If we place these struggles in the context of contemporary political concerns with the frontiers between the self and the seductions of mass phantasy, Milner's theoretical troubles with the self also begin to carry, not only a theoretical, but also a political and ideological premium.

* * *

For both Milner and Smith, the materiality and the artifice of totalitarian fantasy constitutes one of its most powerful seductions. Milner, for example, speaks of the seduction of 'the concreteness of and shape and texture and sound and movement' in totalitarian mythology, while Smith criticizes its 'childish delight in daily use of colour and form'.[30] In these accounts phantasy is both art and political spectacle. For both writers, the possibility of a 'dangerous' collapse of the frontier between political pathology and art is an issue which is inextricably tied to the question of self-narration. The position of the autobiographical 'I' in their first-person narratives is ever-shifting, fragile and subject to an omnipresent risk of seduction by a variety of possible stagings of cultural and political phantasies. Indeed, it is because the autobiographical impulse is so pronounced in these writings that the vertigo associated with tracking down doubles, alter-egos and specular selves is so marked. In her autobiographies Milner, for example, not only narrates her past life, she also offers readings of her own diaries, stories, doodlings, paintings and drawing in order to present, delineate and describe her '"unconscious" self'. In *Over the Frontier*, the recognizably Smith-like English melancholic protagonist of *Novel on Yellow Paper* and Smith's later *The Holiday*, adopts a variety of different masks in keeping with the generic guises of this spy-thriller-cum-*Bildungsroman*. What persists in each as a question is that same tension between the difficulty of self-narration and the seduction of finding a representation, a narrative form within the more encompassing diegesis of phantasy, that we have already seen at work in psychoanalytic theory.

Lacoue-Labarthe and Nancy have argued that the desire for self-representation is inscribed in the pageants, mythemes and narratives that make up the ideological formations and theatricals of totalitarianism. What Hannah Arendt calls the 'total state' that totalitarianism proffers, for example, is one, Lacoue-Labarthe and Nancy suggest, in which 'I' can be just as totally represented to myself as a subject.[31] On the one hand, such phantasies appear to erase the self by transforming identity into a limited set of masks, each wearing the grimace of the common good, and which testify to the uniformity of the 'masses' for whose sake the subject is willing to sacrifice its difference. Yet at the same time, it is nothing less than 'identity' that such phantasies promise, and the desire to 'belong', to be called by one's name, which constitutes their fascination.

There is a chilling echo of this latter logic in one of Milner's final formulations in *An Experiment in Leisure*: 'let purposes have me, watch myself being lived by something that is "other"'.[32] The compulsion to represent oneself to oneself through phantasy, or in Milner's terms to discover oneself through the 'childish confusion between fact and fancy' found in reveries, fairy tales, poetry and myth, drives this seemingly homely and practical study of 'what to do in one's spare time'. Not that Milner's book is without its 'forebodings about fascism': on the contrary, this early example of the popular-psychological genre is, according to its preface, motivated in part by 'a growing uneasiness over anti-intellectual trends in modern life'. Although, as Janet Montefiore points out, Milner's work says little about its historical context, *An Experiment in Leisure* bears the traces of a struggle that is as historical as it is personal.[33] The dilemma the book repeatedly stages is that of distinguishing one's own phantasies from what Milner refers to as 'the distortion of the facts for the sake of arousing and exploiting the feelings of the masses'.[34] In the struggle to keep the two domains separate, the book's innocent therapeutic goals are belied by a kind of interpretative violence which accompanies Milner's compulsion to self-narration.

Auden described Milner's earlier book, *A Life of One's Own*, as being as exciting as a 'detective story'. Detective stories, of course, have their own narrative fantasies. 'The fantasy, then, which the detective story addict indulges', Auden argues elsewhere, 'is the fantasy of being restored to the Garden of Eden, to a state of innocence, where he may know love as love and not as the law. The driving force behind this daydream is the feeling of guilt, the cause of which is unknown to the dreamer.'[35] In *An Experiment in Leisure*, Milner's method of detection is to 'simply let images flow as they would, present or past, fact or phantasy'; the original guilty secret is Milner's own 'crime' against herself – her own masochism ('a study in the use of masochism' is the alternative title she offers for the book). As well as exploring her masochism in reveries, literary texts, diaries and creative writing experiments, Milner also interprets it in terms of religious and pagan mythologies. The cultural phantasies that Freud describes as 'the distorted vestiges of the wishful phantasies of whole nations, the secular dreams of youthful humanity', for Milner are 'the culminating poetic dramatization of the inner processes of immense importance to humanity'.[36] This masochistic and self-abnegating phantasy runs throughout the book and, importantly, also inscribes a form of representational logic within its own thematic. Far from getting rid of the self, the universalist trope of sacrifice to a greater force (such as Milner finds, like Hegel, in the myth of the dying God) provides an already given narrative, context and setting within which the self can be represented and hence mastered. In other words, and according to a well-versed dialectical logic, if this ready-made scenario already determines me from the outside, then, by giving myself up to it, by assimilating it, I master it; self-negation thus returns as self-affirmation. Or as Milner puts it: 'To submit yourself to an alien force that wishes to destroy you, this seems to be the only ultimate security'.[37]

Milner's dream of discovering her self through an omnipotent other, however, irrecoverably collapses in two disturbing moments in the text.[38] The first occurs when she attempts to interpret her masochism through Otto Weininger's ubiquitous *Sex and Character* (1903; trans. 1907). Weininger's quasi-sociology and pseudo-philosophy was well-known at the time, not only for the force of its misogyny and anti-semitism, but also by virtue of its championing of violence and negativity as a means of redemption and regeneration. Weininger is, in many ways, an extremely curious choice of mentor for Milner. Out of all the analysts I have discussed, she is, perhaps, the one who is least interested in contemporary modernism (Keats and Blake are her constant references). To call on Weininger's *Sex and Character* (a text which has been described as an expressionist manifesto) as an aid to female self-discovery is a bit like asking Strindberg if he'd like to take you shopping (it is, perhaps, an act of masochism in itself).[39] It is, infamously and specifically, woman's negativity that Weininger promotes, as is evident from the extract that Milner chooses to quote: 'The meaning of woman is to be meaningless. She represents negation, the opposite pole from the Godhead, the other possibility of humanity'.[40] When Milner recognizes her own masochistic phantasies in Weininger's text, she simultaneously opens up an impossible space between her own drive to self-narration and the intractability of the wider field of gendered representation. For once the dialectic between the self and other is gendered, then the woman, in Weininger's schema at any rate, cannot represent herself through another scene, because *she* is herself 'the terrible mystery' of that scenario. To identify with the female player in this male phantasy, in other words, is to become irredeemably lost within it: the prospect of a return to self-identity, the objectival relation in this phantasy, belongs to someone else, while for the woman there is no specular distance and the relation between her and the phantasy becomes, strictly speaking, impossible.

Milner's response to this impasse is to attempt to neutralize Weininger's instantiations: 'If for the word "woman" one reads "the subjective temperament" then I thought these statements were very illuminating, particularly as a picture of the terror and hatred that an unrecognized tendency to subjectivity in oneself, whether man or woman, could arouse'.[41] What is striking here is the way that Milner also turns Weininger's phobic repudiation of femininity into an indictment of his own theory. Modernist repudiations of femininity and interiority, in the hands of the woman psychologist and autobiographer, are turned into a kind of symptomatology – behind a manifesto that legitimates misogyny and anti-semitism, Milner suggests, there lurks a terror of the self. Milner may be identifying with her aggressor in her choice of Weininger, but this is an identification predicated on a fruitful mis-reading.

This tension between the drive toward self-narration through phantasy and the collapse of such a project within a wider cultural phantasy returns, most hideously, in the final section of the book, with Milner's sudden recognition that her own reveries match exactly those of totalitarian phantasy:

> I had learnt that it was in these images that unrecognized desires express themselves, that when people purported to be talking of external facts, but talked with extreme hatred, then what they said had less reference to the facts than to their own internal needs. I had been most shocked when I found that some of these images which had seemed to grow out of my most intimate and private experiences, and that I had thought represented for me the kernel of the problem of escape from the narrow focus of egoism, were being used by others to foster what seemed to me that most sinister form of egoism – jingoistic nationalism. For I had read in the newspapers that Pagan rituals were being revived in Germany, as part of the movement to glorify violence and discredit the teachings of Christ.[42]

Here, the idea of phantasy as a recognizable space for the staging of the self, or as a field of expression for 'unrecognized desire', turns horribly uncanny with the return of the same phantasy within the mass spectacles being staged in Nazi Germany. This collision between Milner's desire to see phantasy as the product of and means to a self, and the return of this phantasy in the wider field of representation, prompts a form of theoretical panic or vertigo, as she attempts to forestall the consequences of the latter model by an appeal to the former:

> The whole history of popular religions could I thought be looked upon as a materialization of the image; and once it was no longer looked on as a truth of a spirit, but instead a truth of external fact, then it became the instrument of all kinds of exploitation – lustful, political, social, the instrument of the crudest infantile desire to be king of the castle... But the fact that they could be so exploited did not take away the truth of the images in terms of internal experience. The fact that dictators had realized the power of images for political purposes in controlling and unifying a nation need not make me discard my own discovery that they had the power to unify my own chaos of experience.[43]

If there is something disturbing about this attempt to drive a wedge between phantasy in reverie, art, myth and legend, and politics, it is not least because Milner's attempted solution to this dilemma – if it is inside me then it is good, if it is outside it is bad – not only fails to check the implications of the fact that the phantasies through which she stages her 'self' are the same phantasies through which totalitarian subjects are constituted, but also seems to repeat that psychic logic which, for example, Ella Freeman Sharpe identified as supporting fascism – a belief in the good object inside. By displacing the line of severance between what Milner calls 'your own pantheon of visual images, a mythology of one's own' and 'the reach-me-down mass-produced mythology of Hollywood, of the newspapers, or the propaganda of dictators', on to a frontier which differentiates what is inside from what is outside a self, Milner returns us to the same paradoxical logic which we saw earlier: namely, if the self is staged through phantasy, how can that same self then take in or disown the phantasy? How can it represent this relation to itself?

The problem with Milner's autobiographical work of the 1930s is not just that her quest for the self is too cumbersome a project to negotiate the fields of gendered and political representation, but that it is through her encounter with these two fields that the subjective imperative towards self-representation breaks down. Despite the inadequacy of Milner's attempted solution to these impasses, *Experiment in Leisure* forces us to think about the relation of subjectivity and phantasy not in terms of the content of such phantasies, nor in terms of subjective and objective (the destructive element within, for example, versus the destructive element without) but through a different question: if phantasy cannot contain the logic of self-representation, if the drive towards self-narration cannot be purely specular, then what is it that binds the self to phantasy?

An Experiment in Leisure was completed one year before Milner began her analysis and analytic training and the outbreak of war. In her later case histories and theoretical work phantasies of self-negation return. In these texts, what we saw in Milner's autobiographical study as a tension between the difficulty of self-narration and the seductions of finding a representational form within a wider diegesis of mass phantasy is staged within that 'earliest form of phantasy', the psychoanalytic playroom. In some senses Milner's early case histories echo the kind of violent interpretative strategies that Lacan finds so objectionable in Klein's 'symbolization' of little Dick, in which the phantasy in the playroom quite clearly becomes a means of giving narrative form, a 'theatre of representation', to a child who is neither necessarily a subject nor a self.[44] Yet at the same time, what makes these case histories so interesting is the fact that Milner is also attempting to move away from the Kleinian specular theatre of object relations and toward her different 'framing' of the question of phantasy with which I began.

By the time Milner starts practising as an analyst her 'forebodings about fascism' have been realized. But it is not only the punctuation of her case histories with descriptions of falling bombs, absent fathers and the children's war phantasies that link these texts to her earlier work: the question of the line of severance between one's own phantasies and an exterior stage of cruelty also dominates Milner's initial psychoanalytic questioning. In her 1944 membership paper 'A Suicidal Symptom in a Child of 3', for example, Milner interprets the child, Rachel Sheridan's, drive toward self-negation, manifested in an eating inhibition, as 'an inner doubt and inability to separate an external and internal reality': an inner doubt, note, that corresponds precisely to the same dilemma that Milner left us with in her own encounter with totalitarian phantasy.[45] Milner first interprets Rachel's self-negation in terms of Klein's ideas about early oedipal rivalry. Her inhibition in eating is seen as a defence against her own aggression towards her objects and a symptom of a fear of what they might do to her once they are inside. Rachel's cure consists in her getting her to recognize her own suicidal intentions in terms of an objectival desire. The dialectical logic we saw at work in *An Experiment in Leisure* returns here as the cornerstone of analytic interpretation. Rachel's own 'greedy angry' desires, for example, are read as an indication of 'there being something inside her mother which she wanted to get for herself, something she wanted to both destroy and save'.[46] Self-negation, once again (here through a sort of *Aufhebung*) promises a form of self-affirmation, as Rachel's desire is given a role within a *dramatis personae* of the Kleinian drama of insides/outsides, part and whole objects.

But Milner's account of the analysis is by no means as clear-cut as this implies. There is a growing tension in the case-history between the predominantly Kleinian logic to which Milner is trying to get her patient to conform (Klein supervised the case), and another narrative, more contradictory and persistent, which weaves through the text. Rachel is a little too good at playing the parts allotted to her in the phantasy being staged in the analytic playroom. 'She was a gifted little actress', Milner remarks, 'and once, when making me play the part of a crying baby, she was so disgusted with my poor performance that she gave me a demonstration of how I should do it.'[47] Although by the end of the analysis Milner claims to uncover the real Rachel behind the artifice, the extent to which this 'gifted little actress' can play her parts is vividly demonstrated throughout the case-history. '"Stand here! No, here! here!, go downstairs! no, come here!"'; at one point, the little actress turns little totalitarian, in just one of the series of ludic identifications which are played out in scenes of 'a frenzy of dramatic cruelty'.[48] These identifications testify not so much to Rachel's desires or anxieties about *having* her objects, but to a concern about *being*, about identity: '"I'm Rachel Sheridan, you're Mrs. Milner – say that", but when I repeated it she retorted at once, "No you're not"'. Identities are displayed as uncertain and unstable here, I would argue, not just because of the imbroglio of ego identifications at work for Rachel, but because of a powerful identificatory desire – a desire for mimesis – that subtends the narrative within which Milner is simultaneously inviting Rachel to recognize herself.

> When I gave an interpretation beginning 'Whatever I do you say it's wrong...' She interrupted with 'Whatever I do I cut myself' and then 'D'you know, Mrs. Milner, my Mummy got a bleed with a pin'. I then interpreted that the hurt Mummy was inside, like the nasty lady, and she went on pretending to cut her arms and fingers and threw the scissors away and said, 'Let's pretend we're dead, we must take our shoes off'.[49]

The diegetic pull here towards representing Rachel in terms of prohibition and a desire to take in the mother is interrupted by Rachel's *miming* of the analyst's speech ('"Whatever I do..."'). Similarly Milner's interpretation of the 'nasty lady' within compares not with a representation of Rachel 'having' the nasty lady, but with her act of performing her, 'being' her. Running alongside Milner's desire to represent Rachel's self through phantasy, then, is Rachel's own impossible (in both senses of the word) identificatory logic; she cannot represent herself to herself because, like Freud's analysands in 'A Child is Being Beaten', she 'is' the mimetic double in the phantasy provided by the playroom.

In 'A Suicidal Symptom in a Child of 3', Milner returns, with a new urgency, to the problem she was left with at the end of *An Experiment with Leisure*; not because the case-history repeats the dilemma between inner phantasy worlds and outside ones but, more importantly, because Milner's account of Rachel's analysis suggests both the inseparability of the question of identity from phantasy and the impossibility of recovering an adequate distance, a representational space, with which to view, to narrate and contain that relation. Phantasy, as it is staged in ideological formations, invites us to symbolize our desires, to recognize ourselves as subjects within its narratives hence, as Milner dramatizes so well, its dangers. Uncovering the 'blindspot' of the representational logic that propels this encounter between the psyche and the political, revealing the impossibility of the dream of our total representations as subjects, does not check it any more than it offers an alternative model of phantasy. The possibility and impossibility of the representation of self through phantasy are part of the same double-logic. In other words, as soon as the model of phantasy as a vehicle for self-narration collapses then, invariably, the attempt to represent this relation between self and phantasy begins anew, in a seemingly endless interpretative process.

In Milner's case this process points to much more than a theoretical or interpretative vertigo: by changing the terms of phantasy, she also radicalizes the parameters of English psycho-aesthetics. For Leo Bersani, it is precisely Klein's emphasis on the defensive origins of symbol formation and phantasy that constitute what he calls the solipsism of the Kleinian ego: an ego which is founded on a desire not only to have one's objects but to re-create them in one's own image. The specular theatre of Kleinian object relations, seen in this light, subsumes the contingency of history under the universal laws of phantasy. Something very different from this valorization of phantasy happens in Marion Milner's 1952 paper, 'The Importance of Illusion in the Role of Symbolic Formation' written, like Adrian Stokes' 'Form in Art', in honour of Klein's seventieth birthday. As with 'A Suicidal Symptom', the case material in this paper is reminiscent of the totalitarian phantasies that Milner runs up against in *An Experiment in Leisure*. Milner's patient, an eleven-year-old boy suffering from inhibitions in his school work, constructs through his play a phantasy war between two villages in which he, 'god like' and with a 'dictatorship attitude', performs the role of aggressor and victor. To an extent, Milner is an exemplary Kleinian in this case (again the analysis was supervised by Klein). This war in the nursery is traced back to Simon's own anxiety and aggressivity: the bombing of the toy villages is an expression of the extent to which Simon feels the world, and particularly his school, to be a mechanized 'waste land' and his transferential games with Milner are an attempt to repair a damaged maternal body. But as she watches Simon enact this Guernica in the playroom, Milner is increasingly bothered by the weight of her interpretative models. To assume that Simon is entrapped in a vicious circle of violent projective identifications, is to assume that he already has boundaries: 'if I am felt to be inside him then he has a boundary, and the same if a bit of him is felt to be projected into me'.[50] Simon's play, by contrast, concentrates on the obliteration of the boundaries of the self. Less a case of phantastically remaking the objects that were once the targets of his aggression, Simon seems to be telling Milner something about how object relations get made in the first place. So rather than attempt to close Simon's case by interpreting his phantasies within the Kleinian representational framework, Milner changes the terms of the debate. 'Phantasy' becomes 'illusion' and, correspondingly, 'anxiety' becomes 'ecstasy', in a move which allows Milner to construct her 'frame' within which the merging of boundaries between the 'self' and the 'not-self' can be contained, and in which primary objects become equivalent to secondary in a kind of generalized economy of identifications between symbols. This space is propelled by that logic we saw at work earlier in which 'me' and 'not-me' are part of the same continuum. As Winnicott later puts it in a private communication to Milner on her paper, this is not a space for regressive narcissism, rather: 'One could think of separation as the cause of the first *idea* of union; before this there is union, but no *idea* of union, and here the terms good and bad have no function'.[51] It's this kind of space that Simon wants to play in – somewhere where there is no good and bad, no negation, no defensive symbol formation, not anxiety, but ecstasy.

When Milner describes this ectastic space as 'aesthetic' it might look as if she is trying to circumvent Klein's emphasis on reparative symbol formation with a form of mysticism. But something more complex about the relation between phantasy and the social is going on here. Why, asks Milner, should this little boy desire to play in this space? Simon has been an exemplary war child. Sanguine about his father's departure, he has borne the traumas of the Blitz and the birth of his baby brother with mature equanimity. In effect, Simon has developed an ego shaped by the demands of war *too* quickly and *too* competently. By constructing a place for illusion in the playroom, Simon, says Milner, is behaving like the artist who

> is acutely aware of the discrepancy between, on the one hand, all the ways of expressing feeling that are provided by the current development of speech and art, in our particular culture and epoch; and, on the other hand, our changing experiences that are continually outstripping the available means of expression.[52]

The war has rendered Simon out of step with his own illusions; his games are less an expression of the extent to which war fans his destructive impulses than a form of protest against the culture and epoch which insists on his aggressivity. It is not only his culture and epoch which insist on a defensive form of ego construction but also, one might add, psychoanalysis itself. In referring to Simon's behaviour as that of an artist, Milner is paraphrasing the arguments of Christopher Caudwell's *Illusion and Reality* (1937). By citing Caudwell, Milner is not, of course, proposing a historical-materialist conception of phantasy akin to his reading of the development of English poetry; but she is conscious of the extent to which the world must change if the psyche is to create new meanings. For Caudwell, the artist and scientist are 'men who acquire a special experience of life which negates the common ego or the common social world, and therefore require refashioning of these worlds to include new experience'.[53] Simon improves, says Milner, when he persuades his school to refashion its routines. This had happened, Milner concludes 'in response to the vividness of his belief in the validity of his own experience: a vividness of which also had contributed to a refashioning in me of some of my analytic ideas'.[54] In negating the common ego, it might be suggested, Simon and his analyst also negate the Kleinian ego: refusing the imperative to construct the ego out of defensive symbol formations, both challenge the idea that the desire to be a subject is borne out of the ego's own aggression. Small wonder, perhaps, that when Klein reads Milner's paper her main criticism is that Milner does not sufficiently analyse the aggressive and sadistic impulses of Simon's play.[55]

* * *

> There must be a reason for the invention of line. Yes, it is a guide for those who would venture into the formlessness that surrounds on every side; a guide that leads us to the recognition of form and dimension and inner meaning .... Let us then follow the line whither so ever it may go. It may lead to something quite definite and precise – a landscape, or a human face or figure. Or it may lead to the subconscious – the land of Fantasy, where fancy roams where it will.
>
> Georg Grosz[56]

By tracing the line which cuts through the 'formlessness' of perception, for Georg Grosz, fantasy emerges as a space which is 'sub' or adjacent to consciousness. Through art, this 'land of Fantasy' is made present for a subject who, although willing to roam with fancy, nonetheless retains the position of a spectator who can recognize not only 'form', 'dimension' and 'inner meaning', but also the difference between a human face and a fantasy. Mercifully perhaps, Grosz does not invite us to enter into his scenes of the cruelty and savageness of the Weimar Republic: as spectators, we can view the fantasy but maintain the distance – there is, indeed, a reason for the invention of the line. Stevie Smith visited an exhibition of Georg Grosz's work at the Mayor Gallery in June 1934. She submitted an article on his work for the May 1936 edition of John Lehman's *New Writing*. It was rejected.[57] In the same year, Smith began *Over the Frontier*. The novel opens with Pompey, Smith's narrator walking around an exhibition of Grosz paintings, thinking of 'a darker memorial of Georg Grosz that is this dark memorial that is called a Post War Museum where all of the ignobility and shameful pain of war and suffering is set down'.[58] *The Post War Museum* is the title of Grosz' *Criterion* pamphlet published in 1931. Smith owned a copy and clearly found his satire congenial to her own writing practice. By 1936, however, such dark memorials are in danger of erasure; what Pompey discovers in the pictures is the prospect of amnesia, of a 'forgetting to remember the shame and dishonour the power of the cruelty of the high soaring flight of that earlier éclairissement, that was the pale éclair dans une nuit profonde'. This is an accurate reading of Grosz' paintings; it is the precise juxtaposition of smiles, careless leers, satisfied winks and fistfuls of money, with trampled bones, open graves, dismembered bodies and silent screams that make Grosz's satire so effective. One picture in particular, one of Grosz's reworkings of the theme of the 'horseman of the apocalypse', arrests Pompey's attention. Horse and rider make up a contemporary iconography representing, respectively, classicism and something 'a little fin de siècle', power and femininity and nobility and degeneracy. The rider embodies the threat of the forgotten horrors of World War One returning to a Europe overshadowed by totalitarianism. He is, comments Pompey, 'forgetting to remember that rakehell of a beam of light that went showing up in the very sad bones of that earlier situation, this he is very actively forgetting'.[59] Smith's Pompey, then, opens the novel by playing the analytic role of the interpreter of amnesis, of a very active rememberer. Not surprisingly given her enthusiasm, she also desires to possess the picture for herself. But it is too expensive and Pompey is left only with the echo of the gallery assistant's consolatory conversational banter, 'Very witty this painter is he not?' By the end of *Over the Frontier* this distance between Pompey as spectator and prospective purchaser, and Grosz's apocalyptic fantasy has collapsed. Leaving London for a rest cure, Pompey becomes entangled in a bizarre series of events which transform her from melancholic convalescent into soldier and spy. The canvas of Grosz's apocalyptic painting stretches out of its frame and into the narrative fantasies of the text and, by the end of the novel, Pompey 'is' that parodic horseman of the apocalypse.

Smith, then, like Milner and, indeed, many others at the time, is concerned with the aggressor within. To get into one of Grosz' pictures, to lose the distance necessary for critical satire, is a little like identifying oneself within Weininger's *Sex and Character*. Critics have been baffled by Smith's generic hybrid. Valentine Cunningham, for example, suggests that in it Smith demonstrates the same relish for sadism as Lewis. This is to miss the point. Smith is very much concerned with the voyeuristic pleasures of the destructive element (traces of Warner, Auden, Huxley and Lewis can be found throughout the text, as indeed, can references to Milton, Donne and Tourneur). Others, including Naomi Mitchison and Frank Swinnerton, could follow the first part of the novel which portrays Pompey's break-up of her love-affair with Freddy and the boredom of her life as a secretary to Sir Phoebus, pillar of a creaking, preposterous but still dangerously imperialist English establishment, but found the second part of the novel which depicts Pompey's transition to soldier and spy bewildering and confusing. 'Surrealistic' and 'puzzlingly fantastical' are both epithets which have been used to describe this part of the text.[60] But the novel only reads as if it has a broken back if the 'surrealistic' and 'fantastical' are opposed to, or taken as distinct from, the 'realism' of England between the wars. For Smith, they are not and this, to an extent, is precisely the point.

As for Freud in *Civilization*, a destructive and aggressive desire for power emerges as the bottom line in Smith's analysis: 'Is then power and the lust for power the very stuff of our existence?', she asks at the end of the novel,

> And if we cannot achieve in our individualities this power are we any less guilty if we pursue it, or again, abandoning the sweet chase, identify ourselves with a national ethos, take pride in our country, in our country's plundering, or, if the mood takes us, in our country's victories upon other fields less barren, in science, art, jurisprudence, philosophy?[61]

This displacement from an individual desire for power on to an identification with nationalist fantasies is enacted throughout the novel. The frontier of Smith's title not only refers to the novel's themes (the 'frontiers' of mid-Europe, of race and of gender), but is also inscribed within its textual dynamics and organization. It is this frontier that precariously demarcates the line between, on the one hand, the fantasy that the novel stages of a young Englishwoman turned soldier within a pre-war theatricals of cruelty, and a subtext of the narrative logic of the relation that ties her to those scenes. It is through this narrative logic that Smith raises the question of agency. What is so troubling about *Over the Frontier* is not so much Smith's dramatization of the relation between the individual and the seductions of war, but the way her novel points toward the narrative blind-spots of psychic and political identification.

Genette's discussion of modes of literary discourse in an essay appropriately entitled 'Frontiers of Narrative', is pertinent at this point as it re-casts the difference between a mimetic and a diegetic relation to fantasy which we saw at work in Milner's texts in terms of literary discourse. Genette is concerned with what he terms the 'negative limits' of narrative: in other words, he is interested less in what narrative is than in how it has been defined by what it is not. Despite their differences, for both Plato and Aristotle diegesis is what mimesis is not; an incomplete imitation or telling of how things are, rather than a perfect mimetic copy or imitation. For Genette, however, this opposition does not hold because, he argues, literature cannot simply conform to a representational model. In fiction, each action, event, description is not imitated but is constituted through language and hence, is narrated. 'Plato opposed *mimesis* to *diegesis* as a perfect imitation to an imperfect imitation; but ... perfect imitation is no longer an imitation [once it is in discourse], it is the thing itself, and, in the end, the only imitation is an imperfect one. *Mimesis* is *diegesis*'.[62] Mimesis is not an imitation of an event or idea that precedes the text, but an effect of a more general category of discourse and the discursive modalities possible within it. As an effect of discourse, mimesis can no longer be conceived of as purely imitative but emerges as a form of 'originary mimesis' in which the 'thing to be imitated' is revealed only through the act of mimesis itself. For Genette, what is crucial here is not so much what each narrative modality actually is, a seemingly pure description of what takes place as opposed to a more self-conscious mode of narration, as the internal 'frontier' that creates the difference between them.

In *Over the Frontier* this narrative frontier emerges in the form of an oscillation between the relating of scenes of totalitarian fantasy and a staging or repetition of those scenes in which Pompey, the narrative 'I', is a participant. The copy precedes the thing to be imitated, just as Pompey's relating of Georg Grosz's iconography of the threat of totalitarian fantasy precedes those scenes in the novel in which Pompey herself becomes an actor in the same fantasy. One particularly disturbing passage, for example, describes Pompey talking, as she puts it, 'a lot about the Jews and women for a dirge and disturbance of all peace'. Homophobic, anti-feminist ('a pseudo-feminist talk to put you out of your mind with irritation'),[63] and anti-semitic ('"Would but they have survived their persecutions"...O final treachery of the smug goy')[64] utterances fall from Pompey's lips, as she becomes an actor within that grotesque dark memorial she once narrated from a distance. Like Freud's patient in 'A Child is Being Beaten' Pompey does not observe that scene or represent it to herself, she 'is' it. A 'great parabola' is how Pompey later describes this potentially endless return to the same point of convergence:

> Very witty this painter, is he not? What did you say, what did you say there Pompey? Why now, remember to be very careful here, oh please remember to be so careful because this Painter Business circles in the widest outsweeping strong flight to the very first words that you have written. But on what a trajectory, to attain such an encirclement, to this back to the beginning, oh what an enormous great parabola you have described. And on the way, what was there on the way, that has turned your lips so pale, where were you then, where was the colour struck from those two lips, that are not yet much withered? I am back again within the picture gallery, to look and see and wish so much to have the amusing canvases they have hung there. Very witty this painter, is he not?[65]

The novel, then, moves from diegesis to mimesis and back again as if, indeed, this paradoxical, and here inverted, relation between imitated and imitator (Grosz's painting and Pompey) has to be told and narrated and yet, as the structural oscillation of the text implies, cannot ultimately be contained. This narrative knowingness by no means exonerates Pompey's (or Smith's) anti-semitism. As much as Pompey might 'despair for the racial hatred that is running in me. ... Out, out damn tooth', no amount of liberal orthodontics will put right the fact that Pompey will only fight for her friends, and that her friends are not Jews.[66] The latent narrative logic of the text shadows its manifest anti-semitic content, and the treachery of the smug goy lies in the fact that she can become the totalitarian she despises.

It is not only through Grosz's paintings that the internal frontier between performing and telling is played out. The figure of the dream in the novel also repeats and develops this logic. Throughout the text Pompey narrates scenes of militarism and totalitarian pomp; from a man 'in uniform' who, echoing the dichotomy between degeneracy and nobility in Grosz's picture, drunkenly caresses a statue of Venus, to 'the absurd and revolting spectacle of a fascist discipline' and through to the inclusion and analysis of an excerpt from German militaristic memoirs.[67] In two identical dreams, however, the pronoun in the syntax of these militaristic scenarios changes: 'he is in uniform' becomes 'I am in uniform' as, once more, Pompey ceases to represent militaristic fantasy and, donning its costume, becomes a participant within it: 'I am in uniform. But it is a secret, this uniform, it must not for a moment appear that I am in uniform, and to me something that is not perfectly assimilated, why I am here, why I am in uniform.'[68] The meaning of this uniformed identity cannot be 'assimilated', not only because of the internal narrative differentiation between performing and telling, but also because, correspondingly, Pompey's seduction over the frontier seems to resist representation. The between-war prophetic nightmare of totalitarianism and militarism persists, Pompey suggests elsewhere, but it cannot be consciously recalled: 'From what impalpable dream of refusal with no power of refusal am I awakened to palpable dismay and death-driven repudiation? I do not wish to consider, to explore, to recall again the dream that now lives only in effect.'[69]

In *Over the Frontier*, the nightmare of Grosz's 'Post War Museum' lives on only in its 'effects', in mimetic scenes of repetition and performance, because of the failure of interiorizing memory to prevent the recurrence of 'death-driven repudiation'. If the dream cannot be 'recalled' or made present to Pompey, it is because the tie that binds her to that fantasy is not reducible to models of recollection and self-narration. In this sense, the frontier between mimesis and diegesis, between performing and telling, also echoes Freud's differentiation between the 'compulsion to repeat' and the 'impulsion to remember'. Ideally, for Freud, analysis should lead to a recollection of a repressed piece of psychical material. Such a remembering need not necessarily refer to anything that has actually been forgotten; the fantasy or desire may never have been made present to consciousness in the first place.[70] Neither need it be true; what is important is the analysand's conviction of its truth brought about by the analyst's narrative constructions and interpretations of his or her free associations.[71] More often, however, the analysand resists such constructions and repeats the earlier situation, reproducing it not as a memory, but as an action. Such repetition is played out *par excellence* within the psychoanalytic transference where early infantile conflict is repeated, by displacement, onto the figure of the analyst. At its 'negative limits', then, repetition is opposed to verbal recollection but, at the same time, it is only by letting repetition 'into the transference as playground', says Freud,[72] that these copies or facsimiles can lead back to infantile conflict and, hence, finally to recollection. At the frontier between these two modalities lies the enigmatic relation between the analysand and analyst and, arguably, the question of how far the process of representing to the patient the desire that lies beyond his or her repetition can contain, or 'cure', not only a repeated object-cathexis onto the analyst (in which the analyst stands in *absentia* of an original love object) but also, importantly in this context, a repeated identification with his or her person.

It is Pompey's love affair with her 'Tom boy', alias Major Tom Satterthwaite, spy and soldier, that finally propels her 'over the frontier' into the theatricals of war. This affair, however, is by no means a stock romantic narrative fantasy; Pompey does not so much 'get her man', she becomes him (she becomes a 'tom boy'). In this sense, the affair joins up with the mimetic and repetitive series which, as we have seen, runs from Grosz's apocalyptic fantasy, through the figure of a dream, and emerges now as a scene of seduction:

> He forces me to look at him, to stare into his eyes, oddly lighted, light and ferocious in the light of the high full moon, shining down from above the light is thrown up again from the sea, is thrown up again from the surf and shining phosphorescent water, to shine again in the eyes of this exigeant Major Satterthwaite.

> 'Yes', I say, dully, tiredly, I am now getting so-o-o tired, it is amazing how suddenly I am become quite... 'Yes, I remember everything, I have forgotten nothing'.[73]

Like an analyst, Major Tom requires that Pompey tell him everything, that she forgets nothing ('be a good girl and remember to remember all the time').[74] In contrast to Milner's promotion of illusion as a space to explore the relation between 'me' with 'not-me', this quasi-analytic scene does not provide a 'frame' through which identification can be contained or made safe. If the scene refers us to anything at all within psychoanalysis, it is to hypnosis, the early form of therapy that Freud was later to reject on the grounds of its 'mysticism'.[75] Within this hypnotic mode it becomes difficult to read Tom as purely being the other through which Pompey recognizes her own destructive element. Instead Pompey's entranced captivation suggests a lack of distinction between subject and other. 'But have *I* been talking?', asks Pompey at one point in the seduction dialogue. 'But I thought it was you, why it was you, why Tom, it was you telling me, and telling me, and questioning and asking why it was certainly you and not I at all.'[76] This confusion is supported in the text as Tom, in turn, speaks in a recognizably Pompey-like idiom. Pompey's final seduction 'over the frontier' takes place through a relation which is not so much, strictly speaking, a relation between subjects, as the insertion of one identity into another.

'I am in uniform', Pompey repeats again, as she catches with horror her reflection in the mirror after Tom has dressed her in preparation for their trip over the frontier. The scene recalls Marion Milner's equally horrific discovery of the uncanny coincidence between her own phantasies and those of totalitarianism. When her young patients begin to play war-games in the nursery, Milner draws back from interpreting their desires as the psychic parallels of the war raging outside. The boundaries, or frontiers, of the self, she seems to be suggesting, are too fragile for the logic of insides and outsides to work. There is no destructive element within than can be projected outside onto the aggressor, and no destructive element without that fans the flames of infantile aggression: inside and outside run into one another like the surfaces of a Möbius strip. In her 1952 paper, Milner comes close to suggesting that war-time closes this illusion of the 'not-self' down and forces the ego into an integrity predicated on its defensiveness. The dissolution of frontiers and boundaries in Smith's *Over the Frontier* almost suggests the opposite – by the end of the novel, Pompey certainly is not 'herself'. But as with Milner's autobiographical works and case-histories, Smith's novel crosses the frontier between a model of fantasy in which the self is represented as a subject, and the blind-spot of that relation where that dream falters even as its inevitability is revealed. To read between these two models in *Over the Frontier* is also to broach the question of our political destinies – as either selves or subjects.

The imperative which *Over the Frontier* reveals is not so much to discover the self through fantasy, but consistently to note what cannot be said about that relation. This is perhaps where what one might call the ethical imperative of the novel also lies. In one of the novel's most powerful scenes, Pompey, now fully interpellated into the theatricals of war, comes face to face with a figure who represents the threat of the crowd most hideously: 'the smug flat note of that vox humana. *We are so many*. Yes, I have seen it before, this rat face; in London, Berlin, Paris, New York, in the villages of Hertfordshire'.[77] Before murdering him, Pompey notes an uncanny familiarity within this rat-face of the totalitarian masses:

> Rat-face … had something so fleeting-familiar upon his beetle-eyes, something that did not at all belong to the essence of the heart of Rat-face, that was flashed upon his eyes by a thought, it must have been my own, from some far place of a dark memory, to rise up with an impertinent incongruity, an altogether out-of character impertinence; to rise up, to question, to question my commission, with a surge-back to a voice that never spoke, but in a dream of weakness: from whom do you hold your commission?[78]

It is precisely the voice 'that never speaks', except within that repeated mimetic sequence which runs from art, dream to fantasy, which questions Pompey's role as participant in the theatre of war. Smith, like Milner, will not let us forget that even as the encounter with the threat of totalitarian phantasy is revealed as caught within a drive toward self-narration, the relation between self and other is simultaneously exposed at its most impossible. From whom do I hold my commission? From the State? From nationalist phantasy? From the other in the phantasy who symbolizes my desires? But if 'I' am the other in the phantasy, where then does accountability begin and end?

Neither Milner's 'frame' nor Smith's 'frontier' offers a fence to sit on, or a line which would neatly demarcate the space between personal desires and identifications and those of a wider political scenario. Instead both women point uncompromisingly to the fragility of this line of severance. In a postscript to 'A Suicidal Symptom in a Child of 3', Marion Milner refers to a case-history that suggests not the containment of a relation between self and other within a 'frame' but, once again, a collapse of this line of demarcation:

> Seven months after reading this paper I was asked to undertake the analysis of a girl of 23 (I called her Susan) whose analysis, centering around her drawings, I eventually tried to describe in the book *The Hands of the Living God*. During the analysis she told me how she had, a few weeks before, left hospital, where she had been persuaded to have ECT (electroconvulsive therapy) and what she felt it had done to her. She said that since having it she had no boundary at the back of her head and that the world was no longer outside her. This meant that she felt terrified of the bombing, since there were no boundaries; it meant that she was everything so the bombs were bound to fall on her.[79]

Susan is not a participant within a pre-war apocalyptic fantasy, she feels, terrifyingly, as if she 'is' the reality upon which that theatricals of cruelty is now being played out. There is an all-important difference here between the extent to which Milner's analytic technique invites her analysands to toy with illusion and Susan's subjection to ECT, a medically induced form of trauma, which literally leaves her selfless. The horror of such a side of self into other, with no redemption and no agency, is also anticipated by Smith in a different register.

> Then then on the other side of the dividing line of pain-in-art and pain-in-madness-badness is nothing but evvivant viscera, and the Oh no, Oh no, no, no, no, of the undeliberate dream that is to be endured and yet resisted, the horror of refusal with no power of refusal, Oh no, Oh no, no, no, no.[80]

If neither art nor indeed psychoanalysis can redeem the destructive element (the 'pain-in-madness-badness'), this does not mean that we are prevented from insisting, with Smith, on that final 'no, no, no'. It does mean that once we have stated our resistance, we are not fooled into thinking we are somehow safe from the seductions of phantasy. And, being vigilant in this respect, as both Milner and Smith demonstrate, involves questioning the 'commission' of the speaker who utters this protest; the same self who, alongside her resistance, continues to be lost and found in the destructive element.

Notes

Note on the text

The spellings 'phantasy and 'fantasy' are used throughout. 'Phantasy' refers to psychoanalytic, particularly to Kleinian, contexts and usage; 'fantasy' is used when the context is more general and less technical.

PREFACE

1. Stephen Spender, *The Destructive Element: A Study of Modern Writers and Beliefs*, London: Jonathan Cape, 1935, p. 19.
2. I.A. Richards, 'A Background for Contemporary Poetry', *The Criterion*, vol. 3, no. 12, July 1925, p. 520.
3. Valentine Cunningham, *British Writers of the Thirties*, Oxford: Oxford University Press, 1988, p. 58.
4. Erich Auerbach, *Mimesis* (1953), trans. W.R. Trask, Princeton: Princeton University Press, 1968, p. 551.
5. Edward Glover, 'Sublimation, Substitution and Social Anxiety', *International Journal of Psychoanalysis*, (*IJPA*), vol. 12, 1931, pp. 284–5.
6. Jacques Lacan, *Le séminaire livre VII: L'éthique de la psychanalyse, 1959–1960*, ed. Jacques-Alain Miller, Paris: Editions du Seuil, 1986, p. 133 (*The Seminar of Jacques Lacan Book VII: The Ethics of Psychoanalysis*, trans. Dennis Porter, London: Tavistock/Routledge, 1992, p. 111).
7. Sigmund Freud, *The Ego and the Id* (1923), *Penguin Freud Library* PFL 11, p. 396, *Standard Edition of the Complete Psychological Works of Sigmund Freud* SE 19, pp. 54–5.

INTRODUCTION: FROM BOKHARA TO SAMARRA: PSYCHOANALYSIS AND MODERNISM

1. Lionel Trilling, *Freud and the Crisis of our Culture*, Freud Memorial Lectures, Boston: Beacon Press, 1955, p. 40.
2. *Ibid*, p. 53.
3. *Ibid*, p. 33.
4. Leo Bersani, *The Culture of Redemption*, Massachusetts: Harvard University Press, 1990. I discuss Bersani's reading of Klein in detail in Chapter 1.
5. See Perry Meisel, *The Myth of the Modern*, New Haven: Yale University Press, 1987, and Jacqueline Rose, 'Freud and the Crisis of our Culture', inaugural lecture delivered at Queen Mary and Westfield College, October 20, 1994, published in Rose, *States of Fantasy*, Oxford: Clarendon Press, 1996, pp. 133–49.

6. Lionel Trilling, *Freud and the Crisis of our Culture*, p. 40.
7. *Ibid*, p. 54.
8. Perry Meisel, *The Myth of the Modern*, p. 5.
9. For historical and biographical accounts of Anna Freud's work on child analysis see Elisabeth Young-Bruchl, *Anna Freud: A Biography*, London: Macmillan, 1988 and Lisa Appignanesi and John Forrester, *Freud's Women*, London: Weidenfeld and Nicolson, 1992, pp. 272–306.
10. Lionel Trilling, *Freud and the Crisis of our Culture*, p. 54.
11. For a full account of the debate between Anna Freud and Melanie Klein, see *The Freud-Klein Controversies: 1941–45*, ed. Pearl King and Riccardo Steiner, New Library of Psychoanalysis, vol. 11, London: Routledge in association with the Institute of Psycho-Analysis, 1991. For critical readings of the Controversies see Phyllis Grosskurth, *Melanie Klein: Her World and Work*, London: Hodder & Stoughton, 1985; Teresa Brennan, 'Controversial Discussions and Feminist Debate', and Pearl King, 'Early Divergences between the Psycho-Analytic Societies in London and Vienna', both in *Freud in Exile, Psychoanalysis and its Vicissitudes*, ed. Edward Timms and Naomi Segal, New Haven: Yale University Press, 1988, pp. 254–74 and pp. 123–33 and Jacqueline Rose, 'War in the Nursery', in *Why War? Psychoanalysis, Politics and the Return to Melanie Klein*, The Bucknell Lectures in Literary Theory, Oxford: Blackwell, 1993, pp. 191–230.
12. Anna Freud, 'Abstract of "Psychoanalysis and Education", Freud Memorial Lecture 1954', *The Psychoanalytic Study of the Child*, vol. 9, 1954, p. 25.
13. Perry Meisel, *The Myth of the Modern*, p. 1.
14. Anna Freud and Dorothy Burlingham, *Young Children in War-Time: A Year's Work in a Residential War Nursery*, republished in *Infants Without Families: Reports on the Hampstead Nurseries 1939–1945, The Writings of Anna Freud, vol. 3*, New York: International Universities Press, 1973, p. 162.
15. Denise Riley, *War in the Nursery: Theories of the Child and Mother*, London: Virago, 1983, p. 7.
16. See Toril Moi, *Sexual /Textual Politics*, London: Methuen, 1986 and Makiko Minow Pinkney, *Virginia Woolf and the Problem of the Subject*, Brighton: Harvester, 1987.
17. Elisabeth Roudinesco, *Jacques Lacan and Company: A History of Psychoanalysis in France, 1925–1985*, trans. Jeffrey Mehlman, London: Free Association Books, 1990, p. 15.
18. Maud Ellmann, '*The Waste Land*': A Sphinx without a Secret', *The Poetics of Impersonality: T.S. Eliot and Ezra Pound*, Brighton: Harvester, 1987, p. 101.
19. See Jacques Lacan, *Le séminaire livre VII: l'éthique de la psychanalyse*, especially pp. 217–21 (*The Ethics of Psychoanalysis*, trans. Dennis Porter, pp. 182–8). I am indebted to Leo Bersani's brilliant reading of the way in which Freud's *Civilization* presents the social law as complicit with an anti-social primal aggressivity, see Leo Bersani, 'Theory and Violence', *The Freudian Body: Psychoanalysis and Art*, New York: Columbia University Press, 1986, pp. 7–27.

20. Elisabeth Roudinesco, *Jacques Lacan and Company: A History of Psychoanalysis in France 1925–1985*, p. 11.
21. *Ibid*, p. 15.
22. *Ibid*, p. 21.
23. Wyndham Lewis, *The Art of Being Ruled*, London: Chatto and Windus, 1926, p. 400.
24. *Ibid*, p. 404.
25. Wyndham Lewis, *Wyndham Lewis on Art*, ed. Walter Michel and C.J. Fox, London: Thames and Hudson, 1969, p. 249 and p. 456.
26. D.H. Lawrence, *'Fantasia of the Unconscious' and 'Psychoanalysis and the Unconscious'* (1921–1922), London: Heinemann, 1961.
27. For studies of H.D.'s relation to psychoanalysis, see Claire Buck, *H.D. and Freud: Bisexuality and a Feminine Discourse*, Brighton: Harvester, 1991; Diane Chisholm, *H.D.'s Freudian Poetics: Psychoanalysis in Translation*, Ithaca: Cornell University Press, 1992, and Susan Stanford Friedman, *Penelope's Web: Gender, Modernity, H.D's Fiction*, Cambridge: Cambridge University Press, 1990.
28. For indispensable feminist accounts of the return to Freud through Lacan, see Jane Gallop, *Feminism and Psychoanalysis: The Daughter's Seduction*, London: Macmillan, 1982; Juliet Mitchell, *Psychoanalysis and Feminism* (1974), Harmondsworth: Penguin, 1990; Jacqueline Rose and Juliet Mitchell, *Feminine Sexuality – Jacques Lacan and the Ecole freudienne*, London: Macmillan, 1982, and Jacqueline Rose, *Sexuality and the Field of Vision*, London: Verso, 1986. For recent returns to Klein see Elizabeth Abel, *Virginia Woolf and the Fictions of Psychoanalysis*, Chicago: University of Chicago Press, 1989; Briony Fer, 'Bordering on Blank: Eva Hesse and Minimalism', *Art History*, vol. 17, no. 3, September 1994, pp. 424–49; Mary Jacobus, *First Things First: The Maternal Imaginary in Literature, Art and Psychoanalysis*, London: Routledge, 1996; *Reading Melanie Klein*, ed. John Phillips and Lyndsey Stonebridge, London: Routledge, 1998; Mignon Nixon, 'Bad Enough Mother', *October*, 71, Winter 1995, pp. 71–92 and Jacqueline Rose, *Why War? Psychoanalysis, Politics and the Return to Melanie Klein*.
29. Raymond Williams, 'The Bloomsbury Fraction', *Problems in Materialism and Culture*, London: New Left Review Editions, Verso, 1980, p. 167.
30. Joan Rivière, 'On the Genesis of Psychical Conflict in Earliest Infancy' (1936), in Melanie Klein, Paula Heimann, Susan Isaacs and Joan Rivière, *Developments in Psycho-Analysis*, ed. Joan Rivière, London: Hogarth Press and the Institute of Psycho-Analysis, 1952, p. 50.
31. See Joan Rivière, 'The Unconscious Phantasy of an Inner World reflected in Literature', in *New Directions in Psycho-Analysis: The Significance of Infant Conflict in the Pattern of Adult Behaviour* (1955), ed. Melanie Klein, Paula Heimann, R.E. Money-Kyrle, London: Karnac, 1985, pp. 346–69.
32. E.F.M. Durbin and John Bowlby, 'Personal Aggressiveness and War', *War and Democracy: Essays on the Causes and Prevention of War*, E.F.M.

Durbin, John Bowlby, Ivor Thomas, D.P.T. Jay, R.B. Fraser, R.H.S. Crossman and George Catlin, London: Kegan Paul, Trench, Trubner and Co, 1938, p. 12.

33. *Ibid*, p. 41.
34. Elisabeth Roudinesco, *La bataille de cent ans: Histoire de la psychanalyse en France*, vol. 1, Paris: Editions Ramsay, 1982, p. 159 (my translation).
35. Melanie Klein, letter to the Boulagers dated 11 September 1952, Melanie Klein Archives held in the Contemporary Medical Archives Centre at the Wellcome Institute of the History of Medicine (KLE/C.3).
36. Jacques Lacan, *The Seminar of Jacques Lacan, Book 1 Freud's Papers on Technique, 1953–4*, trans. John Forrester, Cambridge: Cambridge University Press, 1988, p. 68.
37. See Jacqueline Rose, 'Negativity in the Work of Melanie Klein', *Why War? Psychoanalysis, Politics and the Return to Melanie Klein*, pp. 137–90.
38. André Green, 'Trop, c'est Trop' in *Melanie Klein Aujourd'hui*, James Gammil *et al.*, Lyon: Césura Lyon Edition, 1985, pp. 93–104.
39. Edward Glover, *Freud or Jung?*, London: George Allen & Unwin, 1950, p. 21.
40. Elisabeth Roudinesco, *La bataille de cent ans: Histoire de la psychanalyse en France*, vol. 1 pp. 159–60.
41. Edward Glover, *War, Sadism and Pacifism: Three Essays*, London: George Allen & Unwin, 1933, p. 31. Note also Glover's preface to the 1946 edition which is revised in the light of World War Two.
42. For Klein's views on phantasy and war, see her unpublished paper 'What does death represent to the individual?' (1940), held at the Melanie Klein Archives at the Wellcome Institute (PP/KLE/C95). For some discussion of this paper, see my 'Anxiety in Klein: The Missing Witch's Letter', in *Reading Melanie Klein*.
43. Glover objected to Klein's 1935 paper 'A Contribution to the Psychogenesis of Manic Depressive States'. For an account of Klein's reception by the British Society, see Pearl King, 'The Life and Work of Melanie Klein in the British Psycho-Analytic Society', *IJPA*, vol. 64, 1983, p. 258.
44. For a recent and original reading of Freud's aesthetics, see Malcolm Bowie, 'Freud and Art, or what will Michelangelo's *Moses* do Next?', *Psychoanalysis and the Future of Theory*, The Bucknell Lectures in Literary Theory, Oxford: Blackwell, 1993, pp. 55–87.
45. Jacques Lacan, *Le séminaire livre VII: L'éthique de la psychanalyse*, p. 128 (*Ethics of Psychoanalysis*, trans. Denis Porter, p. 107).
46. Christopher Lasch, 'Reply to Phyllis Grosskurth, "Melanie Klein: Creative Intellectual of Psychoanalysis"', *Salmagundi*, Spring-Summer, 70–71, 1986, pp. 210–13.
47. See Anton Ehrenzweig, *The Hidden Order of Art*, Berkeley: University of California Press, 1967, and *The Psychoanalysis of Artistic Vision and Hearing*, London: Sheldon Press, 1975.
48. Virginia Woolf, 'Sketch of the Past' in *Moments of Being* (1976), ed. Jeanne Schulkind, London: Grafton, 1982, p. 94.

1 STICKS FOR DAHLIAS: THE DESTRUCTIVE ELEMENT IN LITERARY CRITICISM AND MELANIE KLEIN

1. I.A. Richards, 'A Background for Contemporary Poetry', p. 520.
2. Stephen Spender, *The Destructive Element: A Study of Modern Writers and Beliefs*, p. 224.
3. See 'I.A. Richards interviewed by Reuben Brauer' in *Richards on Rhetoric: I.A. Richards Selected Essays 1929–1974*, ed. Ann B. Berthoff, Oxford: Oxford University Press, 1991, p. 7.
4. I.A. Richards, *Principles of Literary Criticism* (1924), London: Routledge & Kegan Paul, 1967, p. 34.
5. I.A. Richards, 'A Background for Contemporary Poetry', p. 520.
6. I.A. Richards, *Principles of Literary Criticism*, p. 35.
7. *Ibid*, p. 39.
8. Steven Connor, *Theory and Cultural Value*, Oxford: Blackwell, 1992, p. 37.
9. I.A. Richards, *Principles of Literary Criticism*, p. 10.
10. *Ibid*, p. 184.
11. *Ibid*, p. 231.
12. I.A. Richards, *Poetries and Sciences: A Reissue of Science and Poetry (1926, 1935) with Commentary*, London: Routledge & Kegan Paul, 1970, p. 64.
13. I.A. Richards, *Principles of Literary Criticism*, p. 43.
14. *Ibid*, p. 233.
15. *Ibid*, p. 235.
16. T.S. Eliot, 'From The Use of Poetry and The Use of Criticism' (1933), *Selected Prose of T.S. Eliot*, ed. Frank Kermode, London: Faber and Faber, 1975, p. 88.
17. For an excellent account of Eliot and New Criticism see John Guillory, *Cultural Capital. The Problem of Literary Canon Formation*, Chicago: University of Chicago Press, 1993, pp. 134–75.
18. William Empson, *The Structure of Complex Words* (1951), London: Hogarth , 1985, p. 425.
19. William Empson, letter to I.A. Richards, *Argufying: Essays on Literature and Culture*, ed. John Haffenden, London: Chatto and Windus, 1987, p. 552. Steven Connor draws a similar parallel, see Steven Connor, *Theory and Cultural Value*, p. 39.
20. William Empson, letter to I.A. Richards, *Argufying*, p. 552.
21. William Empson, 'Death and Its Desires', *Argufying*, p. 540.
22. *Ibid*, p. 536.
23. See Empson's introduction to the Japanese edition of Eliot's essays, 'Mr Eliot and the East' (1933) for the significance of Nirvana and Buddhism to Eliot and also for Empson's defence of Richards following Eliot's review of *Science and Poetry* (*Dial*, March 1927), *ibid*, pp. 566–70.
24. Joseph Conrad, *Lord Jim* (1900), Harmondsworth: Penguin, 1949, p. 181.
25. William Empson, 'Death and Its Desires', *Argufying*, p. 542.
26. *Ibid*, p. 544.

27. R.E. Money-Kyrle, *The Development of the Sexual Impulses*, London: Kegan Paul, 1932, p. 201.
28. I.A. Richards, *Poetries and Sciences*, p. 40.
29. William Empson, *Seven Types of Ambiguity* (1930), Harmondsworth: Penguin, 1995, p. 226.
30. *Ibid*, p. 226.
31. Sigmund Freud, *Civilization and Its Discontents* (1930[1929]) PFL 12, p. 301, SE 21, p. 111.
32. William Empson, *Seven Types of Ambiguity*, p. 270.
33. *Ibid*, p. 9.
34. Wyndham Lewis, *Men Without Art*, London: Cassell, 1934, p. 87.
35. William Empson, *Seven Types of Ambiguity*, p. 9.
36. Sigmund Freud, *Inhibitions, Symptoms and Anxiety*, (1926[1925]) PFL 10, p. 251, SE 20, pp. 98–9.
37. Hanna Segal, 'A Psycho-Analytical Approach to Aesthetics', *New Directions in Psycho-Analysis*, p. 390.
38. For advocates of Klein's aesthetics see Janet Sayers, *Mothering Psychoanalysis: Helene Deutsch, Karen Horney, Anna Freud and Melanie Klein*, London: Hamish Hamilton, 1990, and Meg Harris Williams and Margot Waddell, *The Chamber of Maiden Thought, Literary Origins of the Psychoanalytic Model of the Mind*, London: Routledge, 1991. For a detractor's view of Klein see Noreen O'Connor, 'Is Melanie Klein the One Who Knows Who You Really Are?', *Women: A Cultural Review*, vol. 1, no. 2, Summer 1990, pp. 180–9.
39. For readings of Klein which work with her contradictions see: Jacqueline Rose, 'Negativity in the Work of Melanie Klein' and 'War in the Nursery', *Why War?*, pp. 137–90 and pp. 191–230; Mary Jacobus, *First Things, The Maternal Imaginary in Literature, Art and Psychoanalysis*, and the essays collected in *Reading Melanie Klein*.
40. Maynard Keynes, *The Economic Consequences of the Peace* (1919), London: Macmillan, 1920, see especially 'The Conference', pp. 24–51.
41. Melanie Klein, 'Love, Guilt and Reparation' (1937), *Love, Guilt and Reparation and other works 1921–1945*, London: Virago, 1988, p. 306.
42. Leo Bersani, *The Culture of Redemption*, p. 11.
43. *Ibid*, p. 14.
44. See William Empson, *The Structure of Complex Words*, p. 425.
45. Leo Bersani, *The Culture of Redemption*, p. 16.
46. *Ibid*, p. 18.
47. *Ibid*, p. 19.
48. *Ibid*, p. 20.
49. *Ibid*, pp. 20–1.
50. *Ibid*, p. 22.
51. Melanie Klein, 'Some Theoretical Conclusions on the Emotional Life of the Infant' (1952), *Envy and Gratitude and other works 1946–1963*: London, Virago, 1988, p. 82.
52. Quoted in Melanie Klein, *The Psychoanalysis of Children* (1932), London: Virago, 1989, p. 138. The quotation is from *The Ego and the Id* (1923), PFL 11, p. 396, SE 19, pp. 54–5.

53. Melanie Klein, 'Notes on Some Schizoid Mechanisms' (1946), *Envy and Gratitude*, p. 3. I have expanded and revised this argument about the role of anxiety in Klein's work in 'The Missing Witch's Letter: Anxiety in Klein' in *Reading Melanie Klein*.
54. Melanie Klein, *Love, Guilt and Reparation*, p. 78.
55. Samuel Weber, 'The Witch's Letter', *Return to Freud: Jacques Lacan's Dislocation of Psychoanalysis*, trans. Michael Levine, Cambridge: Cambridge University Press, 1991, p. 152.
56. Melanie Klein, *The Psychoanalysis of Children*, p. 42.
57. *Ibid*, p. 126.
58. *Ibid*, p. 127.
59. Julia Kristeva, 'The True-Real', trans. Sean Hand, *The Kristeva Reader*, ed. Toril Moi, Oxford: Blackwell, 1986, p. 224.
60. Samuel Weber, *Return to Freud*, p. 152. I am indebted to Jacqueline Rose for this formulation. See 'Negativity in the Work of Melanie Klein', *Why War*, p. 166.
61. Melanie Klein, *Envy and Gratitude*, p. 74.
62. Melanie Klein, *The Psychoanalysis of Children*, p. 150.
63. *Ibid*, p. 115.
64. Melanie Klein, *The Psychoanalysis of Children*, p. 174.
65. *Ibid*, p. 148.
66. Melanie Klein, *Love, Guilt and Reparation*, p. 347.

2 IS THE ROOM A TOMB? ROGER FRY, VIRGINIA WOOLF AND THE KLEINIANS

1. Benedict Nicholson, 'Post-Impressionism and Roger Fry', *The Burlington Magazine*, vol. 93, no. 574, January 10, 1951, p. 15.
2. Melanie Klein, 'Infantile Anxiety Situations Reflected in a Work of Art and in the Creative Impulse' (1929), *Love, Guilt and Reparation*, p. 217.
3. Rosalind E. Krauss, *The Optical Unconscious*, (1993), Cambridge, Massachusetts: MIT Press, 1994, pp. 138–139 (the passage from Woolf is also cited by Krauss).
4. Elaine Showalter, *A Literature of Their Own*, London: Virago, 1978, p. 296.
5. Melanie Klein, 'Infantile Anxiety Situations Reflected in a Work of Art and in the Creative Impulse', p. 218.
6. Letters to Adrian Stokes from Joan Riviere and Melanie Klein dated 10 February, 10 August and 4 September 1952, Adrian Stokes papers, Tate Gallery Archive, TGA 8816. I am most grateful to Mrs Ann Angus for taking the time to discuss the circumstances surrounding the portrait's destruction (telephone conversation, 7 August 1995). I discussed the Coldstream incident in more detail in 'Psychoanalysis, Aesthetics and Kleinian Anger', unpublished paper read at the 'Feminism and the Aesthetics of Difference' Conference, London, September 1995.

7. Steven Connor also picks up on this anomaly. I am indebted to his careful analysis of comparisons between Richards and Fry. Steven Connor, *Theory and Cultural Value*, p. 36.
8. See Sigmund Freud, 'Psychogenic Visual Disturbance According to Psychoanalytic Conceptions' (1910), SE 11, pp. 21–40.
9. Rosalind E. Krauss, *The Optical Unconscious*, p. 119.
10. Roger Fry, 'Post-Impressionism', *The Fortnightly Review*, May 1911, reprinted in Richard Reed (ed.), *A Roger Fry Reader*, Chicago: The University of Chicago Press, 1996, p. 100.
11. Roger Fry, 'The Artist and Psycho-Analysis', *Hogarth Essays Series*, London: Hogarth Press, 1924, p. 8–9.
12. Roger Fry, 'The Artist's Vision' (1919), reprinted in *Vision and Design* (1920), Harmondsworth: Penguin, 1961, p. 46.
13. Roger Fry, 'The Artist and Psycho-Analysis', p. 9.
14. Steven Connor, *Theory and Cultural Value*, p. 37.
15. Roger Fry, 'The Artist and Psycho-Analysis', p. 18.
16. Hanna Segal, 'Freud and Art', *Dream, Phantasy and Art*, London: Tavistock and Routledge, 1991, pp. 80–1.
17. Roger Fry, 'The Artist and Psycho-Analysis', p. 18.
18. Roger Fry, 'An Essay in Aesthetics' (1919), reprinted in *Vision and Design*, p. 37.
19. Barbara Low, review of Charles Mauron's *Aesthetics and Psychology* (trans. Roger Fry and Katherine John), *Life and Letters Today*, vol. 13, no. 2, Winter, 1935–6, pp. 211–14.
20. Walter Benjamin, 'Some Motifs in Baudelaire', *Charles Baudelaire: A Lyric Poet in the Era of High Capitalism* (1969), trans. Harry Zohn, London: Verso, 1989, p. 110.
21. Roger Fry, 'An Essay in Aesthetics', reprinted in *Vision and Design*, p. 30, p.25.
22. For a recent assessment of Woolf's Relation to Fry's formalism, see Rebecca Stott, '"Inevitable Relations": aesthetic revelations from Cézanne to Woolf', in *The Politics of Pleasure: Aesthetics and Cultural Theory*, ed. Stephen Regan, Buckingham: Open University Press, 1992, pp. 87–107.
23. Roger Fry, 'Modern French Art at the Mansard Gallery', *Athenaeum*, 8 August 1919, reprinted in Richard Reed (ed.), *A Roger Fry Reader*, p. 342.
24. See Virginia Woolf's letter to Roger Fry, 21 October 1918, *The Letters of Virginia Woolf, vol. 2*, ed. Nigel Nicholson and Joanne Trautmann, London: Hogarth Press, 1976, 981, p. 285.
25. Virginia Woolf, 'The Mark on the Wall' (1917), *The Complete Shorter Fiction*, ed. Susan Dick, London: Grafton Books, 1991, p. 85–6.
26. *Ibid*, p. 84.
27. *Ibid*, p. 87–8.
28. Patricia Waugh, *Practising Postmodernism/Reading Modernism*, London: Edward Arnold, 1992, p. 107.
29. Virginia Woolf, 'The Mark on the Wall', p. 88.
30. See Sigmund Freud, *Beyond the Pleasure Principle* (1920), PFL, 11, pp. 275–338 and SE, 18, p. 7–64.

31. Virginia Woolf, 'The Mark on the Wall', p. 89.
32. Cleanth Brooks, *Modern Poetry and the Tradition*, Chapel Hill: University of North Carolina Press, 1939, p. 44. Cited in Alan Wilde, *Horizons of Assent: Modernism, Postmodernism and the Ironic Imagination*, Baltimore: Johns Hopkins Press, 1981, p. 24.
33. Alan Wilde, *Horizons of Assent: Modernism, Postmodernism and the Ironic Imagination*, p. 21.
34. Maurice Blanchot, 'L'échec du démon: la vocation', *Le livre à venir*, Paris: Gallimard, 1959, p. 125, 'Outwitting the Demon – A Vocation', *The Siren's Song: Selected Essays by Maurice Blanchot*, ed. Gabriel Josipovici, trans. Sacha Rabinovitch, Brighton: Harvester Press, 1982, p. 89. Translation modified.
35. *Ibid*, p. 122 ('Outwitting the Demon – A Vocation, p. 88).
36. Virginia Woolf, 'Sketch of the Past' (1939–40), *Moments of Being* (1976), pp. 83–4.
37. On catastrophe, Klein and Bion, see Michael Eigen, 'Towards Bion's Starting Point: Between Catastrophe and Faith', *IJPA*, 1985, no. 66, pp. 321–30.
38. Virginia Woolf, 'Sketch of the Past', p. 82.
39. *Ibid*, p. 83.
40. *Ibid*, p. 90–1.
41. See manuscript A5(a), p. 24, in *The Monk's House Collection*, University of Sussex.
42. Virginia Woolf, 'Sketch of the Past', p. 83.
43. Charles Bernheimer, 'A Shattered Globe: Narcissism and Masochism in Virginia Woolf's Life Writing', in *Psychoanalysis and...*, ed. Richard Feldstein and Henry Sussman, London: Routledge, 1990, p. 188.
44. *Ibid*, p. 199.
45. Julia Kristeva, 'About Chinese Women', trans. Sean Hand, *The Kristeva Reader*, p. 157.
46. Elaine Showalter, *A Literature of Their Own*, p. 296. But note that Showalter also recognizes that negation has its own power: 'there is a kind of female power in the passivity of her writing: it is insatiable.' Woolf's tomb, it seems, contains something of a restless corpse.
47. The by now classic refutation of Showalter's reading of Woolf is to be found in Toril Moi's 'Who's Afraid of Virginia Woolf', *Sexual/Textual Politics*. For reasons why feminists should be uncomfortable with categories such as 'womanhood', 'woman' and especially 'women', see Denise Riley, *Am I that Name? Feminism and the Category of 'Women' in History*, London: Macmillan, 1988.
48. Virginia Woolf, 'Sketch of the Past', p. 94.
49. Elizabeth Abel, *Virginia Woolf and the Fictions of Psychoanalysis*, p. 13.
50. *Ibid*, p. 11.
51. Virginia Woolf, 'Sketch of the Past', p. 99.
52. Hanna Segal, 'Freud and Art', p. 81.
53. Tony Pinkney suggests that this is particularly the case with Segal's reading of Klein. See *Women in the Poetry of T.S. Eliot*, London: Macmillan, 1984, p. 11.

54. Freud reprimands Klein in 'Female Sexuality' (1931), PFL , 7, 390–1, and SE, 21, p. 242. See also Juliet Mitchell, 'Introduction 1', in *Feminine Sexuality: Jacques Lacan and the Ecole freudienne*.
55. Melanie Klein, 'The Early Stages of the Oedipus Conflict' (1928), *Love, Guilt and Reparation*, p. 193.
56. *Ibid*, p. 194.
57. Leo Bersani, 'Theory and Violence', *The Freudian Body*, p. 25.
58. See Melanie Klein, 'The Oedipus Conflict in the Light of Early Anxieties' (1945), *Love, Guilt and Reparation*, pp. 370–410.
59. Roger Fry, *Cézanne*, London: Hogarth Press, 1927.
60. Paula Heimann, 'A contribution to the problem of sublimation and its relation to processes of internalization', *IJPA*, vol. 33, part 1, 1942, p. 13.
61. *Ibid*, pp. 12–13.
62. Virginia Woolf, *To the Lighthouse* (1927), London: Grafton, 1987, p. 59.
63. Paula Heimann, 'A contribution to the problem of sublimation and its relation to processes of internalization', p. 14.
64. Compare Woolf's description of the 'Angel' in 'Professions for Women': 'I discovered that if I were to review books I should need to do battle with a certain phantom. And the phantom was a woman, and when I came to know her better I called her after the heroine of a famous poem, The Angel in the House .... I turned upon her and caught her by the throat. I did my best to kill her ... her fictitious nature was of great assistance to her. It is far harder to kill a phantom than a reality. She was always creeping back when I thought I had despatched her. Though I flatter myself that I killed her in the end'. 'Professions for Women', *The Death of the Moth and Other Essays*, London: Hogarth Press, 1942, pp. 150–151. Woolf first delivered 'Professions for Women' as a lecture in 1931. Her essay was published in the same year as Heimann's paper.
65. Paula Heimann, 'A contribution to the problem of sublimation and its relation to processes of internalization', p. 16.
66. Matte Blanco, quoted by Heimann, *ibid*, p. 16.
67. *Ibid*.
68. *Ibid*.
69. Hanna Segal, 'A Psychoanalytical Approach to Aesthetics', p. 388.
70. *Ibid*, p. 395.
71. See Julia Kristeva, 'The True-Real', *The Kristeva Reader*, pp. 214–37.
72. Hanna Segal, 'A Psychoanalytic Approach to Aesthetics', p. 403.
73. *Ibid*, pp. 399–400.
74. *Ibid*, p. 400.
75. Hanna Segal, 'Freud and Art', p. 80.
76. See Roger Fry, 'Art and Life', *Vision and Design*, pp. 11–22.
77. Walter Benjamin, 'Some Motifs in Baudelaire', p. 154.
78. *Ibid*, p. 117.
79. Virginia Woolf, 'Sketch of the Past', p. 114.
80. *Ibid*, p. 114.
81. Virginia Woolf, 'Thoughts on Peace in an Air Raid' (1940), *The Death of the Moth and Other Essays*, p. 155.

82. *Ibid*, p. 157.
83. Virginia Woolf, *Roger Fry: A Biography* (1940), London: Hogarth, 1991, p. 214.

3 RHYTHM: BREAKING THE ILLUSION

1. Virginia Woolf, 'A Letter to a Young Poet' (1932), *The Moment and Other Essays*, ed. Leonard Woolf, London: Hogarth Press, 1947, p. 141.
2. Virginia Woolf, *The Years* (1937), London: Hogarth Press, 1974, p. 464.
3. Virginia Woolf, *The Waves* (1931), London: Grafton, 1989, p. 171–3.
4. Jane Marcus, 'Thinking Back Through Our Mothers', in *New Feminist Essays on Virginia Woolf*, ed. Jane Marcus, London: Macmillan, 1981, p. 9.
5. Virginia Woolf, '"Anon" and "The Reader"' (1939–40), ed. Brenda Silver, *Twentieth Century Literature*, 25, 1979, p. 374.
6. Julia Kristeva, *Revolution in Poetic Language*, trans. Margaret Waller, New York: Columbia University Press, 1984, p. 29.
7. For Kristevan readings of Woolf, see Makiko Minow Pinkney, 'Virginia Woolf "Seen from a Foreign Land"' in *Abjection, Melancholia and Love: The Work of Julia Kristeva*, ed. John Fletcher and Andrew Benjamin, London and New York: Routledge, 1991, pp. 162–77, and her full-length study, *Virginia Woolf and the Problem of the Subject*. See also Rebecca Saunders, 'Language, Subject, Self: Reading the Style of *To the Lighthouse*', *Novel: A Forum on Fiction*, 26, 2, Winter 1993, pp. 192–251.
8. Wyndham Lewis, *Men Without Art*, pp. 167–71.
9. Julia Kristeva, *Powers of Horror: An Essay on Abjection*, trans. Leon S. Roudiez, New York: Columbia University Press, 1982, p. 179.
10. For a suggestive glimpse into what may well have been Sharpe's analysis of Adrian Stephen, see Ella Freeman Sharpe, *Dream Analysis: A Practical Handbook for Psycho-Analysts* (1937), London: Karnac Books, 1978, pp. 122–3. An unnamed dreamer dreams of a 'genealogical table set out [which] showed how characters in Jane Austen's novels were related to one another'. Sharpe's analysis traces the dream back to a family genealogy which corresponds to that of the Stephen family: 'The dreamer as a little boy had this conundrum. X was his sister, Y was his sister and Z was his brother. A was his brother and so was B, but the father of A and B was dead while the boy's own father was alive. Yet his mother was the mother of A and B ... The dreamer chose an eminent woman novelist as a tribute to his own mother who created children who became distinguished in later life .... In the logic of this child's range of facts it was inevitable that the father must die after children had been created'.
11. The temporality of rhythm in Sharpe's work seems to be a marginal issue. For a recent account of the psychic temporalities of rhythm, see Nicolas Abraham, 'Psychoanalytic Aesthetics' Time, Rhythm and the Unconscious', *Rhythms: On the Work, Translation and Psychoanalysis*,

collected and presented by Nicholas T. Rand and Maria Torok, trans. Benjamin Thigpen and Nicholas T. Rand, California: Stanford University Press, 1995, pp. 107–30.

12. Ella Freeman Sharpe, 'Similar and Divergent Unconscious Determinants Underlying the Sublimation of Pure Art and Pure Science' (1934) in *Collected Papers on Psychoanalysis*, ed. Marjorie Brierley, London: Hogarth Press, 1950, p. 104.
13. *Ibid*, p. 144–5.
14. Virginia Woolf, 'Modern Fiction', *The Common Reader: First Series* (1925), London: Hogarth Press, 1942, p. 189.
15. Michael H. Levenson, *A Genealogy of Modernism: A Study in English Literary Doctrine 1908–1922*, Cambridge: Cambridge University Press, 1984, p. 119.
16. Virginia Woolf, *A Room of One's Own* (1929), London: Grafton, 1985, p. 99.
17. Virginia Woolf, 'Thoughts on Peace in an Air Raid' (1940), *The Death of the Moth*, p. 17.
18. Ella Freeman Sharpe, 'Similar and Divergent Unconscious Determinants', *Collected Papers*, p. 148.
19. *Ibid*, p. 144.
20. *Ibid*, p. 147.
21. Ella Freeman Sharpe, 'Certain Aspects of Sublimation and Delusion' (1930), *Collected Papers*, p. 128.
22. *Ibid*, p. 135.
23. Ella Freeman Sharpe, 'Psycho-Physical Problems Revealed in Language: An Examination of Metaphor', *Collected Papers*, p. 168.
24. Nicolas Abraham and Maria Torok, 'Introjection – Incorporation: Mourning or Melancholia', *Psychoanalysis in France*, ed. Serge Lebovici and D. Widlocher, New York: International University Press, 1980, p. 6.
25. Ella Freeman Sharpe, 'Psycho-Physical Problems Revealed in Language', *Collected Papers*, p. 160.
26. See Emile Benveniste, 'La notion de "rythme" dans son expression linguistique', *Problèmes de linguistique générale, vol. 1*, Paris: Gallimard, 1966, pp. 327–35. This translation, *Problems in General Linguistics*, trans. Mary Meek, Florida: University of Miami Press, 1971, p. 287.
27. See Emile Benveniste, 'Semiologie de la langue', *Problèmes de linguistique générale, vol. 2*, Paris: Gallimard, 1974.
28. Ella Freeman Sharpe, 'From *King Lear* to *The Tempest*', *Collected Papers*, p. 124.
29. Jacques Lacan, *Le séminaire livre VII: L'éthique de la psychanalyse*, p. 128 (*Ethics of Psychoanalysis*, trans. Denis Porter, p. 107).
30. Ella Freeman Sharpe contribution to 'First Discussion of Scientific Controversies', Discussion held on January 27th, 1943 on Susan Isaacs' paper 'The Nature and Function of Phantasy', *The Freud-Klein Controversies, 1941–45*, pp. 337–340.
31. See Virginia Woolf, *Roger Fry: A Biography*, p. 232; Leonard Woolf, *After the Deluge: A Study of Communal Psychology*, Harmondsworth: Penguin, 1937 and *Quack, Quack*, London: Hogarth Press, 1935.
32. Ella Freeman Sharpe, *Collected Papers*, p. 95.

33. *Ibid*, p. 97.
34. Virginia Woolf, *A Room of One's Own*, p. 19.
35. Virginia Woolf, *A Reflection of the Other Person: The Letters of Virginia Woolf*, vol. 4, 1929–1931, ed. Nigel Nicholson, London: Hogarth, 1978, p. 204.
36. Virginia Woolf, '"Anon" and "The Reader"', p. 382.
37. *Ibid*, p. 408.
38. *Ibid*, p. 380.
39. *Ibid*, p. 385.
40. William Empson, *Some Versions of Pastoral* (1935), London: Chatto and Windus, 1974.
41. Virginia Woolf, 'The Leaning Tower' (read to the Workers' Educational Association, Brighton, May 1940), *The Moment and Other Essays*, pp. 105–25. Compare the replies to Woolf's essay by Edward Upward, B.L. Coombes and Louis MacNeice in *Folios of New Writing*, Spring 1941, Hogarth. 'As for the Leaning Tower' writes MacNeice, 'if Galileo had not had one at Pisa, he would not have discovered the truth about falling weights. We learned something of the sort from our tower too', p. 41.
42. Virginia Woolf, 'Introductory Letter', *Life As We Have Known It*, ed. Margaret Llewelyn Davies, London: Hogarth, 1931; Virginia Woolf, *The Diary of Virginia Woolf, vol. 5, 1939–1941*, ed. Anne Olivier Bell, Harmondsworth: Penguin, 1988, p. 288; John Mepham, *Virginia Woolf: A Literary Life*, London: Macmillan, 1991, p. 191.
43. Virginia Woolf, *The Diary of Virginia Woolf*, vol. 5, p. 248.
44. Sigmund Freud, *Group Psychology and the Analysis of the Ego* (1921), PFL 12, pp. 134–135 and SE 18, pp. 103–4.
45. Virginia Woolf, *The Diary of Virginia Woolf*, vol. 5, p. 166.
46. *Ibid*, p. 249.
47. J. Hillis Miller, '*Between the Acts*: Repetition as Extrapolation', *Fiction and Repetition: Seven English Novels*, Cambridge, Massachusetts: University of Harvard Press, 1982, p. 240.
48. Virginia Woolf, *Pointz Hall: The Earlier and Later Typescripts of Between the Acts*, ed. Mitchell A. Leaska, New York: University Publications, 1983, pp. 61–2.
49. Alex Zwerdling, *Virginia Woolf and the Real World*, Berkeley: University of California Press, 1986, p. 308.
50. Virginia Woolf, *Between the Acts* (1941), London: Grafton Books, 1988, p. 89.
51. *Ibid*, p. 67.
52. Virginia Woolf, *Between the Acts*, pp. 103–4.
53. See, for example, Nora Eisenberg, 'Virginia Woolf's Last Words on Words: *Between the Acts* and "Anon"', *New Feminist Essays on Virginia Woolf*, p. 259.
54. Makiko Minow Pinkney, 'Virginia Woolf "Seen from a Foreign Land"', pp. 171–2.
55. Mitchell A. Leaska also draws attention to this connection between the cows and Woolf's concern with the 'herd instinct'. See Virginia Woolf, *Pointz Hall*, p. 229.

56. Virginia Woolf, *Between the Acts*, p. 135.
57. *Ibid*, p. 70.
58. Virginia Woolf, *Pointz Hall*, p. 103.
59. *Ibid*, p. 129.
60. Virginia Woolf, *Between the Acts*, p. 127.
61. See Sigmund Freud, *Moses and Monotheism* (1939[1937–1939]), PFL 13, pp. 349–87, and SE 23, pp. 103–37.
62. Julia Kristeva, *Powers of Horror: An Essay on Abjection*, p. 179.
63. Virginia Woolf, *The Diary of Virginia Woolf*, vol. 5, p. 135.
64. Virginia Woolf, *Between the Acts*, p. 133.
65. Lacan first delivered 'La stade du miroir' at the fourteenth International Psychoanalytic Congress, Marienbad in 1936. See Jacques Lacan, 'The mirror stage as formative of the function of the I as revealed in psychoanalytic experience', *Ecrits*, trans. Alan Sheridan, London: Tavistock/Routledge, 1977.
66. Virginia Woolf, *Between the Acts*, p. 135.
67. Elizabeth Abel, *Virginia Woolf and the Fictions of Psychoanalysis*, p. 120.
68. Virginia Woolf, *Between the Acts*, pp. 135–6.
69. *Ibid*, p. 137.
70. John Mepham, *Virginia Woolf: A Literary Life*, p. 198.
71. Virginia Woolf, *Pointz Hall*, p. 116.

4 STONE LOVE: ADRIAN STOKES AND THE INSIDE OUT

1. H.D., *End to Torment*, ed. Norman Holmes Pearson and Michael King, New York: New Directions, 1979, p. 3. I regret that this chapter was completed before I learned of Richard Read's work in a similar area in his new book, *Stokes/Pound/Klein: Poetics versus Psychoanalysis in the Early Art Criticism of Adrian Stokes* (forthcoming).
2. 'Giù son gli archi e combusti i muri/Del letto arcano della divina Ixotta', Ezra Pound, *The Cantos of Ezra Pound*, London: Faber and Faber, 1990, p. 428. Trans. Massimo Bacigalupo, 'Ezra Pound's Cantos 72 and 73', *Paideuma: A Journal of Pound Scholarship*, vol. 20, nos 1–2, p. 13.
3. H.D., *End to Torment*, p. 26.
4. See Claire Buck, *H.D. and Freud: Bisexuality and a Feminine Discourse* and Dianne Chisholm, *H.D.'s Freudian Poetics: Psychoanalysis in Translation*.
5. Adrian Stokes, *Inside Out* (1947), *The Critical Writings of Adrian Stokes, vol. 2*, 3 vols, ed. Lawrence Gowing, London: Thames and Hudson, 1978, p. 158. Henceforth cited as *CW*.
6. For an account of male writers' sojourns 'abroad' see Paul Fussell, *Abroad: British Literary Travelling Between the Wars*, Oxford: Oxford University Press, 1980.
7. Ezra Pound, 'A review of the *Quattro Cento* by Adrian Stokes', *Symposium*, Concord, New Hampshire, October 1932, pp. 528–521, reprinted in *Ezra Pound and the Visual Arts*, ed. Harriet Zinnes, New

York: New Directions, 1980, p. 223. Stokes' strategic use of the phrase 'Quatto Cento' needs to be understood in his own terms. According to Stokes, in fifteenth-century Italy, Renaissance sculptors 'made stone bloom'. 'Such effect in relation to stone [...] are referred to in this book by the symbol 'Quattro Cento', actually as one word the Italian chronological expression for fifteenth century. *I will not use it at all in this its proper sense.* The special content with which I am concerned [...] permeates the spirit and the art of the fifteenth century. But I call 'Quattro Cento' only the direct and manifest expression of this content', *CW1*, p. 34. I have followed this use where appropriate.

8. Adrian Stokes, 'Painting, Giorgione and Barbaro', *The Criterion*, vol. 9, April 1930, p. 489.
9. See Walter Pater, *The Renaissance, Studies in Art and Poetry*, London: Macmillan, 1924. For analogies between writing and sculpture see 'Style' in *Appreciations, with an Essay on Style*, London: Macmillan, 1924, pp.1–36. For a detailed analysis of Stokes' aesthetic inheritance and psychoanalysis, see Stephen Bann, 'Adrian Stokes: English Aesthetic Criticism under the Impact of Psychoanalysis', in *Freud in Exile, Psychoanalysis, and its Vicissitudes*, pp. 134–44, and Richard Read, 'Freudian Psychology and the Early Work of Adrian Stokes', *PN Review: 'Adrian Stokes'*, vol. 7, no. 1, 1980, pp. 37–40.
10. Donald Davie, 'Adrian Stokes and Pound's Cantos', *Twentieth Century*, vol. 260, 957, 1956, p. 424. See also Davie's *Ezra Pound: The Poet as Sculptor*, London: Routledge and Kegan Paul, 1965, and his 'Adrian Stokes Revisited', *Paideuma: A Journal of Pound Scholarship*, vol. 12, nos. 2–3, 1983, pp. 189–97.
11. Adrian Stokes, *The Stones of Rimini* (1935), *CW1*, p. 219.
12. Ezra Pound, *The Cantos of Ezra Pound*, p. 78.
13. Adrian Stokes, *The Stones of Rimini*, *CW1*, p. 219.
14. Joseph Conrad, 'Preface', *The Nigger of Narcissus* (1897), London: Everyman, J.M. Dent, 1960.
15. Adrian Stokes, *CW1*, p. 196.
16. Sigmund Freud, *Civilization and its Discontents*, PFL 12, pp. 256–60, SE 21, pp. 69–71.
17. Adrian Stokes, *The Quattro Cento* (1932), *CW1*, p. 46.
18. *Ibid*, p. 135.
19. *Ibid*, p. 46.
20. Adrian Stokes, *The Stones of Rimini*, *CW1*, p. 231.
21. Friedrich Nietszche, *Ecce Homo: How One Becomes What One Is*, trans. R.J. Hollingdale, Harmondsworth: Penguin, 1992, p. 81. My thanks to Stephen Bann for suggesting this comparison.
22. Adrian Stokes, *The Quattro Cento*, *CW1*, p. 76.
23. Adrian Stokes, *The Stones of Rimini*, *CW1*, p. 235.
24. Peter Nicholls, 'Violence, Recognition and Some Versions of Modernism', *Parataxis*, 4, Summer 1993, pp. 19–35.
25. Tony Pinkney, *Women in the Poetry of T.S. Eliot*, p. 58.
26. Adrian Stokes, *The Stones of Rimini*, *CW1*, p. 230. Compare Gaudier-Brzeska's similar affirmation of modern sculpture: 'the modern sculptor is a man who works with instinct as his inspiring force ... light

voluptuous modelling is to him insipid'. Quoted in Lisa Tickner, 'Now and Then: The Hieratic Head of Ezra Pound', *Oxford Art Journal*, vol. 16, no. 2, 1993, p. 57.

27. Adrian Stokes, *The Stones of Rimini*, *CW1*, p. 259.
28. *Ibid*, p. 214.
29. Lawrence S. Rainey, *Ezra Pound and the Monument of Culture: Text, History and the Malatesta Cantos*, Chicago: University of Chicago, 1991, p. 220.
30. Ezra Pound, 'Frontispiece', *Guide to Kulchur*, London: Faber and Faber, 1938.
31. Ezra Pound, *Jefferson and/or Mussolini*, London: Stanley Nott, 1934, pp. 66–7. As noted by Peter Brooker in 'The Lesson of Ezra Pound', *Ezra Pound: Tactics for Reading*, ed. Ian F.A. Bell, London and Ottawa: Vision and Barnes & Noble, 1982, p. 23.
32. Peter Brooker makes this point about New Critical readings of *The Cantos* in 'The Lesson of Ezra Pound', p. 25.
33. Adrian Stokes, Notebook 4, Adrian Stokes Papers, Tate Gallery Archive, TG8816.
34. Adrian Stokes, *The Quattro Cento*, *CW1*, p. 41.
35. See Alan Durant, *Ezra Pound: Identity in Crisis*, Brighton: Harvester, 1981.
36. Adrian Stokes, *The Stones of Rimini*, *CW1*, p. 232.
37. *Ibid*, pp. 188–9.
38. I understand that the biographical circumstances behind Stokes' split from Pound are discussed in Richard Read's *Stokes/Pound/Klein: Poetics versus Psychoanalysis in the Early Art Criticism of Adrian Stokes*.
39. Paul Smith, 'Adrian Stokes and Ezra Pound', *PN Review: 'Adrian Stokes'*, p. 51.
40. Adrian Stokes, 'Psychoanalytic Reflections on the Development of Ball Games, Particularly Cricket', *IJPA*, 37, 1956, pp. 185–92.
41. Paul Smith, 'Adrian Stokes and Ezra Pound', p. 52.
42. Adrian Stokes, *Painting and the Inner World*, *CW2*, p. 220.
43. Stokes' shift to psychoanalysis was by no means a sudden conversion. Stokes had been in analysis with Klein for two years prior to the publication of *The Quattro Cento*. As Richard Read has demonstrated, in both that text and in his earlier work Stokes had already began to negotiate a psychoanalytic aesthetics. See Richard Read, 'Freudian Psychology and the Early Work of Adrian Stokes'.
44. William Barrett in W.H. Auden, Robert Gorham Davis, Clement Greenberg, Irving Howe, George Orwell, Karl Shapiro, Allen Tate, William Barrett, 'The Question of the Pound Award', *Partisan Review*, vol. 16, no. 5, 1949, p. 522.
45. Karl Shapiro, *ibid*, p. 519.
46. Cited by Karl Shapiro, *ibid*, p. 519.
47. *Ibid*, p. 513.
48. W.H. Auden's 'In Praise of Limestone' was first published in *Horizon*, vol. xviii, 103, July 1948, pp. 1–3 and republished in *Nones*, New York: Random House, 1951. The poem was revised in later printings. This reading refers to the version in *Selected Poems* (1979), ed. Edward

Mendelson, London: Faber and Faber, 1988. Jean-Michel Rabaté, 'Adrian Stokes et Ezra Pound', in *Les Cahiers du Musée national d'art moderne: Adrian Stokes*, 25, Automne, 1988, p. 30.

49. Letter from W.H. Auden to Adrian Stokes, dated 5 June 1932, Adrian Stokes Papers, Tate Gallery Archive, TG8816.
50. W.H. Auden, 'In Memory of Sigmund Freud', *Selected Poems*.
51. Cited in Humphrey Carpenter, *W.H. Auden: A Biography*, London: George Allen and Unwin, 1981, p. 357.
52. See Sigmund Freud, 'Creative Writers and Day-dreaming' (1908[1907]), PFL 14, pp. 131–41, SE 9, pp. 143–53.
53. Terry Eagleton, *The Ideology of the Aesthetic*, Oxford: Blackwell, 1990, p. 87. There is a quarrel to picked here with Eagleton's over-emphasis on the reassuring plenitude of the imaginary, and also with his collapse of Lacan into Althusser, not to say into Kant. On the first point, compare Jacqueline Rose, 'The Imaginary', *Sexuality in the Field of Vision*, pp. 167–99; on the second compare Slavoj Žižek, *The Sublime Object of Ideology*, London: Verso, 1989.
54. Terry Eagleton, *The Ideology of the Aesthetic*, p. 90.
55. If Eagleton's first analogy owes much to Althusser's version of Lacan, the second owes more to the Lacan of *Seminaire VII*. Here identity is structured less through the mis-recognition of plenitude, than through the effects of *das Ding*: the inheritor of Kant's 'thing-in-itself', read through the perverse demands of the id-bound Freudian superego. Because it reveals the unconscious underside to Kant's categorical imperative and hence pushes the subject up against a law it cannot grasp, it is *das Ding* which, for Slavoj Žižek, embodies the structure of the 'sublime object of ideology'.
56. Eagleton seems to overlook the extent to which, as Howard Caygill has cogently demonstrated, Kant *self-consciously* uncovers the 'aporia of judgement' in the relation between the development of civil society and the aesthetic. See Howard Caygill, *The Art of Judgement*, Oxford: Basil Blackwell, 1989.
57. Terry Eagleton, *The Ideology of the Aesthetic*, p. 91.
58. Isobel Armstrong, 'So what's all this about the mother's body? The aesthetic, gender and the polis', in *Intertextuality and Sexuality: Reading Theories and Practices*, ed. Judith Stills and Michael Worton, Manchester: Manchester University Press, 1993, p. 225.
59. *Ibid*, p. 227.
60. *Ibid*, p. 232.
61. Ezra Pound, 'Review of *Stones of Rimini*', *The Criterion*, April 1934, pp. 495–7, reprinted in *Ezra Pound and the Visual Arts*, p. 167.
62. *Ibid*, p. 168.
63. Adrian Stokes, *Inside Out* (1947), CW2, p. 157.
64. *Ibid*, pp. 157–8.
65. *Ibid*, p. 158.
66. Adrian Stokes, *Image in Form: Selected Writings of Adrian Stokes*, ed. Richard Wollheim, Harmondsworth: Penguin, 1972, p. 73.
67. Adrian Stokes, 'Form in Art', *New Directions in Psycho-Analysis*, p. 414.
68. *Ibid*, p. 407.

69. *Ibid*, p. 416.
70. Tony Pinkney, *Women in the Poetry of T.S. Eliot*, p. 12.
71. Adrian Stokes, 'Form in Art', p. 418.
72. Adrian Stokes, 'Primary Process, Thinking and Art', *A Game that Must be Lost*, Cheshire: Carcanet, 1973, p. 124.
73. Adrian Stokes, *Inside Out*, *CW2*, p. 124.
74. Adrian Stokes, *Reflections on the Nude*, *CW3*, p. 305.
75. Adrian Stokes, *CW3*, pp. 321–2.
76. Adrian Stokes, *CW3*, p. 284.
77. Adrian Stokes, 'Freud's views concerning culture in *The Future of an Illusion* and in *Civilization and Its Discontents*, unpublished paper delivered to the Imago Group, Adrian Stokes Papers, Tate Gallery Archive, TG8816.
78. Adrian Stokes, *Inside Out*, *CW2*, p. 162.
79. See George Orwell, *The Lion and the Unicorn: Socialism and the English Genius*, London: Secker and Warburg, 1941, p. 54. I owe this cross-reference to Denise Riley.
80. Lisa Tickner, 'Now and Then: The Hieratic Head of Ezra Pound', p. 59.
81. Adrian Stokes, *CW3*, p. 282.
82. *Ibid*, p. 279.
83. Letters from Osbert Sitwell to Adrian Stokes, undated, Adrian Stokes Papers, Tate Gallery Archive, TG8816.
84. Christian Metz, 'The Imaginary Signifier', trans. Ben Brewster, *Screen*, vol. 16, no. 2, Summer 1975, p. 23.
85. 'Che bell'inverno!/Nel settentrion rinasc la patria,/Ma che ragazza,/che ragazze,/che ragazzi,/portan' il nero!', Ezra Pound, *The Cantos of Ezra Pound*, pp. 434–5. Translation Massimo Bacigalupo, 'Ezra Pound's Cantos 72 and 73', pp. 18–19.
86. Lawrence S. Rainey, *Ezra Pound and the Monument of Culture*, p. 220.
87. H.D., *End to Torment*, p. 6.
88. Adrian Stokes, 'Face and Anti-Face: A Fable', *A Game that Must be Lost*, p. 100.
89. *Ibid*, p. 103.
90. *Ibid*, p. 100.

5 FRAMES, FRONTIERS AND FANTASIES: 'NASTY LADIES WITHIN' – MARION MILNER AND STEVIE SMITH

1. Adrian Stokes, *Inside Out*, *CW2*, p. 141.
2. Stevie Smith, 'Mosaic' (1939), *Me Again: Uncollected Writings of Stevie Smith*, ed. Jack Barbera and William McBrien, London: Virago, 1981, p. 107.
3. Anna Freud and Dorothy Burlingham, *Young Children in War-Time*, p. 183.
4. *British Medical Journal*, 8 January, 1944, vol. 1, p. 50. Unsigned editorial, 'War in the Nursery', cited by Denise Riley, *The War in the Nursery: Theories of the Child and Mother*, p. 113.

5. J. Laplanche and J.B. Pontalis, *The Language of Psychoanalysis*, trans. Donald Nicholson-Smith, London: Karnac Books, 1988, p. 315.
6. See Jacqueline Rose, 'Why War?', *Why War? Psychoanalysis, Politics and the Return to Melanie Klein*, pp. 15–40.
7. Mary Jacobus, 'The Portrait of the Artist as a Young Dog', *First Things: The Maternal Imaginary in Literature, Art and Psychoanalysis*, p. 181.
8. The phrase is Christopher Isherwood's. Isherwood used it in the foreword to Edward Upward's *The Railway Accident* (1949). Reproduced in *The Railway Accident and Other Stories* (1969), Harmondsworth: Penguin, 1972, p. 34. Cited in Peter Widdowson, 'Between the Acts? English Fiction in the Thirties', in *Culture and Crisis in Britain in the '30s*, ed. John Clarke, Margot Heinemann, David Margolies and Carole Snee, London: Lawrence and Wishart, 1979, pp. 133–4.
9. Valentine Cunningham, *British Writers of the Thirties*, pp. 55–6.
10. See Anna Freud, 'Identification with the Aggressor', *The Ego and the Mechanisms of Defence* (1937), trans. Cecil Baines, London: Hogarth Press, 1966, pp. 117–31.
11. Stevie Smith, *Over the Frontier* (1938), London: Virago, 1980, p. 62.
12. J.B. Pontalis, 'The Birth and Recognition of the Self: Introducing Potential Space', *Frontiers in Psychoanalysis: Between the Dream and Psychic Pain*, trans. Catherine and Phillips Cullen, London: Hogarth Press, 1981, pp. 126–7.
13. Marion Milner, *On Not Being Able to Paint* (1950), Oxford: Heinemann, 1989, p. 23.
14. See especially Milner's full-length case-history, *In the Hands of the Living God*, London: Hogarth Press, 1969.
15. Marion Milner, *On Not Being Able to Paint*, p. 153.
16. J. Laplanche and J.B. Pontalis, 'Fantasy and the Origins of Sexuality', in *Formations of Fantasy*, ed. Victor Burgin, James Donald and Cora Kaplan, London: Methuen, 1986, pp. 5–34.
17. Marion Milner, *On Not Being Able to Paint*, p. 136.
18. Sigmund Freud, 'Formulations of the Two Principles of Mental Functioning' (1911), PFL 11, p. 42, and SE 12, p. 224.
19. Sigmund Freud, 'Creative Writers and Day-Dreaming' (1908 [1907]), PFL 14. p. 132 and SE 9, p. 144.
20. J. Laplanche and J.B. Pontalis, *The Language of Psychoanalysis*, p. 447.
21. Jacques Lacan, *The Four Fundamentals of Psychoanalysis*, trans. Alan Sheridan, Harmondsworth, Penguin, 1977, p. 185.
22. J. Laplanche and J.B. Pontalis, 'Fantasy and the Origins of Sexuality', p. 27.
23. Sigmund Freud, 'A Child is Being Beaten (A Contribution to the Study of the Origin of Sexual Perversions' (1919), PFL 10, p. 149–94, and SE 17, pp. 177–204.
24. Mikkel Borch-Jacobsen, 'Dreams are Completely Egoistic', *The Freudian Subject*, trans. Catherine Porter, London: Macmillan, 1989, p. 22.
25. *Ibid*, p. 18.
26. *Ibid*, p. 40.
27. Marion Milner, Some Aspects of Phantasy in Relation to General Psychology' (1945), *The Suppressed Madness of Sane Men: Forty Four*

Years of Exploring Psychoanalysis, London: Tavistock and Routledge, 1987, p. 44. Henceforth cited as *SMSM*.

28. See Anna Freud, 'Beating Fantasies and Daydreams' (1922), *The Writings of Anna Freud*, vol. 1, 1922–35, London: Hogarth, 1974, p. 156.
29. Marion Milner, 'Introduction', *SMSM*, p. 10.
30. Joanna Field (Marion Milner), *An Experiment in Leisure* (1937), London: Virago, 1988, p. 255, Stevie Smith, *Over the Frontier*, p. 207.
31. Philippe Lacoue-Labarthe and Jean-Luc Nancy, 'The Nazi Myth', trans. Brian Holmes, *Critical Inquiry*, Winter, 1990, p. 293.
32. Joanna Field (Marion Milner), *An Experiment in Leisure*, p. 185.
33. Janet Montefiore, 'The pram in the hall: men and women writing the self in the 1930s', *Men and Women Writers of the 1930s: The Dangerous Flood of History*, London: Routledge, 1996, p. 75.
34. Joanna Field (Marion Milner), *An Experiment in Leisure*, p. xx.
35. W.H. Auden, quoted in Joanna Field (Marion Milner), *A Life of One's Own* (1934), London: Virago, 1987, p. 219. W.H. Auden, 'The Guilty Vicarage', *The Dyer's Hand and Other Essays* (1938), London: Faber and Faber, 1962, p. 24.
36. Sigmund Freud, 'Creative Writers and Day-Dreaming', PFL 14, p. 141, and SE 9, p. 152; Joanna Field (Marion Milner), *An Experiment in Leisure*, p. 139.
37. Joanna Field (Marion Milner), *An Experiment in Leisure*, p. 33.
38. Compare Lacan, 'A brief aside – when one is made into two, there is no going back on it. It can never revert to making one again, not even a new one. The *Aufhebung* (sublation) is one of those sweet dreams of philosophy', *Feminine Sexuality: Jacques Lacan and the Ecole freudienne*, p. 156.
39. See Peter Nicholls, 'Sexuality and Structure: Tensions in Early Expressionist Drama', *New Theatre Quarterly*, 26, May, 1991, pp. 162–164.
40. Joanna Field (Marion Milner), *An Experiment in Leisure*, p. 211.
41. *Ibid*, p. 212.
42. *Ibid*, p. 223.
43. *Ibid*, p. 226.
44. See Jacques Lacan, 'Discourse Analysis and Ego Analysis', *The Seminar of Jacques Lacan, Book 1: Freud's Papers on Technique 1953–1954*, pp. 62–89.
45. Marion Milner, 'A suicidal symptom in a child of 3', *SMSM*, p. 25.
46. *Ibid*, p. 27.
47. *Ibid*, p. 26.
48. *Ibid*, pp. 29–31.
49. *Ibid*, p. 31.
50. Marion Milner, 'The role of illusion in symbol formation' (1952), originally entitled 'Aspects of Symbolism in the Comprehension of the Not-self', *SMSM*, p. 94.
51. D.W. Winnicott, private communication to Marion Milner, cited in *SMSM*, p. 112.
52. Marion Milner, 'The role of illusion in symbol formation', p. 99.

53. Christopher Caudwell, cited by Marion Milner, 'The role of illusion in symbol formation', p. 99. See also Christopher Caudwell, *Illusion and Reality* (1937), London: Lawrence and Wishart, 1977.
54. Marion Milner, 'The role of illusion in symbol formation', *SMSM*, p. 105.
55. Melanie Klein, letter to Marion Milner, printed in *SMSM*, pp. 109–110.
56. Georg Grosz, 'On My Drawings' (1944), *Georg Grosz*, ed. Herbert Bittner, London: Peter Owen, 1965, p. 29.
57. See Frances Spalding, *Stevie Smith: A Critical Biography*, London: Faber and Faber, 1988, p. 134.
58. Stevie Smith, *Over the Frontier*, p. 16.
59. *Ibid*, p. 17.
60. For accounts of these and other reviews of *Over the Frontier* see Jack Barbera and William McBrien, *Stevie: A Biography of Stevie Smith*, London: Heinemann, 1985, pp. 110–16.
61. Stevie Smith, *Over the Frontier*, p. 271.
62. Gérard Genette, 'Frontiers of Narrative', *Figures of Literary Discourse*, trans. Alan Sheridan, Oxford: Basil Blackwell, 1982, p. 133.
63. Stevie Smith, *Over the Frontier*, p. 151.
64. *Ibid*, p. 159.
65. *Ibid*, p. 163.
66. *Ibid*, pp. 158–9.
67. *Ibid*, p. 90.
68. *Ibid*, p. 135.
69. *Ibid*, p. 61.
70. Sigmund Freud, 'Remembering, Repeating and Working-Through: Further Recommendations on the Technique of Psychoanalysis II' (1914), SE 12, p. 14.
71. Sigmund Freud, 'Constructions in Analysis' (1937), SE 23, p. 226.
72. Sigmund Freud, 'Remembering, Repeating and Working-Through', p. 154.
73. Stevie Smith, *Over the Frontier*, p. 168.
74. *Ibid*, p. 170.
75. See Sigmund Freud, 'Being in Love and Hypnosis', *Group Psychology and the Analysis of the Ego* (1921), PFL 12, pp. 144–7, SE 18, pp. 111–16. For a discussion of the mimetic logic that underpins hypnosis, and the persistence of this logic in psychoanalysis, see Mikkel Borch-Jacobsen, 'Hypnosis in Psychoanalysis', *Representations*, 27, Summer 1989, pp. 92–110.
76. Stevie Smith, *Over the Frontier*, p. 173.
77. *Ibid*, p. 249.
78. *Ibid*, p. 252.
79. Marion Milner, *SMSM*, p. 37.
80. Stevie Smith, *Over the Frontier*, p. 70.

Selected Bibliography

(Full bibliographical information is given in the chapter notes)

Abel, Elizabeth. *Virginia Woolf and the Fictions of Psychoanalysis*, Chicago: University of Chicago Press, 1989.

Appignanesi, Lisa and John Forrester. *Freud's Women*, London: Weidenfeld and Nicholson, 1992.

Auerbach, Erich. *Mimesis* (1953), trans. W.R. Trask, Princeton: Princeton University Press, 1968.

Armstrong, Isobel. 'So what's all this about the mother's body? The aesthetic, gender and the polis', in Judith Stills and Michael Worton (eds), *Intertextuality and Sexuality: Reading Theories and Practices*, Manchester: Manchester University Press, 1993.

Auden, W.H. *Nones*, New York: Random House, 1951.

—— *The Dyer's Hand and Other Essays* (1938), London: Faber & Faber, 1962.

—— *Selected Poems* (1979), ed. Edward Mendelson, London: Faber & Faber, 1988.

Bell, Clive. *Art*, London: Chatto and Windus, 1914.

—— 'Dr Freud on Art', *Nation and Athenaeum*, 35, 1924, pp. 690–1.

Benjamin, Walter. *Charles Baudelaire: A Lyric Poet in the Era of High Capitalism* (1969), trans. Harry Zhon, London: Verso, 1989.

Benveniste, Emile. *Problèmes de linguistique générale, vol. 1*, Paris: Gallimard, 1966.

—— *Problèmes de linguistique générale, vol. 2*. Paris: Gallimard, 1974.

Bersani, Leo. *The Freudian Body: Psychoanalysis and Art*, New York: Columbia University Press, 1986.

—— *The Culture of Redemption*, Massachusetts: Harvard University Press, 1990.

Bion, Wilfred R. *Experience in Groups and Other Papers*, London: Tavistock, 1961.

Blanchot, Maurice. *Le livre à venir*, Paris: Gallimard, 1959.

Borch-Jacobsen, Mikkel. *The Freudian Subject*, trans. Catherine Porter, London: Macmillan, 1989.

Bott Spillius, Elizabeth (ed). *Melanie Klein Today – Developments in Theory and Practice, vol. 1, Mainly Theory* and *vol. 2, Mainly Practice*, London: Routledge in Association with the Institute of Psycho-Analysis, 1988.

Buck, Claire. *H.D. and Freud: Bisexuality and a Feminine Discourse*, Brighton: Harvester, 1991.

Caudwell, Christopher. *Illusion and Reality* (1937), London: Lawrence and Wishart, 1977.

Connor, Steven. *Theory and Cultural Value*, Oxford: Blackwell, 1992.

Chisholm, Diane. *H.D.'s Freudian Poetics: Psychoanalysis in Translation*, Ithaca: Cornell University Press, 1992.

Clarke, John, Margot Heinemann, David Margolies and Carole Snee (eds), *Culture and Crisis in Britain in the '30s*, London: Lawrence and Wishart, 1979.

Conrad, Joseph. *Lord Jim* (1990), Harmondsworth: Penguin, 1949.
Cunningham, Valentine. *British Writers of the Thirties*, Oxford: Oxford University Press, 1988.
Davie, Donald. 'Adrian Stokes and Pound's Cantos', *Twentieth Century*, vol. 260, 1956, pp. 419–36.
—— *Ezra Pound: The Poet as Sculptor*, London: Routledge and Kegan Paul, 1965.
—— 'Adrian Stokes Revisited', *Paideuma: A Journal of Pound Scholarship*, vol. 12, 1983, pp. 189–97.
Doolittle, Hilda (H.D.). *End to Torment*, Norman Holmes Pearson and Michael King (eds), New York: New Directions, 1979.
Durbin, E.F.M., John Bowlby, Ivor Thomas, D.P.T. Jay, R.B. Fraser, R.H.S. Crossman and George Catlin. *War and Democracy: Essays on the Causes and Prevention of War*, London: Kegan Paul, Trench, Trübner and Co., 1938.
Eagleton, Terry. *Ideology of the Aesthetic*, Oxford: Blackwell, 1990.
Eliot, T.S. *The Waste Land* (1922), *The Waste Land and Other Poems*, London: Faber and Faber, 1940.
—— 'A Note on Poetry and Belief', *The Enemy*, 1, 1927, pp. 16–18.
—— *After Strange Gods: A Primer of Modern Heresy*, London: Faber and Faber, 1941.
—— *Selected Prose of T.S. Eliot*, ed. Frank Kermode, London: Faber and Faber, 1975.
Ellmann, Maud. *The Poetics of Impersonality: T.S. Eliot and Ezra Pound*, Brighton: Harvester, 1987.
Empson, William. *Seven Types of Ambiguity* (1930), Harmondsworth: Penguin, 1995.
—— *Some Versions of Pastoral* (1935), London: Chatto and Windus, 1974.
—— *The Structure of Complex Words* (1951), London: Hogarth Press, 1985.
—— *Argufying: Essays on Literature and Culture*, ed. John Haffenden, London: Chatto and Windus, 1987.
Flugel, J.C. *The Psycho-Analytic Study of the Family* (1921), London: Hogarth Press and the Institution of Psycho-Analysis, 1948.
Ferenczi, Sandor. *Thalassa: A Theory of Genitality*, London: Karnac, 1989.
Freeman Sharpe, Ella. *Dream Analysis: A Practical Handbook for Psycho-Analysts* (1937), London: Karnac: 1978.
—— *Collected Papers on Psycho-Analysis*, ed. Marjoire Brierley, London: Hogarth Press, 1950.
Freud, Anna. *The Writings of Anna Freud, Volumes 1–7*, New York: International Universities Press, 1961–81.
—— 'Beating Fantasies and Daydreams' (1922), *Introduction to Psychoanalysis. Lectures for Child Analysts and Teachers, 1922–35* in *Early Writings vol. 1*, New York: International Universities Press, 1974.
—— *The Ego and the Mechanisms of Defence* (1937), trans. Cecil Baines, London: Hogarth Press, 1966.
—— and Dorothy Burlingham. 'Young Children in War-Time: A Year's Work', reprinted in *Infants Without Families: Reports on the Hampstead Nurseries 1939–1945, Writings vol. 3*, New York: International Universities Press, 1973.

—— 'Abstract of "Psychoanalysis and Education", Freud Memorial Lecture 1954', *The Psychoanalytic Study of the Child*, vol. 9, 1954, pp. 10–31.
Freud, Sigmund. 'Creative Writers and Day-dreaming' (1908[1907]). PFL 14, SE 9.
—— 'Remembering, Repeating and Working-Through: Further Recommendations on the Technique of Psychoanalysis II' (1914). SE 12.
—— 'On Narcissism: An Introduction' (1914). PFL 11, SE 14.
—— 'Formulations of the Two Principles of Mental Functioning' (1911). PFL 11, SE 12.
—— *The Ego and the Id* (1923). PFL 11, SE 19.
—— 'A Child is Being Beaten (A Contribution to the Study of the Origin of Sexual Perversions)' (1919). PFL 10, SE 17.
—— *Beyond the Pleasure Principle* (1920). PFL 11, SE 18.
—— *Group Psychology and the Analysis of the Ego* (1921). PFL 12, SE 18.
—— *Inhibitions, Symptoms and Anxiety* (1926[1925]). PFL 10, SE 20.
—— *Civilization and Its Discontents* (1930[1929]). PFL 12, SE21.
—— 'Female Sexuality' (1931). PFL 7, SE 21.
—— 'Constructions in Analysis' (1937). SE 23.
—— *Moses and Monotheism* (1939[1937–1939]). PFL 12, SE 23.
Fry, Roger. *Vision and Design* (1920), Harmondsworth: Penguin, 1961.
—— 'The Artist and Psycho-Analysis', *Hogarth Essays Series*, London: Hogarth Press, 1924.
—— *Cézanne: A Study of his Development*, London: Hogarth Press, 1927.
—— *Reflections on British Painting*, London: Faber and Faber, 1934.
—— *Last Lectures* (1939), Boston, Massachusetts: Beacon Press, 1962.
—— *A Roger Fry Reader*, ed. Richard Reed. Chicago: University of Chicago Press, 1996.
Gammil, James (*et al.*) *Mélanie Klein Aujourd'hui*, Lyon: Césura Lyon Edition, 1985.
Genette, Gérard. *Figures of Literary Discourse*, trans. Alan Sheridan, Oxford: Basil Blackwell, 1982.
Glover, Edward. 'Sublimation, Substitution and Social Anxiety', *IJPA*, vol. 12, 1931, pp. 263–97.
—— *War, Sadism and Pacifism: Three Essays*, London: George Allen & Unwin, 1933.
—— 'The Position of Psycho-Analysis in Great Britain', *The British Medical Bulletin*, vol. 6, 1949, pp. 27–31.
—— *Freud or Jung?*, London: George Allen & Unwin, 1950.
—— *Selected Papers on Psycho-Analysis vol. 1: On the Early Development of the Mind*, London: Imago, 1956.
Grosskurth, Phyllis. *Melanie Klein: Her World and Work*, London: Hodder & Stoughton, 1985.
Grosz, Georg. *Georg Grosz*, Ed. Herbert Bittner, London: Peter Owen. 1965.
Guillory, John. *Cultural Capital. The Problem of Literary Canon Formation*, Chicago: University of Chicago Press, 1993.
Hegel, G.W.F. *Phenomenology of Spirit*, trans. A.V. Miller, Oxford: Clarendon Press, 1977.
—— *Introductory Lectures on Aesthetics*, trans. Bernard Bosanquet, Harmondsworth: Penguin, 1993.

Heimann, Paula. 'A contribution to the problem of sublimation and its relation to processes of internalization', *IJPA*, vol. 33, 1942. pp. 8–17.

Isaacs, Susan. *Social Development in Young Children* (1933), London: George Routledge & Sons, 1948.

Jacobus, Mary. *First Things: The Maternal Imaginary in Literature, Art and Psychoanalysis*, London: Routledge, 1996.

Jones, Ernest. *Papers on Psycho-Analysis*, London: Maresfield Reprints, 1948.

Kant, Immanuel. *The Critique of Judgement*, trans. James Creed Meredith. Oxford: Clarendon Press, 1992.

Keynes, Maynard. *The Economic Consequences of the Peace* (1919), London: Macmillan, 1920.

King, Pearl and Riccardo Steiner (eds). *The Freud-Klein Controversies: 1941–1945*, New Library of Psychoanalysis, vol. 11, London: Routledge in association with the Institute of Psycho-Analysis, 1991.

Klein, Melanie. *The Psychoanalysis of Children* (1932), London: Virago, 1989.

—— and Joan Rivière. *Love, Guilt and Reparation*, London: Hogarth Press, 1937.

—— Paula Heimann, Susan Isaacs and Joan Rivière. *Developments in Psycho-Analysis*, ed. Joan Rivière, London: Hogarth Press and the Institute of Psycho-Analysis, 1952.

—— Paula Heimann, R.E. Money-Kyrle (eds). *New Directions in Psycho-Analysis: The Significance of Infant Conflict in the Pattern of Adult Behaviour* (1955), London: Karnac, 1985.

—— *Narrative of a Child Analysis*, London: Hogarth Press, 1961.

—— *Our Adult World*, London: Hogarth Press, 1963.

—— *The Writings of Melanie Klein, 4 vols*, ed. R.E. Money-Kyrle in collaboration with B. Joseph, E. O'Shauhnessy and H. Segal, London: Hogarth Press and the Institute of Psycho-Analysis, 1975.

—— *The Selected Melanie Klein*, (ed.) Juliet Mitchell, Harmondsworth: Penguin, 1986.

—— *Love, Guilt and Reparation and other works 1921–1945*, London: Virago, 1988.

—— *Envy and Gratitude and other works 1946–1963*, London: Virago, 1988.

Kohon, Gregorio (ed). *The British School of Psychoanalysis: The Independent Tradition*, London: Free Association Books, 1986.

Krauss, Rosalind E. *The Optical Unconscious* (1993), Cambridge, Massachusetts: MIT Press, 1994.

Kristeva, Julia. *La révolution du langage póetique*, Paris: Seuil, 1974, translated (in part) as *Revolution in Poetic Language*, trans. Margaret Waller, New York: Columbia University Press, 1984.

—— *The Kristeva Reader* (ed.), Toril Moi. Oxford: Blackwell, 1986.

—— *Powers of Horror: An Essay in Abjection*, trans. Leon S. Roudiez, New York: Columbia University Press, 1982.

Lacan, Jacques. *Ecrits*, trans. Alan Sheridan, London: Tavistock/Routledge, 1977.

Lacan, Jacques. *Four Fundamentals of Psychoanalysis*, trans. Alan Sheridan, Harmondsworth: Penguin, 1977.

—— *The Seminar of Jacques Lacan, Book 1, Freud's Papers on Technique 1953–54*, trans. John Forrester, Cambridge: Cambridge University Press, 1988.

—— *Le séminaire livre VII: L'éthique de la psychanalyse, 1959–1960*, ed. Jacques-Alain Miller, Paris: Editions du Seuil, 1986 (*The Seminar of Jacques Lacan Book VII: The Ethics of Psychoanalysis*, trans. Dennis Porter, London: Tavistock/Routledge, 1992).

Lacoue-Labarthe, Philippe and Jean-Luc Nancy. 'The Nazi Myth', trans. Brian Holmes, *Critical Inquiry*, Winter, 1990, pp. 271–98.

Laplanche, J. *Life and Death in Psychoanalysis*, trans. Jeffrey Mehlman, Baltimore: Johns Hopkins University Press, 1985.

—— and J.B. Pontalis. *The Language of Psychoanalysis*, trans. Donald Nicholson-Smith. London: Karnac, 1988.

—— 'Fantasy and the Origins of Sexuality' in *Formations of Fantasy*, Victor Burgin, James Donald and Cora Kaplan (eds), London: Methuen, 1986, pp. 5–34.

Lebovici, Serge and D. Widlocher (eds). *Psychoanalysis in France*, New York: International Universities Press, 1980.

Lewis, Wyndham. *The Art of Being Ruled*, London: Chatto and Windus, 1926.

—— *Men Without Art*. London: Cassell, 1934.

Levenson, Michael H. *A Genealogy of Modernism: A Study in English Literary Doctrine 1908–1922*, Cambridge: Cambridge University Press, 1984.

Meisel, Perry. *The Myth of the Modern*, New Haven: Yale University Press, 1987.

Meltzer, Donald. *The Kleinian Development, Parts 1–3*, Perthshire: Cluny Press, 1978.

Mepham, John. *Virginia Woolf: A Literary Life*, London: Macmillan, 1991.

Milner, Marion (Joanna Field). *A Life of One's Own* (1934), London: Virago, 1987.

—— *An Experiment in Leisure* (1937), London: Virago, 1988.

—— *On Not Being Able to Paint* (1950), Oxford: Heinemann, 1989.

—— *In the Hands of the Living God*, London: Hogarth Press, 1969.

—— *The Suppressed Madness of Sane Men: Forty-Four Years of Exploring Psychoanalysis*, London: Tavistock and Routledge, 1987.

Mitchell, Juliet and Jacqueline Rose (eds). *Feminine Sexuality – Jacques Lacan and the Ecole freudienne*, trans. Jacqueline Rose, London: Macmillan, 1982.

Money-Kyrle, R.E. *The Development of the Sexual Impulses*, London: Kegan Paul, 1932.

Montefiore, Janet. *Men and Women Writers of the 1930s: The Dangerous Flood of History*, London: Routledge, 1996.

Nicholls, Peter. *Ezra Pound: Politics, Economics and Writing: A Study of the Cantos*, New Jersey: Humanities Press, 1984.

—— 'Violence, Recognition and Some Versions of Modernism', *Parataxis*, 4, Summer 1993, pp. 9–15

—— *Modernisms: A Literary Guide*, London: Macmillan, 1995.

Oligivie, Betrand. *Lacan, le sujet*, Paris: PUF, 1993.

Phillips, John and Lyndsey Stonebridge (eds). *Reading Melanie Klein*. London: Routledge, 1998.

Pick, Daniel. *War Machine: The Rationalisation of Slaughter in the Modern Age*, New Haven: Yale University Press, 1993.

Pinkney, Tony. *Women in the Poetry of T.S. Eliot*, London: Macmillan, 1984.
Pontalis, J.B. *Frontiers in Psychoanalysis: Between the Dream and Psychic Pain*, trans. Catherine and Phillip Cullen. London: Hogarth Press, 1981.
Pound, Ezra. *Jefferson and/or Mussolini*, London: Stanley Nott, 1934.
—— *Guide to Kulchur*, London: Faber & Faber, 1938.
—— *Ezra Pound and the Visual Arts*, ed. Harriet Zinnes, New York: New Directions, 1980.
—— *The Cantos of Ezra Pound*, London: Faber & Faber, 1990.
Rainey, Lawrence S. *Ezra Pound and the Monument of Culture: Text, History and the Malatesta Cantos*, Chicago: University of Chicago, 1991.
Richards, I.A. *Principles of Literary Criticism* (1924), London: Routledge & Kegan Paul, 1967.
—— 'A Background for Contemporary Poetry', *The Criterion*, vol. 3, no. 12, July 1925, pp. 511–28.
—— 'Psychopolitics', *Fortune*, vol. 24, September, 1942, pp. 108–16.
—— *Poetries and Sciences: A Reissue of Science and Poetry (1926, 1935) with Commentary*, London: Routledge & Kegan Paul, 1970.
—— *Richards on Rhetoric: I.A. Richards Selected Essays 1929–1974*, ed. Ann B. Berthoff, Oxford: Oxford University Press, 1991.
Riley, Denise. *War in the Nursery: Theories of the Child and Mother*, London: Virago, 1983.
Rivière, Joan. 'Womanliness as Masquerade', *IJPA*, 10, 1929.
Rose, Jacqueline. *Sexuality and the Field of Vision*, London: Verso, 1986.
—— *Why War? Psychoanalysis, Politics and the Return to Melanie Klein*, The Bucknell Lectures in Literary Theory, Oxford: Blackwell, 1993.
—— *States of Fantasy*, Oxford: Clarendon Press, 1996.
Roudinesco, Elisabeth. *La bataille de cent ans: Histoire de la psychanalyse en France, vol. 1*, Paris: Editions Ramsay, 1982.
—— *Jacques Lacan and Company: A History of Psychoanalysis in France, 1925–1985*, trans. Jeffrey Mehlman, London: Free Association Books, 1990.
Segal, Hanna. *Introduction to the Work of Melanie Klein*, London: Hogarth Press, 1978.
—— *The Work of Hanna Segal, A Kleinian Approach to Clinical Practice: delusion, creativity and other psychoanalytic essays*, London: Free Association Books and Maresfield, 1986.
—— *Klein*, London: Karnac and The Institute of Psycho-Analysis, 1989.
—— *Dream, Phantasy and Art*, London: Tavistock and Routledge, 1991.
Smith, Stevie. *Over the Frontier* (1938), London: Virago, 1980.
—— *Me Again: Uncollected Writings of Stevie Smith*, ed. Jack Barbera and William McBrien. London: Virago, 1981.
Spender, Stephen. *The Destructive Element: A Study of Modern Writers and Beliefs*, London: Jonathan Cape, 1935.
Steiner, Riccardo. 'Some Thoughts about the Tradition and Change Arising from and Examination of the British Society's Controversial Discussions (1943–44)', *International Review of Psycho-Analysis*, 12, 1985, pp. 27–71.
Stokes, Adrian. 'The Sculptor Agostino Di Ducio'. *The Criterion*, vol. 9, October 1929, pp. 44–60.

'Painting, Giogione and Barbaro', *The Criterion*, vol. 9, April 1930, pp. 482–500.

—— 'Psychoanalytical Reflections on the Development of Ball Games, Particularly Cricket', *IJPA*, 37, 1956, pp. 185–92.

—— *The Invitation in Art*, London: Tavistock, 1965.

—— *Image in Form: Selected Writings of Adrian Stokes*, ed. Richard Wollheim, Harmondsworth: Penguin, 1972.

—— *A Game that Must be Lost*, Cheshire: Carcanet, 1973.

—— *The Critical Writings of Adrian Stokes, vols 1–3*, ed. Lawrence Gowing. London: Thames and Hudson, 1978.

—— 'Freud's views concerning culture in *The Future of an Illusion* and in *Civilization and its Discontents*' (undated and unpublished paper), Adrian Stokes Papers, Tate Gallery Archive, TG8816.

—— *PN Review: 'Adrian Stokes'*, vol. 7, 1980.

—— *Les Cahiers du Musée National d'Art Moderne: Adrian Stokes*, ed. Yves Michaud, 25, Automne 1988.

Sutherland, J.D. ed. *Psychoanalysis and Contemporary Thought*, by W.D. Winnicott ... (*et al.*), London: Hogarth Press, 1958.

Timms, Edward and Naomi Segal (eds). *Freud in Exile, Psychoanalysis and its Vicissitudes*, New Haven: Yale University Press, 1988.

Trilling, Lionel. *Freud and the Crisis of our Culture* Freud Memorial Lectures. Boston, Massachusetts: Beacon Press, 1955.

Weber, Samuel. *Return to Freud: Jacques Lacan's Dislocation of Psychoanalysis*, trans. Michael Levine, Cambridge: Cambridge University Press, 1991.

White, Allon. *The Uses of Obscurity*, London: Routledge Kegan Paul, 1981.

Wilde, Alan. *Horizons of Assent: Modernism, Postmodernism and the Ironic Imagination*, Baltimore: Johns Hopkins Press, 1981.

Williams, Raymond. *Problems in Materialism and Culture*, London: New Left Review Editions, Verso, 1980.

Winnicott, Donald. *Collected Papers: Through Paediatrics to Psychoanalysis*, London: Tavistock, 1971.

Wollheim, Richard. *Art and Its Objects* (1968), Harmondsworth: Penguin, 1970.

—— *On Art and the Mind*, Massachusetts: Harvard University Press, 1974.

Woolf, Virginia. 'The Mark on the Wall' (1917), *The Complete Shorter Fiction*, ed. Susan Dick, London: Grafton, 1991.

—— *The Common Reader: First Series* (1925), London: Hogarth Press, 1942.

—— *To the Lighthouse* (1927), London: Grafton, 1987.

—— *A Room of One's Own* (1929), London: Grafton, 1985.

—— '"Anon" and "The Reader"' (1939–40), ed. Brenda Silver, *Twentieth Century Literature*, 25, 1979, pp. 356–435.

—— 'A Sketch of the Past' (1939–1940), unpublished manuscripts A5(a), A5(b), A5(c). *The Monk's House Collection*, University of Sussex and in *Moments of Being* (1976), ed. Jean Schulkind, London: Grafton, 1982.

—— *Roger Fry: A Biography* (1940), London: Hogarth Press, 1991.

—— *Between the Acts* (1941), London: Grafton, 1988.

—— *Pointz Hall: The Earlier and Later Typescripts of Between the Acts*, ed. Mitchell A. Leaska. New York: University Publications, 1983.

—— *The Death of the Moth and Other Essays*, London: Hogarth Press, 1942.

—— *The Moment and Other Essays*, ed. Leonard Woolf, London: Hogarth Press, 1947.

—— *The Letters of Virginia Woolf, vol. 2*, ed. Nigel Nicholson and Joanne Trautmann, London: Hogarth Press, 1976.

—— *The Letters of Virginia Woolf, vol. 4*, ed. Nigel Nicholson, London: Hogarth Press, 1978.

—— *The Diary of Virginia Woolf, vol. 5, 1939–1941*, ed. Anne Olivier Bell, Harmondsworth: Penguin, 1988.

Young-Bruehl, Elisabeth. *Anna Freud: A Biography*, London: Macmillan, 1988.

Žižek, Slavoj. *The Sublime Object of Ideology*, London: Verso, 1989.

Index